Also by Katherine Ashenburg

Going to Town: Architectural Walking Tours in Southern Ontario

The Mourner's Dance: What We Do When People Die

THE DIRT ON

CL

Katherine Ashenburg

An

UNSANITIZED

HISTORY

NORTH POINT PRESS
A division of Farrar, Straus and Giroux
New York

North Point Press

A division of Farrar, Straus and Giroux

19 Union Square West, New York 10003

Copyright © 2007 by Katherine Ashenburg

Printed in the United States of America

Originally published in 2007 by Alfred A. Knopf Canada

Published in the United States by Farrar, Straus and Giroux

First American edition, 2007

Owing to limitations of space, all aknowledgments for permission to reprint
previously published material can be found on pages 355–56.

Library of Congress Cataloging-in-Publication Data

Ashenburg, Katherine.

The dirt on clean : an unsanitized history / by Katherine Ashenburg. —
1st American ed.

    p.   cm.

"Originally published in 2007 by Alfred A. Knopf, Canada."

Includes bibliographical references and index.

ISBN-13: 978-0-86547-690-5 (hardcover : alk. paper)

ISBN-10: 0-86547-690-X (hardcover : alk. paper)

1. Bathing customs.   2. Hygiene.   I. Title.

GT2845.A84 2007

391.6'4—dc22

2007032334

Designed by Kelly Hill

www.fsgbooks.com

3   5   7   9   10   8   6   4   2

For Kate and John,
who love their bath,
and for Alberto,
always immaculate

CONTENTS

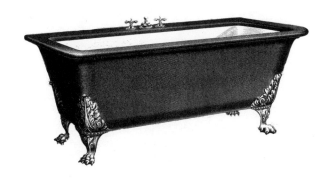

"BUT DIDN'T THEY *SMELL*?"

For the modern, middle-class North American, "clean" means that you shower and apply deodorant each and every day without fail. For the aristocratic seventeenth-century Frenchman, it meant that he changed his linen shirt daily and dabbled his hands in water but never touched the rest of his body with water or soap. For the Roman in the first century, it involved two or more hours of splashing, soaking and steaming the body in water of various temperatures, raking off sweat and oil with a metal scraper, and giving himself a final oiling—all done daily, in company and without soap.

Even more than in the eye or the nose, cleanliness exists in the mind of the beholder. Every culture defines it for itself, choosing what it sees as the perfect point between squalid and over-fastidious. The modern North American, the seventeenth-century Frenchman and the Roman were each convinced that cleanliness was an important marker of civility and that *his* way was the royal road to a properly groomed body.

It follows that hygiene has always been a convenient stick with which to beat other peoples, who never seem to get it right. The outsiders usually err on the side of dirtiness. The ancient Egyptians thought that sitting a dusty body in still water, as the Greeks did, was a foul idea. Late-nineteenth-century Americans were scandalized by the dirtiness of Europeans; the Nazis promoted the idea of Jewish uncleanliness. At least since the Middle Ages, European travellers have enjoyed nominating the continent's grubbiest country—the laurels usually went to France or Spain. Sometimes the other is, suspiciously, *too* clean—which is how the Muslims, who scoured their bodies and washed their genitals, struck Europeans for centuries. The Muslims returned the compliment, regarding Europeans as downright filthy.

Most modern people have a sense that not much washing was done until the twentieth century, and the question I was asked most often while writing this book always came with a look of barely contained disgust: "But didn't they *smell*?" As St. Bernard said, where all stink, no one smells. The scent of one another's bodies was the ocean our ancestors swam in, and they were used to the everyday odour of dried sweat. It was part of their world, along with the smells of cooking, roses, garbage, pine forests and manure. Twenty years ago, airplanes, restaurants, hotel rooms and most other public indoor spaces were thick with cigarette smoke. Most of us never noticed it. Now that these places are usually smoke-free, we shrink back affronted when we enter a room where someone has been smoking. The nose is adaptable, and teachable.

The North American reader, schooled on advertisements for soap and deodorants, is likely to protest at this point: "But body odour is different from smoke. Body odour is innately disgusting." My own experience tells me that isn't true. For the first seven years of my life, I spent countless hours with my maternal grandmother, who came from Germany. She lived only a few houses down the street from us in Rochester, New York, and she often took care of us grandchildren. She was a cheerful, hard-working woman, perpetually cooking, cleaning, sewing, crocheting or knitting. Two smells bring my grandmother vividly to mind. One is the warm amalgam of yeast and linen, from the breads she shrouded in tea towels and set to rise on her dining-room radiators. The other smell came from my grandmother herself. As a child, I never thought to describe it or wonder what it was—it was just part of my grandmother. Whom I loved, so the smell never troubled me.

When I married, my husband and I went to Germany on our honeymoon, staying in bed-and-breakfasts in small, clean-swept Bavarian towns. There, unexpectedly, memories of my grandmother came flooding back. The industrious Bavarian women who cleaned our rooms and made our breakfasts didn't just act like my grandmother; they *smelled* like her. By then, as an adult raised in cleaner-than-clean North America, I knew what the smell was—the muffled, acrid odour of stale sweat—and for the first time, I consciously connected my grandmother's characteristic smell to its cause. She cleaned her house ferociously but not her body, or not very often. (It was a northern European habit I would later read about, when travellers from other European countries, as far back as the sixteenth and seventeenth centuries, would marvel at the cleanliness of Swiss, German and Dutch houses and even streets, but note that it did not extend to their bodies.)

I had to learn that my grandmother's smell was not "good," as determined by twentieth-century North American standards. My natural, uncultivated reaction was that it was neutral or better. Similarly, there are tribes that consider the odour of menstrual blood pleasant because it signifies fertility; others that find it repulsive, because their taboos include blood or secretions; and still other tribes that remain indifferent to it. When it comes to feelings about our bodies or those of other people, much depends on the assumptions of our group.

To modern Westerners, our definition of cleanliness seems inevitable, universal and timeless. It is none of these things, being a complicated cultural creation and a constant work in progress. My grandmother kept her Old Country notions of cleanliness until she died, in the late 1970s. Her daughter, my mother, left Germany when she was six, in 1925. Growing up in Rochester, she went to college and became a nurse. She also became an American, watching with the immigrant's ever-vigilant eye as her adopted country ratcheted up the cleanliness standards in the 1930s and '40s.

She remembered the advertising campaigns, launched by razor manufacturers, inculcating the novel idea that women's hairy legs and underarms were bad and, in the case of underarms, encouraged body odour. She remembered when she first heard of a newfangled product known as deodorant and when she realized that something called shampoo worked better than the boiled-down soap her mother produced for washing hair. She never wore perfume because, as she liked to say, "That's what Europeans use instead of soap." (Not that perfume had ever touched her no-nonsense mother's body.) Her own regime involved plenty of soap and Mitchum's, a clinically packaged deodorant "for problem perspiration."

In my generation, standards reached more absurd levels. The idea of a body ready to betray me at any turn filled the magazine ads I pored over in *Seventeen* and in *Mademoiselle* in the late 1950s and early '60s. The lovely-looking girls in those pages were regularly baffled by their single state or their failure to get a second date or their general unpopularity, and all because their breath, their hair, their underarms or—the worst—their private parts were not "fresh." A long-running series of cartoon-style ads for Kotex sanitary napkins alerted me to the impressive horrors of menstrual blood, which apparently could announce its presence to an entire high school.

The most menacing aspect of the smells that came with poor-to-middling hygiene was that, as we were constantly warned, we could be guilty of them *without even knowing it!* There was no way we could ever rest assured that we were clean enough. For me, the epitome of feminine daintiness was the model who posed on the cover of a Kotex pamphlet about menstruation, titled *You're a Young Lady Now.* This paragon, a blue-eyed blonde wearing a pageboy hairdo and a pale blue shirt-waist dress, had clearly never had a single extraneous hair on her body and smelled permanently of baby powder. I knew I could never live up to her immaculate blondness, but much of my world was telling me I had to try.

While ads for men told them they would not advance at the office without soap and deodorant, women fretted that no one would want to have sex with them unless their bodies were impeccably clean. No doubt that's why the second-most-frequent question I heard during the writing of this book—almost always from women—was a rhetorical "How could they bear to have sex with each other?" In fact, there's no evidence that the birthrate ever fell because people were too smelly for copulation. And although modern people have a hard time accepting it, at least in public, the relationship between sex and odourless cleanliness is neither constant nor predictable. The ancient Egyptians went to great lengths to be clean, but both sexes anointed their genitals with perfumes designed to deepen and exaggerate their natural aroma. Most ancient civilizations matter-of-factly acknowl-edged that, in the right circumstances, a gamy, earthy body odour can be a powerful aphrodisiac. Napoleon and Josephine were fastidious for their time in that they both took a long, hot, daily bath. But Napoleon wrote Josephine from a campaign, "I will return to Paris tomorrow evening. Don't wash."

Early in my reading about the history of cleanliness, I began talking one day at a lunch about some of the extremes, in both directions, that I was discovering. Another guest, a journalist, was astonished. "I just assume everyone is like me," she said, "showering every single day, no more, no less." Her assumption, even about educated North Americans like her, is not true, but most people are loath to admit that they deviate from the norm. As I went on reading about cleanliness, people began taking me aside and confessing things: several didn't use deodorant, just washed with soap and water; some didn't shower or bathe daily. Two writers told me separately that they had a washing superstition: as the end of a long project neared, they stopped washing their hair and didn't shampoo until it was finished. One woman confided that her husband of some twenty years takes long showers at least three times a day: she would love, she said wistfully, to know what he "really" smells like, as opposed to deodorant soap.

Something similar happened during the writing of my last book, which was about mourning customs. Most of the traditional customs were obsolete and considered primitive or sentimental—or both—by a world interested in "moving on" as quickly as possible. But while I worked on that book, people would tell me privately about a mourning observance that was acutely important for them, even if it didn't seem quite right in the twenty-first century—how they wore their father's old undershirts, for example, or had long talks with their dead wife. Now that people were confiding their washing eccentricities—usually on the side of less scrupulosity rather than more—I was amused. Is a failure to meet the standards of the Clean Police as bizarre as full-blown mourning in the modern world? The surreptitious way people revealed their deviations to me indicates how thoroughly we have been conditioned: to risk smelling like a human is a misdemeanour, and the goal is to smell like an exotic fruit (mango, papaya, passion fruit) or a cookie (vanilla, coconut, ginger). The standard we read about in magazines and see on television is a sterilized and synthetic one, "as if we're not on this earth," a male friend remarked, but it takes some courage to disregard it.

What could be more routine and apparently banal than taking up soap and water and washing yourself? At one level and almost by definition, personal cleanliness is superficial, since it involves only the surface. At the same time it echoes, and links us to, some of the most profound feelings and impulses we know. In almost every religion, water and cleansing are resonant symbols—of grace, of forgiveness, of regeneration. Worshippers around the world wash themselves before prayer, whether literally, as the Muslims do, or more metaphorically, as when Catholics dip their fingers in holy-water fonts at the entrance to the church.

The archetypal link between dirt and guilt, and cleanliness and innocence, is built into our language—perhaps into our psyches. We talk about dirty jokes and laundering money. When we step too close to something morally unsavoury at a business meeting or a party, we say, "I wanted to take a shower." Pontius Pilate washed his hands after condemning Jesus to death, and Lady

Macbeth claims, unconvincingly, "A little water clears us of this deed," after persuading her husband to kill Duncan. Baths and immersions also have a natural kinship with rites of passage, the ceremonies that mark the transition from one stage of life to the next—from being an anonymous infant to a named member of the community, from singlehood to marriage, from life to death. Being submerged in water and emerging from it is a universal way of declaring "off with the old, on with the new." (My writer friends who finally shampoo when their projects are finished are signalling that a passage has been accomplished.) Brides, and often grooms, from ancient Greece to modern-day Africa, have been given a celebratory prenuptial bath; young women in Renaissance Germany made a "bath shirt" for their husbands-to-be, a token of this custom. The Knights of the Bath were so called because they took a ritual bath the night before their formal investiture, as do men and women in many religious orders on the night before their final vows.

One of the most widespread rites of passage involves bathing the dead, an action that serves no practical purpose but meets deep symbolic ones. The final washing given to Jewish corpses is a solemn ceremony performed by the burial society, in which the body is held upright while twenty-four quarts of water are poured over it. Other groups—the Japanese, the Irish, the Javanese— enlist the family and close neighbours to wash the dead. All have a sense that respect for the dead means that he or she must be clean for the last journey, to the last resting place. This is a ritual whose power is by no means exhausted: in one of the most moving episodes in the television series *Six Feet Under*, the mother and brother of Nate Fisher wash his corpse, slowly and methodically, in the family funeral parlour in twenty-first-century Los Angeles.

Rites of passage and religion are not the only domains in which washing extends its reach beyond the bathroom. Until the late nineteenth century, therapeutic baths played a significant part in the Western medical repertoire, and they still do in eastern Europe. Observers often connect a culture's cleanliness to its technological muscle. It's true that plumbing and other engineering feats have made our modern standard of cleanliness possible, but technology usually follows from a desire rather than leads it: the Roman bathhouses had sophisticated heating and water-delivery systems that no one cared to imitate for centuries because washing was no longer a priority.

Climate, religion and attitudes to privacy and individuality also affect the way we clean ourselves. For many in the modern West, few activities demand more solitude than washing our naked bodies. But for the ancient Romans, getting clean was a social occasion, as it can still be for modern Japanese, Turks and Finns. In cultures where group solidarity is more important than individuality, nudity is less problematic and scrubbed, odourless bodies are less necessary. As these values shift, so does the definition of "clean."

Because this book is a history of Western cleanliness, it only glances at the rich traditions of other cultures, usually as they revealed themselves to astonished European travellers, missionaries or colonizers. Before the twentieth century, Europeans usually found that prosperous Indian, Chinese and Japanese people washed themselves far more than was usual in the West. (In the case of Japan, every social level was well washed.) For their part, Indians and Asians considered Westerners puzzlingly dirty. To some extent, it was a matter of merocrine sweat glands, which Caucasians have in profusion while Asians have few or none. (Because of this, they can still find even clean Westerners very smelly.) Partly it was that Christianity's emphasis on the spirit encouraged a certain neglect and disparagement of the physical side of life, and Christian teachings, unlike those of Hinduism, Buddhism and Islam, ignored hygiene. And partly the difference between West and East was that much of Europe took a long hiatus when it came to regular washing, roughly from the late Middle Ages to the eighteenth or nineteenth century, and non-Westerners who encountered Europeans in those centuries were often stunned by their abysmal hygiene.

The story of that hiatus was the germ of this book. Until a few years ago, I had a vague notion that after the Roman baths petered out, everyone was more or less filthy until perhaps the end of the nineteenth century. The world I imagined was very like Patrick Süskind's description of eighteenth-century Paris in his novel *Perfume*, except that it went on unchanged for fifteen hundred or so years—an overwhelming, rank palimpsest of rotten meat, sour wine, grimy sheets, excrement and, above all, the look and smell of dirty human flesh. Then, one day in the Royal Ontario Museum in Toronto, I paused in front of a picture of an eighteenth-century crowd. The caption underneath read, "The aristocrats in this picture are as dirty as the peasants. Press the button and learn more."

That seemed to confirm my assumptions about the history of cleanliness, but I was willing to learn more, so I pressed the button. The story turned out to be more complicated than I had imagined. The aristocrats were dirty, according to the audiotape, because of an undulating chain of events that began in the eleventh century. When the Crusaders returned from the East, they brought with them the news of Turkish baths, and for a few centuries medieval people enjoyed warm water, communal baths and plentiful opportunities for sexual hijinks. Although ecclesiastical disapproval and the threat of syphilis cast a shadow over the bathhouses, it was the devastating plagues of the fourteenth century that closed their doors in most of Europe. The French historian Jules Michelet called the years that followed "a thousand years without a bath"—in fact, four hundred years without a bath would be more accurate. At least until the mid-eighteenth century, Europeans from the lowliest peasant to the king shunned water. Instead, they convinced themselves that linen had admirable cleansing properties, and they "washed" by changing their shirts.

For me, the medieval interlude of cleanliness and its end were startling and absorbing news. Personal cleanliness, even during the relatively few centuries detailed in the museum's audiotape, suddenly had ups and downs I had never suspected, and it connected to far more than soap and water. I needed to know more about all the tentacles—social, intellectual, scientific, political and technological—that found their way in and out of a condition we call "clean." Following those twists and turns led me from Homer's Greece to the American Civil War, from Hippocrates to the germ theory, and through a handful of revolutions—French, Industrial and the sexual one of the 1960s and '70s. Cleanliness played a part in all of them.

The evolution of "clean" is also a history of the body: our attitudes to cleanliness reveal much, occasionally too much, about our most intimate selves. Benjamin Franklin said that to understand the people of a country, he needed only to visit its graveyards. While there's truth in that, I suggest a smaller and likelier place. Show me a people's bathhouses and bathrooms, and I will show you what they desire, what they ignore, sometimes what they fear—and a significant part of who they are.

ONE

THE SOCIAL BATH

GREEKS AND ROMANS

dysseus, his wife, Penelope, and their son, Telemachus, were a notably well-washed family, and the reasons would have been obvious to the first audience of *The Odyssey*. Greeks in the eighth century B.C. had to wash before praying and offering sacrifices to the gods, and Penelope frequently prays for the return of her wandering husband and son. A Greek would also bathe before setting out on a journey, and when he arrived at the house of strangers or friends, etiquette demanded that he first be offered water to wash his hands, and then a bath. This is a book full of departures and arrivals, as Odysseus struggles for a

Washing in Greece, fifth century B.C. The young woman is about to pour water into the *labrum*, or washstand.

decade to return home to Ithaca after the Trojan War, and Telemachus searches for his father. Their journeys are the warp and weft of this great adventure story.

When Odysseus visits the palace of King Alcinoos, the king orders his queen, Arete, to draw a bath for their guest. Homer describes it in the deliberate, formulaic terms reserved for important customs: "Accordingly Arete directed her women to set a large tripod over the fire at once. They put a copper over the blazing fire, poured in the water and put the firewood underneath. While the fire was shooting up all round the belly of the copper, and the water was growing warm . . . the housewife told him his bath was ready."

Then the housekeeper bathes Odysseus, probably in a tub of brass or polished stone, rubbing his clean body with oil when he steps out of the tub. Here it is the head servant who washes the stranger, but when the guest was particularly distinguished, one of the daughters of the house might do the honours. When Telemachus travels to the palace of King Nestor, his youngest daughter, Polycasta, bathes him and massages him with olive oil. Telemachus emerges from her ministrations "as handsome as a young god."

More than the most lyrical copywriter extolling the wonders of a modern bathroom, Homer stresses the transforming power of the bath—partly because *The Odyssey* is a tall tale but partly because travellers in the wilds of ancient Greece did no doubt look remarkably better after soaking in hot water. Not only does a bath turn nicelooking young men into near-divinities, but Odysseus gains height, strength and splendour when his old nurse bathes him. With his clean hair curling like hyacinth petals, he too "came out of the bathroom looking more like a god than a man."

The most poignant transformation achieved by a bath in *The Odyssey* happens at the end of the book. Odysseus, who has been away from home for twenty years, comes upon his old father, Laertes, digging in his vineyard. Laertes' clothes are dirty and

Let not your hands be unwashed when you pour a libation
Of flaming wine to Zeus or the other immortal gods.

—Hesiod, *Works and Days*

SYBARITIC STEAM

The Sybarites, a luxury-loving people who lived in southeastern Italy from around 720 to 510 B.C., are credited with inventing the soup spoon, the chamber pot and the steam bath.

patched, and "in the carelessness of his sorrow," as Homer puts it, he is wearing a goatskin hat, an emblem of rustic poverty. Before he reveals his identity, Odysseus tells his father that he looks like a man who deserves better—namely, "a bath and a good dinner and soft sleep." Laertes explains that his son is missing, probably devoured by fishes or beasts, and "a black cloud of sorrow came over the old man: with both hands he scraped up the grimy dust and poured it over his white head, sobbing." It is a potent image of desolation, one repeated by mourners from many cultures—dirtying oneself, whether by daubing one's face with mud or covering one's head, as Laertes does, with dust. Misfortune and dirtiness are natural companions, as are cleanliness and good fortune.

MURDER IN THE BATH

In Aeschylus' *Agamemnon*, Agamemnon's wife, Clytemnestra, kills him in the bath by striking him twice with an axe.

At this point, Odysseus reveals his identity and takes an overjoyed Laertes back to his house. The neglected old man has a bath, which once again works its magic: "Athena stood by his side and put fullness into his limbs, so that he seemed stronger and bigger than before. When he came out of the bathroom his son was astonished to see him like one come down from heaven, and he said in plain words: 'My father! Surely one of the immortal gods has made a new man of you, taller and stronger than I saw you before!'"

The ancient Greeks cleaned themselves for the reasons we do: to make themselves more comfortable and more attractive. They also bathed for reasons of health, since soaking in water was one of the major treatments in their physicians' limited arsenal. Hippocrates, the great fifth-century doctor, was a champion of baths,

believing that a judicious combination of cold and hot immersions could bring the body's all-important humours, or constituent liquids, into a healthy balance. Warm baths also prepared the body, by softening it, to receive nourishment and supposedly helped a variety of ailments, from headaches to the retention of urine. Those suffering from painful joints were prescribed cold showers, and female ills were treated with aromatic steam baths.

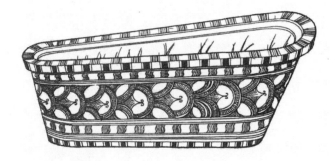

The world's earliest known bathtub—painted terra-cotta—dates from about 1700 B.C. and was found in the queen's apartments at the Palace of Knossos on Crete.

As *The Odyssey* makes clear, washing was a necessary prelude to prayer and libations. Sanctuaries normally had fonts of water at their entrances—not that intercourse with the gods required greater cleanliness than with humans, but the Greeks believed that any respectful relationship demanded neatness and cleanliness.

And, like almost all peoples, they bathed as part of a rite of passage. The first bath of the newborn and his mother was an important event, with the water sometimes brought from a propitious spring. Both the Greek bride and groom took a ceremonial bath on the eve or the morning of the wedding, washing off their single state and preparing to take on a married identity. And when someone died, not only was the body formally washed and anointed, but the chief mourners and attendants on the dead also needed purifying, and they washed after the funeral. Contact with the dead and with grief made you dirty, always symbolically and sometimes actually. When Achilles, in *The Iliad*, hears that his friend Patroclus has been killed, he acts out that connection: "Taking grimy dust in both his hands he poured it over his head, and befouled his fair face." He refuses to wash until Patroclus has received a proper funeral.

With an abundant coastline, long, sunny summers and mild winters, the Greeks must have bathed in the sea from the time they first settled in the southeastern tag end of Europe, around four thousand years ago. As early as 1400 B.C., they had invaded Crete, an advanced civilization with running water, drains and (at least in the royal palace at Knossos) bathtubs. No doubt Crete influenced their bathing customs, as did the other, more shadowy cultures they met in the course of their trading and colonizing, which extended into North Africa and Asia Minor.

By the Athenian golden age, in the fifth century B.C., the bathing habits the Greeks had forged from native and foreign sources were in place. An upper-

"Eureka!" ("I have found it!") cried the Greek scientist Archimedes in the third century B.C., jumping naked from a public bath and running exultantly through the streets of Syracuse. What he'd discovered in his bath—by noting that the water level rose when he entered it—was the formula needed to measure the volume of King Hieron II's crown.

middle-class or patrician Greek—let us call him Pittheus—could clean himself in various ways. His house would probably have a bathroom, more accurately a washing room, next to the kitchen. The essential equipment was a washstand, called a *labrum*, rather like a big birdbath on a base, positioned roughly at hip height. A servant would be sent to the household cistern or the nearest well for water and might be enlisted to pour it over Pittheus or his wife. The room might also include a terra-cotta hip bath—big enough for the bather to sit in with legs extended, but not to lie down. The bath was set into the floor and drained by a channel to the outside. Pittheus gave himself a speedy stand-up wash in the morning and reserved the time before dinner for a more thorough cleansing.

A poor man without a bathroom at home might use the nearest well for a daily wash and make an occasional visit to the public bath. Some of these baths were run by the government, others by private businessmen; they either were free or had a very low admission price. Water was warmed over a fire, as in *The Odyssey*, and the rooms were heated, when necessary, with braziers. At its most lavish, the public bath had separate rooms for cold, warm and steam baths—basic by later Roman standards but more than the prosperous Pittheus had at home. He, as well as his wife, patronized the public bath—for the steam bath, perhaps, or for the primitive showers, in which streams of water from spouts mounted on the wall doused his head and shoulders. (A servant on the other side of the wall poured the water into the spouts.) There were no hard and fast rules about the frequency of bath-house visits; some customers appeared daily, others once or twice a month.

The sociable Greek public bath, with individual hip baths arranged in a circle.

Another advantage of the public bath was its sociability. Pittheus bathed there in an individual hip bath, one of up to thirty arranged around the perimeter of a circular room. (It's an odd image, more like the bathing room of an orphanage or an infirmary than one intended for healthy adults.) The bath assistant, or bath man, provided customers with a cleansing substance, wood ashes or the absorbent clay called fuller's earth. Pittheus, who could afford it, brought his own perfumed cleansers. Games such as dice or knucklebones were available, as were wine and probably snacks. What was to become unimaginably sumptuous in the Imperial baths of Rome was modest and intimate in Pittheus's bathhouse, but the essentials—baths in a variety of temperatures in a public, recreational setting—were here.

HERODOTUS ON THE EGYPTIANS IN THE FIFTH CENTURY B.C.

"They always wear freshly washed linen clothes. They make a special point of this. They have themselves circumcised for reasons of cleanliness, preferring cleanliness to a more attractive appearance. Priests shave their bodies all over every day to keep off lice or anything else dirty."

In addition to home and bathhouse, Pittheus had a third place in which to wash—the gymnasium. One of the central Athenian institutions, the gymnasium was intended primarily as a place for middle- and upper-class young men to develop their physical strength and for older men to maintain it. Its rooms were arranged around an outdoor exercise field, with a running track nearby. Either after exercise or instead of it, men used the rooms and nearby groves (the original gymnasiums were outside the town centre) for discussions and lectures. The motto *mens sana in corpore sano*—a sound mind in a sound body—is Roman, but the Greeks were even more passionately devoted to the cult of the well-trained body and mind. To us it sounds incongruous that Plato's Academy and Aristotle's Lyceum, two of the earliest schools of philosophy, both founded in the fourth century, were part of working gymnasiums, but to the Greeks it was a natural combination.

In the gymnasium, bathing was a humble adjunct to exercise. Greek athletes, who exercised in the nude—gymnasium literally means "the naked place"—first oiled their bodies and covered them with a thin layer of dust or sand to prevent chills. After wrestling or running or playing ball games, the men and boys removed their oil and dust, now mingled with sweat, with a curved metal scraper called a strigil. After using the strigil, athletes could wash, either standing up at a basin or in a shower or a tub. Although hot water would have made their oil and grit much easier to remove, there is no evidence that the gymnasiums offered hot water before the Roman period. The manly rigour of cold-water bathing suited the gymnasium's spirit and reassured those Athenians who brooded about the weakening and feminizing effects of hot water.

And brood they did. The playwright Aristophanes makes fun of the perennial tug-of-war between austerity and luxury in his fifth-century comedy *The Clouds*. Strepsiades, an older man who remembers fondly his sloppy youth in the countryside—then there was "no bother about washing or keeping tidy"—has fallen under the sway of Socrates and the philosophers. Strepsiades likes the fact that they never shave, cut their hair or wash at the baths. He prefers their ways to those of his citified son, Phidippides, who is "always at the baths, pouring my money down the plug-hole." A character called Fair Argument agrees with the father, harking back to the good old days when boys sang rousing military melodies, sat up straight and would have scorned to cover their bodies in oil. That kind of no-frills upbringing, he insists, produced the hairy-chested men who fought at the battle of Marathon. These days, boys who indulge in hot baths shiver in the cold and waste their time gossiping like sissies.

A Greek's position on hot-water bathing spoke volumes about his values, and one of the most enduring debates in the history of cleanliness centres on the merits of cold versus hot water. Edward Gibbon, the eighteenth-century chronicler of the decline and fall of the Roman Empire, was convinced that hot baths were one of the principal reasons Rome weakened and fell. Victorian men, influenced by their classical Greek studies, believed that the British Empire was built on the bracingly cold morning bath. It's a prejudice with staying power, as indicated by the modern German expression for a man short on masculinity—a *Warmduscher*, or warm-showerer. Plato, who in *The Laws* reserves hot baths for the old and ill, would have sympathized with those judgments. But, in spite of Plato, young and healthy men became accustomed to warm water at the bathhouses, if not in the gymnasiums.

Young and healthy Athenians, that is, but not the militaristic, ascetic Spartans, who bathed their newborns in wine (perhaps with some sense that it acted as an antiseptic) but took baths infrequently after that. The biographer Plutarch tells the story of a Spartan who watched in disbelief as a slave drew water for the bath of Alcibiades, the Athenian general, and commented that he must be exceedingly dirty to need such a quantity of water. (That remark, always attributed to people who saw little need for washing, surfaces again and again over the centuries.) The Spartans' ninth-century lawgiver Lycurgus ordered the Spartans to eat in public mess halls in order to avoid dining at home on couches. If they grew accustomed to that self-indulgence, he warned, they would soon be in need of "long sleep, warm bathing, freedom from work, and, in a word, of as much care and attendance as if they were continually sick." Warm bathing keeps company in Lycurgus' list with the other mollycoddling tendencies he saw as threatening his city-state's military severity. Spartan self-discipline remained uncompromised by hot water, and Lycurgus' grim forecast never came true.

Theophrastus was an Athenian philosopher whose most enduring legacy is *The Characters*, a collection of thirty merciless portraits of irritating types, such as Pretentiousness, Officiousness and Buffoonery. Through them we get a keen sense of grooming standards at the beginning of the Hellenistic period, near the end of the fourth century B.C., as well as a satirical sketch of a society still rough and ready in many ways. Nastiness, for example, typifies "a neglect of the person which is painful to others" and goes about town in stained clothes, "shaggy as a beast," with hair all over his body. The parts not covered with hair display scabs and scaly deposits. His teeth are black and rotten. He goes to bed with his wife with unwashed hands (hands were to be washed after supper, which was eaten without forks or spoons), and when the oil he takes to the baths is rancid and thickened, he spits on his body to thin it.

Repulsive as Nastiness is, Theophrastus is no more fond of his foppish opposite, Petty Pride, who gets his hair cut "many times in the month," uses costly unguent for oil and has white teeth (a rarity and considered over-fussy). The middle way between the extremes of sloven-liness and vanity, Theophrastus suggests, is best. (So do the arbitrators of almost every period, at least in theory, but that prized middle ground shifts considerably.)

Public baths have always been a godsend to painters—lots of naked flesh and water—and to satirists—ample opportunity for bad behaviour. The baths as Theophrastus describes them are a flourishing institution with well-defined rules, all the better for unsocialized types to flout. Water and resonant surfaces must have been as tempting to the bathroom baritone 2,300 years ago as they are now, but it takes an oaf like Boorishness to give in to the temptation to sing in the bathhouse. It goes along with his other loutish, attention-seeking behaviour, such as confiding too much in servants and wearing shoes with clattering hobnails on the soles.

Disingenuously, Meanness complains that the oil his slave has brought to the baths is rancid, so that he can help himself to another man's. The Unconscionable, or tight-fisted, man is similar, always trying to get some-thing for nothing. That includes the drenching at the baths, for which the bath man was customarily paid. Unconscionable grabs the ladle, dips it into the cauldron of water, douses himself and runs off, shouting to the infuriated bath man, "I've had my bath, and no thanks to you for that!"

The Greeks appreciated water, but the Romans adored it. In their gymnasiums, the Greeks bathed as a necessary conclusion to exercise. The Romans reversed the priorities: they exercised because it made their baths even more enjoyable. "Hedonist" and "sybarite" come to us from the Greek—perhaps because the Greeks so distrusted those types—but the terms were better suited to the Romans, who inspired and enjoyed the over-the-top luxuries of the great Imperial baths.

But first, the characteristic Roman bath—heated and communal, as opposed to cold and individual—had to be born. It probably evolved in the region of Campania, in southern Italy on the Tyrrhenian Sea, sometime in the third century B.C. The area was a lively meeting place for Greek, Etruscan, Italian and Roman influences, and it was here that the Greek bath mingled with local and imported traditions. By the second century B.C., the Roman bath had become an ordinary, expected part of everyday life. As Roman customs insinuated themselves into the Hellenistic world, the Roman-style bath triumphed even in Greece. By the first century B.C., gymnasiums, the symbols of stoic Greek athleticism, were adding hot water.

"Baths, wine, and sex ruin our bodies, but they are the essence of life—baths, wine, and sex."
—Epitaph on the tomb of Titus Claudius Secundus, first century A.D.

The oldest more-or-less intact Roman baths are the Stabian Baths at Pompeii, dating from around 140 B.C. Pompeii had a population of 20,000 when Vesuvius erupted in A.D. 79, so the Stabian's small-windowed, cave-like changing room must have been crowded during peak hours. Here the bather stored his street clothes in one of the cubicles, to be guarded either by a personal slave or a member of the bathhouse staff. (Even so, theft was common.) Outside the changing room is the exercise yard, a big grassy space ringed on three sides by a portico. In this space, which was not for women, male bathers, oiled and usually naked, would work up a light sweat playing ball, wrestling or running. After his exercise, the bather would proceed to a moderately warm room, where he continued to perspire. Usually in the warm room, he would scrape off the accumulated oil, dirt and perspiration with his strigil. An attendant or fellow bather would strigil his back. In the next chamber, the hot room, he might plunge into a pool of hot water or might just sprinkle water on himself from a basin on a pedestal. Finally came a room with a shockingly cold plunge pool. That could be followed by another oiling, a massage and a final scraping with the strigil. Oils and perfumes are frequently mentioned as accessories to the bath, but not soap. In any case, a thorough scraping of oiled and sweaty skin with a strigil and

Rather than using soap and a washcloth, the Greeks and Romans scraped oil and sweat off their bodies with a metal implement called a strigil. The small canister held oil.

a rinse with hot water probably removed as much dirt as would soap and warm water.

With its waters of contrasting temperatures, the Roman bath has more than a passing likeness to another social bath, the Finnish sauna, where the sauna takers alternately sweat and cool down with hot air, cold water and, in season, snow. The Roman bath and the *hamam*, or Turkish bath, have an even closer family resemblance since, as we shall see, the *hamam* descends directly from its Roman parent.

A basic Roman bathhouse needed a warm room, a hot room and a cold room. More elaborate ones might include a chamber with intense dry heat, and a separate chamber for oiling and massage. A special scraping room and an open-air swimming pool were also possibilities, but these were frills. In theory (and unlike the Greeks' baths, which followed no special order), a Roman bath proceeded from warm to hot to icy cold, with exercise at the start and at least one scraping. In reality, the bather could modify the order as he wished. The architecture of the later Imperial baths reflected the ideal progression. But in the more modest bathhouses of the Roman republic, up to the end of the first century B.C., rooms were added haphazardly as a new treatment became popular or as the clientele grew.

Roman men adopted the Greek habit of bathing after work, which meant about two or three in the afternoon, corresponding to the eighth or ninth hour in the Roman time scheme. (The Roman workday began early in the morning, certainly by six o'clock, and was effectively over by mid-afternoon.) In the Republic, when the sexes were more reliably segregated for bathing than they were in the Empire, women would have either separate bath chambers or separate hours, usually in the morning. Slaves and servants, too, often bathed in the morning so they would be available to escort their masters to the bathhouse in the afternoon. The typical price for men was the smallest copper coin, called the *quadrans*, a quarter of a cent. Women might pay twice that amount, but children, soldiers and sometimes slaves were admitted free of charge.

Close to the Stabian Baths was Pompeii's biggest brothel. The combination of warm water, nudity and relaxation meant that baths and brothels tended to be near neighbours; sometimes prostitutes offered their services on the second floor of a bath. In another Pompeiian bathhouse, the Suburban Baths, the link between bathhouses and sex is literally painted on the wall. In the intimate, ochre-coloured changing room of these first-century A.D. baths, the wooden compartments where bathers left their clothes are long gone. But on the wall above where they stood are eight unblushingly bawdy frescoes—a woman, brandishing a fish, about to be penetrated by a man; women giving and receiving oral sex; a threesome (two men and a woman) locked in close conjunction; and other similarly frisky scenes. They may be advertising services available nearby, or perhaps they were simply meant to contribute to the baths' pleasure-loving, sensuous atmosphere. The frescoes, dashed off with charm and style, are disarmingly direct—and utterly unlike our idea of suitable

THE STORY OF SOAP, PART I

A mixture of animal fats and ashes sounds neither clean nor pleasant, but that is how soap was made for most of human history. Clay cylinders dating from about 2800 B.C., discovered during excavations in Babylon, contain a soapy substance, and the writing on the cylinders confirms that fat and ashes were boiled together to produce it. What actually got washed with soap is less clear. The Egyptians, whose soap contained milder vegetable oils as well as animal fats, used it for washing their bodies. The Greeks and Romans did not: they preferred coating themselves with sand and oil and scraping it off with a strigil. Although soap, probably made with olive oil, was a regular part of the Turkish bath, or *hamam*, that aspect of washing did not travel to Europe when the bath returned in the Middle Ages. Europeans were still boiling animal fats and ashes together to make a soap that was used to wash clothes and floors but was too harsh for bodies. Toilet soap, made from olive oil, was manufactured in small batches in pioneering soap businesses in Marseilles, Italy and Spain (where the soap made in Castile was so prized that eventually all fine white soap made with olive oil was called Castile soap), but it was a luxury and beyond the budgets of most people in the Middle Ages. They made do with plain water, to which they sometimes added herbs believed to have cleansing or medicinal qualities.

decoration for a commercial building used by men, women and probably children.

The Romans considered cleanliness a social virtue. (Up to a point, so did the Greeks, as Theophrastus makes clear, but the Romans were more preoccupied with grooming, and they raised the bar when it came to hygienic standards.) The Latin word for "washed" or "bathed" is *lautus*, which became by extension the adjective for a refined, grand or elegant person. And more and more, as the daily bath was knitted tightly into their schedules, cleanliness—achieved *their* way—became a *Roman* virtue. Modern-day Japanese people report that what they miss most when living abroad is not familiar food or language or people: it is the Japanese bath, with its particular protocol of pre-washing before a communal soaking in extraordinarily hot water. Similarly, the Roman bath became one of the defining marks of Roman-ness, one of the central ways they separated themselves from outsiders, and one of the first civilities with which they welcomed conquered peoples into the far-flung Roman family. When Agricola became governor of cold, foggy Britain in A.D. 76, he knew what the shaggy and unkempt natives needed. He introduced them, in short order, to public buildings, togas, Latin and baths. It was the essential shortcut to Romanization.

FIRST-CENTURY A.D. GRAFFITI
"Two companions were here and, since they had a thoroughly terrible attendant called Epaphroditus, threw him out on the street not a moment too soon. They then spent 105½ sesterces most agreeably while they fucked."

—At the Suburban Baths, Herculaneum, in a room off the vestibule (possibly a brothel)

As in Greece, some of the baths of the Roman Republic were private enterprises and some were owned by the city. The unassuming Republican bath was a beloved institution but no marvel. The Imperial bath, a grandiose pleasure palace built and maintained by the government, left even jaded Romans slack-jawed with awe. The great age of Imperial baths began around 25 B.C., when Agrippa, the designated successor of Augustus, opened the baths that bore his name. Set in gardens that included an artificial lake and a canal, the Baths of Agrippa were notable for their size (the buildings measured at their largest about 400 feet by 330 feet) and their splendour. When Agrippa died in 12 B.C., he left the baths to the people of Rome. All this—scale, grandeur and the bequest to the Romans—was new, and it set the standard for the Imperial baths to come. Agrippa's were the first *thermae*, as the dazzling, multi-functional Imperial baths came to be called, to distinguish them from a *balneum*, a plainer, more workaday bathhouse.

At the same time as the *thermae* grew more and more extravagant, the satirist Juvenal coined the phrase "bread and circuses" to describe the government's attempts to buy the people's favour with cheap food and mindless entertainment. Vastly more expensive than bread and circuses—they required not only building but costly maintenance—the *thermae* were like them on some levels but, to the Roman

BATHROOM BARITONE

"Then he sat back as though exhausted, and enticed by the acoustics of the bath, he opened his drunken mouth as wide as the ceiling, and began to murder the songs of Menecrates—or so those who could catch the words said."

—Petronius, *Satyricon*

mind, far more substantial. Becoming *lautus,* or bathed, was essential to a person's self-respect, as well as his health.

An emperor would usually build his *thermae* at the start of a dynasty or after a civil war to signal his magnanimity and his ability to provide the best of Roman lives for his people. Nero built ambitious *thermae,* famous for their very hot water, around A.D. 60. Impressive as they were, it was only in 109, when the Baths of Trajan were built, that successive emperors began to pull out all the stops. In the Baths of Trajan, the central bath block was surrounded by a perimeter of buildings that included club rooms, libraries, lecture halls and exercise rooms. It was a virtual village, the most complete bath domain Rome had seen.

The two biggest *thermae,* the Baths of Caracalla (216–17) and the Baths of Diocletian (298–306), were reckoned among the wonders of Rome and the fate of their remains gives some idea of their magnificence. When Pope Paul III ransacked the Baths of Caracalla in the sixteenth century to decorate his Farnese Palace, the spoils—marbles, medals, bronzes and bas-reliefs— were enough to furnish a museum (the Farnese Collection, now mainly in the Naples Archaeological Museum). In the twentieth century, the ruins of the hot room alone housed productions of Verdi's opera *Aida* that included chariots, horses and camels, as well as the cast and audience. Even more colossal, Diocletian's *thermae* were estimated to hold three thousand bathers. In 1561, Michelangelo converted the cold room into the nave of the Basilica Santa Maria degli Angeli. The ruins of the *thermae* are now home as well to the

A nineteenth-century re-creation of the Baths of Diocletian, the many-splendoured
Imperial bath, which also functioned as a gymnasium, club and town square.

National Roman Museum and the Oratory of Saint
Bernard.

As baths and their facilities grew more elaborate,
Romans often spent most of their leisure hours there.
With pools, exercise yards, gardens, libraries, meeting
rooms and snack bars, the bath became a multi-purpose
meeting point, a place to make connections, do business,
flirt, talk politics, eat and drink. Prostitutes, healers and
beauticians often had premises in the bath complex or in
the shops around its perimeter, so it was possible to have
sex, a medical treatment and a haircut as part of a regular
visit. Although well-born men used their favourite bath
as English aristocrats would later use their London club,
the bathhouse was also the most democratic Roman
institution. Unlike the Greek gymnasium, which was
limited to middle-class and upper-class men, the Roman

bath accommodated men and women, slaves and freedmen, rich and poor. A Roman, at least by the first century B.C., when there were 170 baths in the capital, had plentiful choice but usually settled on one as a regular haunt. It was common, when meeting a man, to ask where he bathed.

The purposes that cafés, town squares, clubs, gymnasiums, country clubs and spas served in other societies, including ours, were fulfilled here. Imagine a superbly equipped YMCA that covered some blocks, with gyms, pools, ball courts and meeting rooms. Then add onto it the massage and treatment rooms of a fancy spa and the public rooms and grounds of a resort. Finally, give it a fee structure that would allow the poorest people to use its facilities. That approximates, but does not equal, an Imperial bathhouse.

Although the emperors had lavish baths in their palaces, most of them bathed in one of the bathhouses occasionally, if only for the sake of public relations. The most famous anecdote about an emperor at the bathhouse involves Hadrian, in the second century A.D. One day, the story goes, he recognized an old army crony in the hot room. The veteran was rubbing himself up against the marble wall, and when Hadrian asked why, he explained that he lacked the money to hire an attendant to strigil him. Hadrian immediately gave him money and slaves. The next day, when the bathers heard that the emperor was in the baths, a

BATHHOUSE CAMARADERIE

"Skinship" is the approving Japanese expression for the close relationship that is built by bathing together. In Japan, work groups often bathe communally as part of a professional retreat. In Finland, where the sauna is a national institution, when government leaders cannot agree on an issue, they continue their discussion in the sauna.

number of them began rubbing themselves ostentatiously against the walls. Hadrian suggested that they take turns strigiling each other.

The rosy-coloured vision of the baths in which slave and emperor soak side by side before consulting the bathhouse libraries and discussing philosophy in the lecture rooms, called *exedrae,* is largely wishful thinking. The libraries and *exedrae* were smaller and less frequented than the ball courts. The baths were notorious (some more than others) for the stealing, drunkenness and unsavoury sex that went on under their roofs. Social distinctions naturally persisted there, in that the rich could pay extra for the use of particular rooms or services. They could and did flaunt their wealth, swanning in with a retinue of servants bearing costly flagons and perfume dispensers, finely wrought strigils and sumptuous towels.

But for the men and women who lived in Rome's dark apartment blocks, without water or toilets or much space, an afternoon at the bathhouse was a delight. Even the relatively modest quarters of a Republican bath were luxurious to them, while the huge, light-filled Imperial baths gave them an intimate experience of Rome at its most splendid. Besides, poverty was not always a disadvantage at the baths. Far from making everyone equal, nudity imposed

The accumulated sweat, dirt and oil that a famous athlete or gladiator strigiled off himself was sold to his fans in small vials. Some Roman women reportedly used it as a face cream.

Three technological innovations allowed the sturdy
Republican bath to evolve into the sybaritic Imperial one. The
early baths obtained their water from wells, cisterns and
springs, but by 100 B.C., nine aqueducts provided each
Roman with 300 gallons of water a day, four times the average
consumed by a modern North American. The baths were
among the aqueducts' most demanding and privileged users,
served from mains connected to the bottom of the tank,
where the water flowed with greatest force.

From the bath's reservoir, water was sent, by means of
pumps and lead pipes, to the furnace and then to the bath's
various chambers. The pools and the rooms were heated by
the second innovation, a system called a hypocaust.
Developed at the end of the second century B.C., the
hypocaust heated a hollow space underneath the floors and
behind the walls with hot air generated from a furnace. The
floor, supported over the cavity by short piles of bricks or
tiles, could become so hot that bathers needed sandals to
protect their feet. The bath's hottest rooms were positioned
directly over the furnace, with the cold room and the dressing
room placed farthest away.

An early bath could be made of squared stones. By the first
century B.C., the invention of Roman concrete, an amalgam
of brick fragments and stones in a mortar of lime, sand and
volcanic dust, made increasingly large, sophisticated
buildings possible. The development of the concrete vaulted
roof, in particular, led to the untrammelled spaces that made
a visit to the Imperial baths such an impressive experience.

its own hierarchy, one that frequently favoured the toned body of the poorest freedman or slave over that of the indulged, unexercised rich man.

Prosperous Romans also built private baths in their townhouses and, more frequently, in their country villas. Although lodged in private houses, these too were public, in that family and guests bathed together in a suite of rooms that usually included tepid, hot and cold chambers. Far from being a private hideaway, the bath suite was often positioned near the main entrance of the villa—a reception room as public as the dining room.

A bath at home had obvious advantages, but a family that owned one would also use the public baths for their greater size and variety of facilities. Pliny the Younger had baths in his Laurentine villa, but he was pleased that the nearest village had three public baths, "which is a great convenience if you arrive unexpectedly, or if you are staying such a very short time that you do not feel inclined to have the fires in your own bath lit." Few Romans wanted to deprive themselves of the convivial fun of the public bath. After his outrageous, wine-sodden dinner party, Trimalchio and his guests, in Petronius' novel *Satyricon*, retreat to his private baths to sober up, but before dinner, he had gone, as usual, to the public baths.

A bathhouse in the first century A.D. appealed to all the senses—the smell of the oils and perfumes as well as of the bathers before and after their baths; the feel of the waters, the strigil, the massage, the towels; the taste

GROOMING ADVICE FOR WOMEN
I was about to warn you against rank
  goatish armpits
And bristling hair on your legs,
But I'm not instructing hillbilly girls
  from the Caucasus. . . .
—Ovid, *Art of Love*

of the wine, oysters, anchovies, eggs and other foods that were for sale; the sight of the architecture, with its arches, domes and endless spaces lined with marble and works of art, as well as of the humans, either nude or decked out to impress the crowds. As for the noise, Seneca's famous account of the bathhouse hubbub brings its cacophony to life.

> I live over a public bathhouse. Now imagine to yourself every type of sound which can make you sick of your ears: when hearty types are exercising by swinging dumb-bells around—either working hard at it or pretending to—I hear their grunts, and then a sharp hissing whenever they let out the breath they've been holding. Or again, my attention is caught by someone who is content to relax under an ordinary massage and I hear the smack of a hand whacking his shoulders, the sound changing as the hand comes down flat or curved. If on top of all that there is a game-scorer beginning to call out the score, I've had it! Then there's the brawler, the thief caught in the act, the man who likes the sound of his voice in the bath, the folk who leap into the pool with an enormous splash. Besides those whose voices are, if nothing else, natural, think of the depilator constantly utter-ing his shrill and piercing cry to advertise his services: he is never silent except when pluck-ing someone's armpits and forcing him to yell instead. Then there are the various cries of

the drink-seller; there's the sausage seller and the pastry-cook and all the eating-house pedlars, each marketing his wares with his own distinctive cry.

The scene at Seneca's *balneum* sounds like a vivid human comedy but not necessarily a decadent one. Still, the anxieties about effeminacy and softness that dogged the Greeks worried the Romans too. Writers in the Empire often looked back nostalgically to the Republic, when manly men would have scorned a hot bath that stole hours out of every day. Seneca visited the seaside villa of Scipio Africanus, the general who had defeated Hannibal and the Carthaginians in the Second Punic War, some 250 years earlier. The letter in which he describes the war hero's bath contrasts Scipio's hardy habits with the self-indulgent preciousness of his own time.

The baths of Seneca's Rome glistened with vaulted glass roofs, silver faucets and marble finishes imported from Egypt and Africa. Scipio, who was dirty from the plowing and other farm work he did when not at war, cleaned himself in a narrow, dark bath, designed to conserve heat. "Who is there nowadays who could bear to bathe in such a place?" Seneca asks.

> Some people nowadays condemn Scipio as being extremely uncouth because he did not let the daylight into his hot water tub through wide windows, because he did not boil himself in a well-lit room, and because he didn't linger in the hot tub until he was stewed. "What an

unfortunate man!" they say. "He didn't know how to live well. He bathed in water which was unfiltered, which in fact was often murky and, after a heavy rain, was almost muddy." But it didn't matter much to Scipio whether he bathed in murky water, because he came to the baths to wash off sweat, not oily perfumes!

Even more unsavoury to Seneca's contemporaries, Scipio didn't take a daily bath. In his time, people washed their arms and legs, which got dirty from farm labour, every day, and their whole bodies only once a week. "Of course," Seneca continues, "someone will at this point say, 'Sure, but they were very smelly men.' And what do you think they smelled of? Of the army, of farm work, and of manliness!'"

The poet Martial was a few generations younger than Seneca, born in about A.D. 40, and less inclined to berate his era for self-indulgence. He's an unflaggingly racy guide to the baths, with his own satirical hobbyhorses—chiefly social climbing and sex, the latter of which often involves descriptions of the physical attributes of his fellow bathers. As they did for Theophrastus four centuries earlier, the baths afforded Martial excellent views of people's foibles and peccadilloes. His portrait of Aper is typically etched in acid. Before he inherited money, Aper decried the drinking of wine in the baths. A bow-legged slave carried his towel there and a "a one-eyed old crone" guarded his clothes in the changing room. Now that he's rich, the formerly abstemious man leaves the baths drunk every night. And the homely servants are a thing of the past:

Aper insists on handsome slaves and delicately chased gold cups.

Above all, the bath for Martial is a place to meet people, cadge a dinner invitation or offer one, and judge others as they do the same things. Poor pathetic Selius, one of Martial's targets, would do anything rather than dine at home. He darts from fashionable shops to the temple of Isis to no fewer than seven baths, all the while angling for a dinner invitation. Another man is equally assiduous in his invitation-seeking efforts:

> I defy you to escape him at the baths.
> He'll help you arrange your towels;
> While you're combing your hair, scanty as it
>   may be,
> He'll remark how much you resemble Achilles;
> He'll pour your wine and accept the dregs;
> He'll admire your build and spindly legs,
> He'll wipe the perspiration from your face,
> Until you finally say, "Okay, let's go to my place."

Because the baths took up so much of a Roman's day, vignettes from the bathhouse appear again and again in Martial's poems—anecdotes of ladies bathing with their male slaves, of drunken bathing parties, of persistent worries about the cleanliness of the bathwater, of the dinner one Aemilius made at the baths, including lettuce, eggs and lizard-fish. When the poet gripes about a too-demanding friend, one of his offences is to expect an exhausted Martial to accompany him to the Baths of Agrippa at the tenth hour, or later, even though Martial regularly bathes earlier, at the Baths of Titus. In one of Martial's funniest protests, addressed to his friend Ligurinus, who is "too much of a poet," we meet a man who can't stop reading his work to his friends—while they're running, while they're walking, while they're using the latrine or sitting in the dining room. "I fly to the warm baths," Martial sighs, "you buzz in my ear; I make for the swimming bath: I am not allowed to swim."

The intimate, revealing work of caring for one's body is made to order for Martial's satirical purposes. Take poor Thais, who smells dreadful and tries to cover her "reek" with other odours. Stripped, she enters the bath "green with depilatory, or is hidden behind a plaster of chalk and vinegar, or is covered with three or four layers of sticky bean-flour [to remove wrinkles]." It's to be hoped that Thais stays out of plunge and swimming baths when she is so bedaubed, but in any case, when it comes to her unfortunate odour, it is all fruitless: "Thais, do what she will, smells of Thais."

The baths are also a fine place to assess the other patrons' physical attributes. A well-endowed man is cause for comment:

> It's easy to tell
> by the roar of applause
> in which of the baths
> Maron is bathing.

To some extent, nudity was optional when men and women bathed together in Martial's day, but he complains when a woman is clothed. When he compliments Galla on her hands and legs, she promises him, "Naked I shall please you more." Still, she resists bathing with him, and he asks, "Surely you are not afraid, Galla, that I shall not please you?" Similarly, Saufeia says she wants to have a liaison with him but shies away from a bath. He wonders, do her breasts sag, is her belly lined with furrows, or is there some other imperfection? Or, worst of all, is she beautiful—and hence stupid?

The old strictures against men and women bathing together in the nude seem to have retained some latent force, even if they were often not honoured. Martial writes teasingly to a matron that up to this point, his book has been written for her. But now, he warns her, he's writing for himself: "A gymnasium, warm baths, a running ground are in this part of the book; depart, we are stripping; forbear to look on naked men." Then he says, mischievously, that he knows he's piqued her interest.

Martial's voice is usually cynical and ironical. But his famous definition of the good life is sincere. He needs, he writes, "a taverner, and a butcher and a bath, a barber, and a draught-board and pieces, and a few books—but to be chosen by me—a single comrade not too unlettered, and a tall boy and not early bearded, and a girl dear to my boy—warrant these to me, Rufus, even at Bututi, and keep to yourself Nero's warm baths."

The needs of the body come first—the means to drink, eat, bathe (at a *balneum*) and be barbered. Then social and mental life—a game, books and a compatible friend. With these and a servant boy and girl, he is content, even in Bututi, an obscure town in Calabria. The two words Martial uses for "bath" are significant: Nero's grandiose *thermae* count for nothing, compared with his necessary and beloved *balneum*, a humble, non-Imperial, neighbourhood bathhouse. Martial's unpretentious *balneum* was in a tradition that stretches back to the Greeks' simple bathhouses, while the *thermae* were bravura demonstrations of the Romans' mechanical skill and taste for luxury. Luckily for Martial, he died around A.D. 103 without realizing that the days of both kinds of bath were numbered.

A larger, even more unimaginable future event was the end of the mighty Roman Empire, as well as the appearance of an obscure Galilean preacher who became the founder of a world religion. The decline of the baths was due more directly to the fall of Rome than to the rise of Christianity, but there is no denying that the three events—one apparently mundane but close to the heart of Roman civilization, and two with vast, long-term consequences—were intertwined.

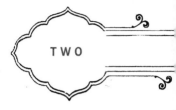

BATHED IN CHRIST

200-1000

An Arab gardener in *A Thousand and One Nights* accounted quite simply for the dirtiness of the Christians: "They never wash, for, at their birth, ugly men in black garments pour water over their heads, and this ablution, accompanied by strange gestures, frees them from all obligation of washing for the rest of their lives." Of course, the Arab's claim that baptism absolved Christians from further cleansing was partly a joke, but it suggests how Christians were seen by medieval Muslims.

Outsiders to the Christian tradition have frequently been puzzled by what they see as its indifference to cleanliness. When the twentieth-century English writer Reginald Reynolds was in India, an observant Hindu once asked him about the Christian teaching on personal hygiene. Reynolds answered that there was no such thing. The Hindu protested that that was impossible:

> For every religion has a code for the closet, how cleansing is to be performed, when and in what manner the hands shall be washed, also concerning baths and the cleaning of teeth. Nevertheless, I told him . . . we have none such. How so, then, says he, have you no teachings at all in these matters? To which I replied that our priests taught theology, but left hygiene to the individual conscience.

The Hindu's surprise was justified, for Christianity's unconcern with cleanliness is unusual among world religions. There is no single obvious reason for that omission. The first Christians were Jews, people who were expected to be clean for reasons of health as well as out of respect for others. But their laws were much more specific about ritual purity than about physical cleanliness. Jews were obliged to wash away in a ritual bath the pollution caused by immoral acts, such as adultery, homosexuality and murder, as well as by innocent activities and conditions such as sexual intercourse with their spouse, contact with the dead, genital discharges and childbirth. During the time of Christ, that web of obligatory purifications was tightening and expanding.

> **MORE MURDER IN THE BATH**
>
> "Odious to himself and to mankind, Constans [ca. A.D. 323–50] perished by domestic, perhaps by episcopal, treason in the capital of Sicily. A servant who waited in the bath, after pouring warm water on his head, struck him violently with the vase. He fell, stunned by the blow and suffocated by the water; and his attendants, who wondered at the tedious delay, beheld with indifference the corpse of their lifeless emperor."
>
> —Edward Gibbon, *The Decline and Fall of the Roman Empire*

The Jesus who appears in the gospels was either rebellious or indifferent when it came to some of the most important of these impure states. In the course of his healing, he touched the dead, as well as people with leprosy-like conditions and a woman with a "bloody issue" (vaginal discharge)—all forbidden. He scandalized the Pharisees, one of the strictest groups when it came to ritual purification, by belittling one of their

Detail from *The Birth of the Virgin*, by Pietro Lorenzetti. Bathing a newborn baby, whether the Virgin Mary, Jesus or a saint, was a favourite theme in medieval religious painting.

central practices, washing their hands before eating. Mark's gospel describes their dismay when Jesus' disciples eat bread with unwashed hands: "For the Pharisees, and all the Jews, except they wash their hands oft, eat not, holding the tradition of their elders" (Mark 7:1–23). In Luke's version of the story, it is Jesus who sits down to eat without washing, shocking his Pharisee host (Luke 11:37–54). Jesus' response in both accounts is to belittle the custom and accuse the Pharisees of hypocrisy. A man is not defiled by what goes into him, he says in Mark's gospel, only by what comes out of him. "Now do ye Pharisees make clean the outside of the cup and the platter," he retorts in Luke's account, "but your inward part is full of ravening and wickedness" (Luke 11:39). It's the familiar Christian dichotomy between outer and inner, between flesh and spirit, between the letter of the law and its essence, applied to ritual handwashing. The handwashing stories were traditionally read by Christians as examples of the Pharisees' badgering Jesus with the minutiae of the law, but they also point to what became a telling separation between Judaism and Christianity.

Scholars have advanced various reasons to explain Jesus' indifference to ritual purity. His thinking may have been influenced by his origins in a rural, Galilean branch of Judaism that was relatively unconcerned with ritual purity. His teachings on morality may also have inclined him away from ritual cleansing, for he does not seem to have believed that the innocently "impure," menstruating women or men with a discharge, for example, needed purification. Nor were the morally culpable absolved, in Jesus' view, by immersing themselves in a ritual pool—they also had to repent. As a further

St. John baptizes Jesus. Baptism is one of Christianity's rare ritual washings, and until the seventh century it involved a full immersion. Because pagan rituals marking the summer solstice often included water and immersion, the Church christianized them by celebrating the feast of St. John the Baptist near the solstice, on June 24.

complication, the speech and actions of the Jesus we meet in the gospels may well have been doctored to suit the attitudes of the early Church.

So the reasons behind Jesus' attitude to ritual purification remain stubbornly opaque. And whatever they were, they do not lead in a straight line to a Christian devaluation of cleanliness. Ritual purity is not the same as cleanliness. You can be physically clean and ritually impure, just as you can be physically dirty and ritually pure. But it is mostly anthropologists who place ritual purity and physical cleanliness in watertight containers. To the average person, purity, which was good, simply felt more like cleanliness than like uncleanliness; impurity, on the other hand, almost inevitably had connotations of uncleanliness. Also, since people emerged from a ritual immersion or even a ritual handwashing cleaner than before, there was a natural connection between the symbolic act and the physical result.

Jesus' indifference to ritual purity accorded with what became a wider Christian distrust or neglect of the body. Somewhat paradoxically, the Jewish purity laws, especially at the time of Christ, emphasized the body's importance: the purity or impurity of the body at any given moment was a significant matter. Within a few hundred years of Christ's death, Christianity had gone in a different direction. It discounted the body as much as possible, devaluing the flesh so as to concentrate on the spirit.

By the end of the first century, the Christians began to pull away from distinctive Jewish laws about forbidden foods, circumcision and the keeping of the Sabbath. Gradually, too, they distanced themselves from the Jewish laws of purification. Some of the Jewish obligations survived longer than others in Christian communities. Early Christian brides continued to take a ceremonial bath before the wedding, as did Jewish women, but this particular custom has a psychological, worldwide appeal. As late as the third century, Christians in Palestine and Syria had to be told that a ritual bath was unnecessary after intercourse—an indication that the Talmudic law was still being followed in those places. The Christian "churching" ceremony, in which a woman received a special blessing some weeks after childbirth, was an option in the Catholic church until the 1960s, and is a vestige of the ritual purification bath Jewish women took after childbirth. Similarly, Greek Orthodox women do not receive communion when they are menstruating, another remnant of the Jewish belief that menstruation renders a woman impure.

As the Arab gardener wryly noted, baptism is a ritual washing—the most thorough one that Christians undergo, which until the seventh century involved a full immersion (as it still does for some denominations). The Catholic custom of dipping the fingers in holy water on entering a church and blessing oneself echoes purificatory handwashing, as does the priest's ceremonial handwashing during the mass. Aside from that, Jewish ritual purification left few lasting echoes in Christianity.

YET MORE MURDER IN THE BATH
Fausta, the wife of Constantine, was accused of having an affair with a slave. On Constantine's orders, she was suffocated by the extraordinarily hot steam of her bath in about A.D. 326.

The early Christians lived under the rule of the Romans, whose baths presented a more obvious dilemma for the early Church. The Roman bath had nothing to do with ritual purity and much to do with hedonism, if not downright sin. And yet it was woven so firmly into everyday life that it seemed impossible to do without it. When the second-century theologian Tertullian wanted to persuade the pagans in Carthage how normal and unthreatening the Christians were, he began with their participation in three central Roman institutions. "We live with you in the world," he wrote, "abjuring neither forum nor shambles [market] nor bath." Before and after his conversion to Christianity, the baths were a routine part of St. Augustine's life in fourth-century North Africa. In its first centuries, depending on local conditions and the beliefs of the current bishop or pope, Christianity negotiated a tentative coexistence with the Roman custom.

Naturally enough, mixed nude bathing was forbidden, although this was not immediately clear to everyone. Cyprian, the bishop of Carthage, scolded a devout Christian woman who patronized a mixed bath, which was apparently an unremarkable practice in third-century Carthage. The woman, who had taken a vow of chastity, responded stoutly that she was not responsible for the motives of people who might look upon her nudity: "As for me," she wrote, "my only concern is to refresh and bathe my poor little body." Nonsense, Cyprian answered: "Such a bath sullies; it does not purify and it does not cleanse the limbs, but stains them. You gaze upon no one immodestly, but you yourself are looked at immodestly. You do not corrupt your eyes with foul delight, but in delighting others, you yourself are corrupted." In other words, Christians were responsible for the lust they excited in others.

PUBLIC CONVENIENCE
In the fourth century, St. Melania, the abbess of a women's monastery on the Mount of Olives in Jerusalem, successfully petitioned for a bath in the nunnery. Until then, her nuns had been walking down into the city and washing in the public bathhouses.

Most church authorities did allow Christians to patronize single-sex baths for the proper motives. Clement of Alexandria was a second-century teacher and writer whose views on most subjects were balanced and moderate for his time. In his guide to Christian thought and behaviour, the *Paedagogus* (Instructor), he writes that there are four reasons for visiting the baths—cleanliness, warmth, health and pleasure. Christians may not bathe for pleasure, nor (although this is a less serious objection) for warmth. Women may bathe for cleanliness and health, and men only for health—probably because men could wash in the river, which would be immodest for women. Clement prized the democratic nature of the baths, chiding ostentatious customers who arrived with a parade of servants, "because the bath [has] to be common and the same for everybody." For the same reason, bathers should wash their own bodies, not relying on the care of an attendant.

Even the austere St. John Chrysostom (ca. 344–407) classed bathing, like eating, with the necessities of life. Chrysostom's ascetic credentials were impeccable: he had lived for four years as the disciple of a hermit, and then for two years alone in a cave, where he fasted and studied the Bible. Only the gastric difficulties caused by fasting brought him back to Antioch. But when the emperor Theodosius punished Antioch by closing its bathhouses in 387, Chrysostom protested that giving up bathing was too great a hardship and that he worried about the old, the sick, children and nursing mothers who relied on the bathhouse to safeguard their health.

Bishop Sissinius was asked why he bathed twice. "Because I couldn't bathe three times," he answered.

When his outspoken reforms as the archbishop of Constantinople angered the emperor, who sent him into exile, the priests loyal to Chrysostom staged a protest in the public baths. It was customary to baptize new

Christians on the eve of Easter, and the baths were convenient for a ceremony that was still performed at this date with a full immersion. To this annual event, the priests gathered large numbers of laypeople sympathetic to Chrysostom, and they spent the Easter vigil reading from the Scriptures as well as baptizing the converted. During Chrysostom's three-month journey into exile, his sadistic guard knew that refusing the prisoner the "refreshment of a bath" whenever they reached a city with a bathhouse would be a particular torment, and Chrysostom was forced to travel unbathed. But even a saint who appreciated the baths recognized that they held abundant temptations. Chrysostom expected Christians to make the sign of the cross when entering one, to guard against its dangers, and crosses were placed over bathhouse doors with the same aim in mind.

Christianity's relationship to the body and so to cleanliness was complicated. On the positive side, the body was intended to be a temple of God. Parts of it—the saliva of saints, for example, or the fluid that magically sprang from their breasts—could work miracles, or be worshipped, in the form of relics. At the same time, the body's potential for temptation provoked suspicion, if not hostility. A darker, more self-denying strain surfaced early in the Christian era, although opposition to the baths began in earnest only in the third century.

Spartan types, such as St. Jerome (ca. 340–420), shrank even from the most virtuous private baths. One

BLESSED BODIES
St. Lutgard's saliva healed the sick, as did the crumbs chewed by St. Colette of Corbie. A man sent from England to the Netherlands for St. Lidwina's washing water; he wanted to apply it to his afflicted leg. The water from St. Eustadiola's face- and handwashing cured the blind and healed other illnesses.

of Jerome's crusades was the encouragement of lifelong virginity for women. To that end, he urged a low-stimulus life, with a meagre diet of mostly vegetables and mild herbs. Because heat was thought to be conducive to sexual desire, wine (which heated the blood) and hot baths were forbidden to virgins.

Clement of Alexandria forbade Christians to entertain in their private baths. Even without guests, another problem remained: the bathers "strip naked before their slaves, and are rubbed by them, giving to the crouching menial liberty to lust, by permitting fearless handling."

In addition to the heat-sex connection, bathing was suspect because it might provoke a young woman's interest in her appearance. The right-thinking virgin, as St. Jerome puts it, "by a deliberate squalor . . . makes haste to spoil her natural good looks." His dear friend Paula, the head of a convent near his own monastery in Bethlehem, was a kindred spirit on the subject of feminine cleanliness: "A clean body and a clean dress," she warned her nuns, "mean an unclean soul."

If baths struck ordinary virgins (or their advisors) as dangerous, more than a few saints rejected them entirely. Particularly in the East, in the fourth and fifth centuries, dirtiness became a uniquely Christian badge of holiness. This particular mortification of the flesh was known as *alousia,* "the state of being unwashed," and was largely chosen by hermits, monks and saints. For them, the only acceptable cleansing was baptism, which was sometimes called "the washing of regeneration," as opposed to the more normal washing, which signified vanity and worldliness.

Many early saints embraced filth enthusiastically and ingeniously. St. Agnes never washed any part of her body during her admittedly short life of thirteen years.

St. Francis Receiving the Stigmata, by Taddeo Gaddi. Although he praised a dirty body as "a stinking badge of piety," St. Francis demonstrated his charity by washing lepers.

Godric, an English saint, walked from England to Jerusalem without washing or changing his clothes. (On this fragrant pilgrimage, he subsisted on minimal amounts of water and barley bread, but only after it had grown stale.) At home in his hermitage in the woods near Durham, he wore a hair shirt which, when combined with summertime sweat, supported abundant lice.

St. Francis of Assisi revered dirt and was said to have appeared after his death to compliment friars on their grubby cells.

Alousia punished the body so that the better part, the soul, could flourish. St. Olympias, a friend and patroness of St. John Chrysostom, lived her life according to those priorities. Beautiful, rich and noble, she seemed destined for pleasure but thwarted it at every turn. Born in Constantinople around 360 and married when she was a teenager, Olympias was widowed by the age of twenty. Female saints often refused to marry or mysteriously managed to live a celibate life within marriage, and Olympias falls into both categories. Somehow, "adorned with the bloom of youth," as her anonymous fifth-century biographer puts it, she had remained a virgin throughout her marriage. When pressed to remarry, "like a gazelle, she leapt over the insufferable snare of a second marriage." The young widow explained that if Jesus had wished her to live with a man, he would not have conveniently removed her husband. Since Christ knew that she was "unsuited for the conjugal life and was not able to please a man," he freed her from the "burdensome yoke" of servitude to a husband and rewarded her with the pleasing yoke of chastity.

Giving her considerable money and real estate to Chrysostom so that he could dispense it to the needy and the Church, Olympias founded a monastery for women and became its deaconess. Her clothing was "contemptible," as her biographer records admiringly:

THE ODOUR OF SANCTITY
A monk came upon a hermit in a cave in the desert, and humbly reported a piece of good fortune: "I, Pambo, this least one, smelt the good odour of that brother from a mile away."

"For there could be found nothing cheaper than her clothing; the most ragged items were coverings unworthy of her manly courage." (To call a woman manly, or virile, was a significant compliment.) At the same time, "her whole intolerable life was spent in penitence and in a great flood of tears"—nothing was more unlikely than that the virile Olympias, "always gazing on Christ, [would] leave off crying for a while."

Predictably, this paragon ate no meat and "for the most part she went without bathing. And if a need for a bath arose through sickness (for she suffered constantly in her stomach), she came down to the waters with her shift on, out of modesty even for herself." Olympias took care not to scandalize anyone, including herself. Most tellingly, her biographer praises her for her "immaterial body"—not literally true, but an accurate statement of her wish to disregard her physical being.

With their denial of normal bodily wants, saints such as Olympias represented one extreme of the Christian continuum. At the same time, while they remained heroically dirty themselves, saints frequently washed other people. The biblical precedent was Christ, who washed the apostles' feet at the Last Supper and commanded them to do likewise. One who obeyed this order was St. Radegund, a sixth-century queen of the Franks and the founder of a convent at Poitiers. She had resumed a celibate life after separating from her husband, Clotaire, the king of France—an understandable decision, since he had murdered her parents and her brother. When lepers arrived at her convent, St. Radegund set a table for them, washed their hands and faces with warm water, and kissed them. To her attendant, who asked, "Most holy lady, when you have embraced lepers, who will kiss you?" she answered that this did not worry her. Every Thursday and Saturday, Radegund bathed paupers. Her medieval biographer describes the scene:

> Girding herself with a cloth, she washed the heads of the needy, scrubbing away whatever she found there. Not shrinking from scurf, scabs, lice or pus, she plucked off the worms and scrubbed away the putrid flesh. Then she herself combed the hair on every head she had washed. As in the gospel, she applied oil to their ulcerous sores that had opened when the skin softened or that scratching had irritated, reducing the spread of infection. When women descended into the tub, she washed their limbs with soap from head to foot.

Two standards were operating here, one a radical asceticism and the other a more normal understanding that we live in bodies that require a certain amount of care and tending. Self-punishing as they were about their own bodies, Olympias, Radegund and other early saints recognized that their choices were not for everyone. For ordinary Christians, cleanliness was a good, bringing comfort, a sense of well-being and a measure of healthfulness. Humility and charity demanded that the most scrupulously filthy saints help others to be clean.

The Roman bath culture died slowly, fizzling out at various times and places in the waning empire. Ironically, as political and economic troubles made it difficult to maintain the great *thermae* where the people bathed, bishops, popes and emperors continued to build and enlarge lavish baths in their residences.

From being a resource for all, the baths declined into an aristocratic preserve. In the sixth century, Bishop Victor of Ravenna renovated the baths that adjoined his episcopal palace with mosaics and marbles. On Tuesday and Friday, he graciously allowed the lesser clergy to bathe there. As late as the ninth century, Pope Gregory IV redecorated the splendid baths of the Lateran Palace.

These privileged enclaves were far from representative of their society as a whole. In Italy and the western part of the Byzantine Empire in general, the Lombardic invasions in the mid-sixth century led to a period of confusion and breakdown. After the Goths disabled the Roman aqueducts in 537, the *thermae* never recovered. Even if the aqueducts had been repairable, Rome was in too much disarray to manage the complex operations that furnished the *thermae* with water. That still left more than eight hundred *balneae* in the city, simple neighbourhood baths of perhaps three rooms, and it is possible that they carried on for some generations. So, undoubtedly, did smaller baths all over the Byzantine Empire.

Although the invading Germanic tribes admired many Roman institutions, the baths were not among them. Their preference was for a manly dip in a stream, at least in warm weather. (The Romans thought the invaders smelled vile, in part because they dressed their hair with rancid butter.) By the eighth and ninth centuries, mistrusted by the Christians and neglected by the Germanic conquerors, the baths in the West had fallen into disrepair and were finally abandoned. Extraordinary achievements in engineering, architecture, public health and city planning that stretched from Italy to Britain to North Africa, they mostly lay in ruins for centuries. Some, as at Bath in England, later returned to full use; others, like the Baths of Caracalla, were never restored.

The baths lasted longer in the eastern part of the Byzantine Empire. In sixth-century Alexandria, one-third of the city's budget was spent in heating the baths. In the eastern provinces of Syria, Judaea and Arabia, places of cross-fertilization between Christian, Roman and Islamic traditions, the bath, usually a small one, evolved into a Roman-Islamic hybrid. The exercise yard disappeared, and the room with the cold plunge pool became much smaller and less important. In its place, a large social hall developed, a combination of changing room and lounge. Ultimately that hybrid, adopted by the Turks as they encountered it in Byzantine cities across Asia Minor and in the Arabic-Islamic baths in Egypt and Syria, became the Turkish bath, or *hamam*. Except when the *hamam* was built at the site of mineral springs, customers at a Turkish bath washed at basins rather than in communal pools, and attendants gave them an energetic soaping and rub-down with a coarse-fibred mitten instead of the Roman oiling and strigiling. But the *hamam* remains the only living descendant of the Roman bathing tradition, and it was via the *hamam* that the Roman custom would return to medieval Europe.

No bathtubs have survived from the early medieval period, but large wooden ones were probably used in monasteries and infirmaries. Letters and diaries, songs and epic poems, chronicles and other official records from the time rarely refer to people's dirtiness or cleanliness. We don't know how and how often people washed, but given the difficulty of procuring water and an apparent unconcern about cleanliness, the plausible estimates are "not thoroughly" and "seldom."

The early medieval hygiene we know most about was that practised by monks, who were not only literate but eager to document the monastic life, which was something new under the sun. Besides, a monastery had to provide healthy living conditions for sometimes hundreds of men, and monks were in a better position to understand the Romans' engineering feats than most. They devised complicated gravity-based water systems, which could, in the case of some English monasteries, deliver water from a distance of several miles, through pipes of lead or wood. Controlled by taps, the water flowed into kitchen sinks, laundry tubs and the basins or stone troughs that were de rigueur for washing hands and face before meals. (Such a trough can still be seen in the cloisters at Gloucester Cathedral in England.)

Following Christ's example, monks greeted guests to the monastery by washing their hands and feet. For themselves, they performed their ablutions—in some monasteries, a painstaking cleaning each Saturday—without resorting to a full bath except on rare occasions. Monks troubled with carnal desires were prescribed cold baths, and warm ones were given to the sick. The ninth-century monastery of St. Gall, in Switzerland, provided baths in the infirmary as well as a bathhouse in the cloister. But baths and the monastic code of virile abstinence made an uncomfortable pairing. The Rule of St. Benedict, written about 528 for an order that combined manual work with contemplation, reserved them for the old and ill: "Let baths be granted to the sick as often as it shall be expedient, but to those in health, and especially to the young, they shall seldom be permitted."

"As to our baths, there is not much that we can say, for we only bathe twice a year, before Christmas and before Easter."

—Ulrich, a monk of Cluny, ca. 1075

The baths taken before Christmas at the Canterbury monastery sound more tense than festive. The monks gathered in the cloister and were summoned to the bathhouse in groups. They bathed in silence, alone, in a cubicle surrounded by a curtain, and as quickly as possible. "When he has sufficiently washed," according to the monastery constitution, "he shall not stay for pleasure, but rise, dress and return to the cloister." Other orders allowed three baths a year, before the feasts of Christmas, Easter and Pentecost, but monks whose holiness trumped cleanliness could decline any or all baths. Three a year represented a level of cleanliness that was probably below the upper-class standard of the day but above that of the peasantry.

According to that rule of thumb, some of the cleanest people in early medieval Europe were married Jewish

women below the age of menopause. A *niddah*, as a menstruating woman was called, had to purify herself by immersing herself in a ritual bath called a *mikveh*. That happened seven days after the end of her period, and only after that was she able to resume a sexual life with her husband. (The *mikveh* had other uses—converts were immersed during the initiation ceremony, and especially religious Jews took a ritual bath on the eve of the Sabbath and holidays. Glass and metal dishes and pots that had been made by non-Jews also had to be purified in the *mikveh* before they touched food.)

The *mikveh* itself did not make the woman using it clean so much as did the preliminary bath in warm water that had to be taken before the *mikveh*. The *niddah*, including her hair and nails, had to be physically immaculate when she entered the ritual pool so that nothing came between her skin and the *mikveh* waters. Barring infrequent periods, pregnancy and lactation (and the prescribed resumption of sex midway through a woman's monthly cycle must have ensured a high rate of pregnancy and lactation), that meant that a woman took a minimum of twelve serious baths a year—an impressive number for the day. It seems that many women developed a liking for baths and took them even more frequently: a rabbi in the Ashkenazic community of northern France and the Rhineland complained that women had made washing a "permanent practice," not

A sixteenth-century painting of Bathsheba and her servants at a *mikveh*. The placement of the ritual bath in a basement is accurate, but the headdresses worn by the bathers would have been forbidden, as nothing could come between the water and the woman being purified.

the scrupulous, pre-*mikveh* cleansing but an altogether more carefree endeavour. And because they had washed a few days before the *mikveh*, the rabbi wrote, they assume it's sufficient, but meanwhile "all their scales and scabs have dried on to them and block the water of immersion from reaching their skin, and thus their immersion is not valid."

Although Jewish women had the most clear-cut obligation to bathe, all Jews were commanded by the Talmud to keep clean. The Talmud lists ten things a city needed to have before a scholar could live there, including public baths, a court of justice, a schoolteacher, a circumciser and a public toilet. Jews particularly relied on public baths because Jewish men were often forbidden to bathe in the river, where Gentile men cleaned themselves. If a town had no bath of its own, or if the public bath was closed to them or otherwise uncongenial, the Jews would build their own bathhouse.

But far more than the Jewish quarter or the best-equipped monastery, the cleanest corner of early medieval Europe was Arab Spain. Unlike in Christianity, cleanliness was an important religious requirement for the Muslim, and a ninth-century observer described the Andalusian Arabs as "the cleanest people on earth." While the Christians in the north of Spain "wash neither their bodies nor their clothes which they only remove

A MIKVEH AT FRANKFURT IN 1705

In the cold tub, "twenty Women watch to see, that she, who baths herself, Plunges over Head and Ears into the Water; for their ancient Laws ordain that every Hair be purified. However that be, I am sure one can't stay long in this Bath without perishing; for we but just looked into it, and were almost frozen with Cold."

—Jean de Blainville, *Travels*

when they fall into pieces," a poor man in the Arab south would reportedly spend his last coin on soap rather than on food. Arab Spain sparkled with water—in pools, fountains and *hamams*. Every neighbourhood had its public bath. When the Christians recaptured Cordoba in 1236, the city had three hundred *hamams* as well as hot and cold water in private bathrooms.

In Moorish Spain the sexes always bathed separately. The town bath in Teruel, in Aragon, for example, followed a typical pattern, being reserved for men on three days of the week, for women on two and for Jews and Muslims of both sexes at different hours on Friday. The admission fee was low, and children and servants bathed free.

Healthy and progressive as these arrangements sound, to the Christians they were decadent and damnable. There had been a time, during the Roman period, when the Spaniards had had their own popular hot baths. Martial, the poet laureate of the baths, was born in Spain and retired there at the end of his life, to a small farm in Aragon; it is impossible to imagine Martial leading a life without baths. But when the Visigoths conquered Spain in the fifth century, they entertained the familiar suspicions that lolling about in hot water made strong men effeminate, and they demolished the baths.

Only when the Moors invaded the country in 711 did baths return. But now the Spaniards associated washing with the hated Moors' heretical beliefs, and their own dirty ways with the True Faith. Historians have connected what they see as a long-standing Spanish tradition of distaste for water and washing to ancestral memories of the Moorish baths. According to Richard

Ford, a nineteenth-century English traveller who knew Spain well, "The mendicant Spanish monks, according to their practice of setting up a directly antagonistic principle [to the Arabs], considered physical dirt as the test of moral purity and true faith; and by dining and sleeping from year's end to year's end in the same unchanged woolen frock, arrived at the height of their ambition, according to their view of the odor of sanctity, the *olor de santidad*. This was a euphemism for 'foul smell,' but it came to represent Christian godliness, and many of the saints are pictured sitting in their own excrement." One of the Spaniards' first actions during the Reconquest was to destroy the Moorish baths.

But the *hamam* had a robust longevity. The Crusaders were about to discover it and return it to its European birthplace.

THREE

A STEAMY INTERLUDE

1000–1550

he thirteenth-century Old French poem *The Romance of the Rose* is full of advice for lovers, from the achievement of mutual orgasm ("One should not abandon the other, nor should either cease his voyage until they reach port together") to the strategic use of fakery ("If she feels no pleasure, she should pretend to enjoy the experience and simulate all the signs that she knows are appropriate to pleasure; in this way, he will imagine that she is glad of it, when in fact she cares not a fig"). Enormously influential throughout France, Italy, England and the Netherlands for the next two centuries, the poem is partly an allegory about the code of chivalry, partly the kind of compendium of learning and lore that medieval readers loved.

The lore includes plenty of counsel about the relationship between cleanliness and romance. "Do not allow any dirt upon your person," a character named Love tells a young man, "wash your hands and clean your teeth, and if any speck of black appears in your nails, do not let it stay there. Lace up your sleeves and comb your hair, but do not paint your face or wear make-up: only women do that, and those of evil reputation." A young woman, for her part, is advised to make love in the dark, to prevent her lover from spotting a blemish or worse on her body: "She should beware lest he find anything dirty there, for if he did, he would be on his way at once, and take to flight with his tail in the air, which would be shameful and distressing for her." Even more bluntly, the woman is reminded that she must keep her "chamber of Venus" clean.

The *Romance* conjures up a world of pleasure, in which dainty ladies and elegant gentlemen dance to the music of viols and drums, court over games of dice, backgammon and chess, and feast on exotic new foods such as apricots and oranges. Idealized as it is, the society described in the poem reflects a shift that was noticeable as early as the eleventh century. As Europe organized itself into fiefs and kingdoms, no longer prey to marauding bands of barbarians, and as Christianity's dominion looked more and more unassailable, both church and state could afford to relax. The new stability made travel less dangerous, and this spurred the develop-

An "arsewisp" was what genteel people cleaned themselves with after defecating— a fistful of hay or straw.

ment of roads and inns and the importation of luxury goods from afar. Domestic life became more comfortable. Some of the old, austere habits of the early Middle Ages, such as a neglect of personal hygiene, began to strike both clergy and laity as not only unnecessary but undesirable.

Compare St. Benedict's sixth-century restrictions of baths to old and sick monks with the counsel given in the *Ancrene Wisse*, in the first half of the thirteenth century. Writing for religious women who had chosen a life of solitude and simplicity, often in small cells positioned near churches, the English author, who may have been a Dominican friar, advises, "Wash yourself whenever there is need as often as you want, and your things, too—filth was never dear to God, though poverty and plainness are pleasing." There was a revolution of sorts in the quiet phrase "filth was never dear to God." Scores of early hermits, monks and saints, who cultivated dirt, would have been aghast at this dangerous claim.

CARE OF THE TEETH
"To brush them with urine is a custom of the Spaniards. Food particles should be removed from the teeth, not with a knife or with the nails, in the manner of dogs or cats, and not with a napkin, but with a toothpick of mastic wood, or with a feather, or with small bones taken from the drumsticks of cocks or hens."
—Erasmus, "On Good Manners for Boys"

Basic behaviour, of course, did not change overnight. Both for laypeople and for those in religious life, hands remained the part of the body washed most reliably during the Middle Ages. It was a sensible practice when food was still eaten with the hands, without forks, but its point was also symbolic, as a mark of civility that dated at least to Homer's day. Medieval paintings of interiors often show a ewer, a basin and a cloth for drying hands in a corner of the room. Encountering people who did not wash their hands was worthy of remark: Sone of Nansay, the wandering hero of a thirteenth-century French romance, for example, notes with dismay that Norwegians neglected to wash at the end of a meal.

Medieval people apparently liked being told how to conduct themselves, whether they were religious women, as in the *Ancren Wisse*, or young people hoping for success in love, as in *The Romance of the Rose*. Manuals proliferated on genteel behaviour, the care of babies, health and education for boys, written by authorities who ranged from senior servants to the great humanist Erasmus. Naturally, etiquette books order handwashing before as well as after meals, but the practice also appears, with a frequency that borders on obsession, in poetry. Poets found it hard to describe a banquet or even a meal without affirming that everyone washed their hands. In *The Romance of Flammenca*, a thirteenth-century Provençal novel in verse, Flammenca's husband gives a feast for three thousand knights and ladies. At the start of the meal, the poet writes, "When they had washed, they sat down." At the end of the meal, he duly notes, "When they had eaten, once again / They washed themselves." At points, the repeated attention to handwashing sounds like a Continental hygiene campaign, but more than that, it was a formulaic reiteration of the characters' refinement. After the hands, the cleanest part of the body was the face, including the mouth. Etiquette books recommended washing the face upon rising, and rinsing out the mouth with water.

In theory, infants were kept fairly clean during this period: medieval baby-care manuals recommend bathing them in warm water at least once and sometimes three times a day. Clearly, they were bathed more than adults or older children because they were not yet chamber-pot-trained, but also because it was much easier to draw, heat and transport the water for a baby's bath than for an adult's. (A gallon of water weighs eight pounds, and the average medieval tub for an adult held at least ten gallons, which meant that eighty pounds of water had to be procured, heated and disposed of after an adult's bath.) In reality, the infants of peasants and the urban poor, who were also unlikely to be reading manuals about their children's care, were probably not bathed so frequently, nor were their swaddling clothes changed often.

The medieval world was immeasurably less deodorized than ours. In general, people were accustomed to that, but the rankest odours did not pass unnoticed. So spiritual a character as St. Thomas Aquinas approved of incense in church because it masked the prevailing body odour, which, he admitted, "can provoke disgust." At least in the upper levels of secular society, ideas about courtly love and gentility were drawing attention to a personal attractiveness that was based on cleanliness. Poor grooming was commented upon, especially among the gentry. A contemporary wrote of Brun, the brother of the tenth-century Holy Roman Emperor Otto the Great, "When he took a bath, he hardly ever used any soap or preparations to make his skin shiny, which is even more surprising, since he was familiar with such cleansing methods and royal comforts since early childhood."

In Boccaccio's fourteenth-century collection of stories, *The Decameron*, the characters are highly conscious of the odour of their bodies and their breath. The latter was cause for keen concern, and in one of the tales, a deceitful woman named Lydia first convinces two serving boys that because they "stank at the mouth," they must serve with their heads held as far backward as possible. She then persuades her husband that the cause for their strange posture was *his* halitosis. The point stressed in *The Romance of the Rose* and *The Decameron*, as well as other romances and manuals of the time—that intimacy is often more pleasant when the beloved is clean and sweet—may seem obvious to us, as it would have been to the Romans. But for medieval readers it was a new idea, slowly percolating down through the social classes.

PRIVY MATTERS

In 1518, John Colet, the head of St. Paul's School, London, furnished only urinals for the boys who went to his prestigious school. "For other causes," he wrote, the boys should go down to the River Thames.

The most momentous change in personal cleanliness during the Middle Ages was the return of the public bath. In most of western Europe, the institution had been defunct or seriously diminished since the fifth century or so. It reappeared thanks to the Crusaders, who arrived home from their failed campaigns in the East with the news of a delightful custom—the *hamam*, or Turkish bath. Ironically, Christianity, which was at least partly responsible for the demise of the Roman baths, was now, incidentally, responsible for their revival, in this modified Eastern incarnation. Probably as early as the eleventh century, Europeans added the bath to the list of luxuries—including

Rudimentary tooth-cleaning included, in medieval Wales, the use of green hazel twigs and woollen cloths.

damask, glass mirrors, silk and cotton—that they discovered in the Arab world.

The first medieval bathhouses, which were stripped-down adaptations of the *hamam*, combined a steam bath and, usually in a separate room, round wooden bathtubs, bound with iron, that might seat six. Although the Turkish bath did not usually include sitting in tubs, the European version—perhaps inspired by memories of Roman baths—did. The *hamam* in Turkey never became a daily habit as it had been with the Romans; it was frequented once a week or every two weeks. It doesn't seem likely that medieval Europeans used the bathhouse more often than that. In some cases, Roman baths were rehabilitated and, where baths were positioned at hot springs, as at Baden in Switzerland, large outdoor pools were built, holding scores of people. Occasionally bathhouse owners and bakers joined forces, with the bakers making use of the surplus heat from the bath furnaces. As bathhouses became better established, rooms for private baths and rooms with beds for resting after the bath were added.

THE KING TAKES A TURKISH BATH
"Abu Sir came to him and rubbed his body with the bag-gloves, peeling from his skin dirt-rolls like lamp-wick, and showing them to the King, who rejoiced therein . . . after which thorough washing, Abu Sir mingled rose-water with the water of the tank, and the King went down therein. When he came forth, his body was refreshed, and he felt a lightness and liveliness such as he had never known in his life."

—*A Thousand and One Nights*

Such extras were not within everyone's means, but the medieval bathhouses were democratic institutions where all classes would meet. Much as modern bosses may tip their employees with a massage or day at the spa as Christmas presents, medieval employers rewarded servants and workers with a session at the bathhouse. In

Germany, *Badegeld*, or bath money, was a regular part of a salary, and bathhouse taxes provided free baths for the poor. Within a century or so of its reintroduction, the bath had changed from an exotic novelty into an expected part of town and city life.

Once the baths reappeared, they spread rapidly. Fourteenth-century London had at least eighteen bath-houses; in Florence three or more streets were lined with baths. In 1292, with a population of 70,000 people, Paris had twenty-six bathhouses, and the owners formed their own guild. Public baths enjoyed a particular popularity in Germany, where communal washing in at least one form had enjoyed some popularity even before the days of the returning Crusaders. The so-called Russian or vapour bath had entered Germany from the north, and as early as 973, Ibrahim ben Yacub, a diplomat and geographer who visited Saxony and Bohemia, described the saunas he saw there.

Writing in the 1920s, Marcel Poète, the historian of Paris, noted of its medieval inhabitants, "The Parisians of that time had at least one point of superiority to those of to-day: they bathed much more."

The acceptance of mixed bathing waxed and waned through much of Europe during the Middle Ages, rather like the Romans' on-again, off-again flirtation with the practice, and completely unlike the strict segregation of the *hamam*. When public opinion dictated, separate days, times or premises for men and women would be ordered or reinstated. Unlike the south, the countries north of the Alps had an ease about undress that began with the journey to the baths. A miniature in a German manuscript from 1405 shows a woman entering a bathhouse from its exterior staircase, casually holding a sheet to her front,

A Swiss picture of an outdoor bath at Baden shows bathers in various stages of dress and undress (but always hatted), and their onlookers.

with her derrière fully exposed. Hippolyt Guarinonius, an Italian doctor who lived in Germany, scolded his neighbours for allowing families, including adolescent children, to walk naked and near-naked through town on their way to the baths. Laws were enacted to ensure more decorum in the streets, and sometimes they were obeyed.

German and Swiss nonchalance about nudity shocked travellers from Mediterranean countries. In 1414, a sophisticated Florentine writer and collector of ancient manuscripts named Gian-Francesco Poggio journeyed to the Swiss baths of Baden, near Zurich. He describes a prosperous city in a valley, where the central square was ringed with thirty magnificent buildings, all public or private baths. To the Italian's amazement, although segregated into a men's section and a women's, naked bathers were clearly visible to those of the opposite sex. In this Edenic scene of apparently innocent pleasure, bathers "contemplate, chat, gamble, and unburden the mind, and they stay while the women enter and leave the water, their full nakedness exposed to everyone's view." Windows had been cut into the grilles that nominally separated the sexes, so that bathers on both sides could admire and even touch one another. Torn between surprised laughter, lascivious thoughts and admiration, Poggio marvels at husbands who take no offence as their wives are touched by strangers, and at men who mingle in the nude or near-nude with female relatives or friends. "Every day they go to bathe three or four times," he rhapsodizes, "spending the greater part of the day singing, drinking, and dancing. . . . And it is charming to see young girls, already ripe for marriage, in the fullness of their nubile forms, their faces striking with nobility, standing and moving like goddesses."

Contemporary illustrations corroborate Poggio's goggle-eyed description of the baths at Baden. A French manuscript illuminated for the Duke of Burgundy in the late fifteenth century pictures a more elegant scene, a bathhouse that caters to couples. Turbaned men and women, otherwise unclothed, eat and drink in two-seater tubs. Another couple, still in their turbans, have already gone to bed in an adjoining room. A Polish

A woman wants to go to Baden,
But does not want her husband to follow her.
—Traditional Swiss song

drawing provides a rougher, satirical look at another side of bathhouse life. A tonsured monk lies in a tub, having his head and body massaged by two young bath maids in diaphanous gowns. A second monk lies at his ease on a bench, his hand on a maid's breast while she holds a ewer of water.

At its most refined, a bathhouse became a watery banquet hall, where troubadours played music and the patrons, nude but wearing elaborate headdresses, jewellery and makeup in the case of the women, ate and drank on floating trays or on boards spread across the bath. Bathhouses were inevitably titillating, and they quickly became known as good places for dalliance. Poggio summed up the erotic possibilities at Baden: "All who want to make love, all who want to marry or who otherwise look for pleasure, they all come here where they find what they are looking for."

PRIESTS AT THE STEWS
Methinks it must be a bad Divinitie
That with the stews hath such affinitie.
—Fourteenth-century English ballad

In medieval poems and stories, men and women bent on adultery often use the baths as their meeting place, their alibi or both. In *The Romance of Flammenca*, which takes place in the French spa of Bourbon-l'Archambault, baths provide the cover for an extramarital love affair. Interesting for its realistic detail of a spa town and thirteenth-century manners, the Provençal verse-novel is also a study of pathological jealousy.

Maddened with suspicions about his wife Flammenca's virtue, the local lord, Archambault, gives up grooming himself: "With unwashed head, unshaven beard, / An ill-bound oat-sheaf he appeared." (Significantly, when Archambault recovers his senses at the end

Medieval Polish monks enjoying the bathhouse amenities.

of the story, he washes his head.) Kept under lock and key by Archambault, Flammenca is charmed by a handsome, *soigné* stranger named William whom she encounters at mass. When he urges her to meet him in the bathhouse, she tries the usual excuse with her husband—she has a racking pain that only the baths can relieve. Archambault first suggests a daily dose of nutmeg, but eventually he relents and orders the bath owner, "Clean out your baths and make them fresh." The baths are drained, flushed and filled with water; Flammenca's maids pack basins and ointments. Flammenca assumes that her rendezvous with William will take place in a private room in the baths. But William, staying in one of the hotels that sprang up around mineral springs, has cleverly had a tunnel dug from the baths to his hotel room, and there the lovers meet daily.

Flammenca and William never use the baths, but her maids and his servants, conveniently two apiece, do. Flammenca sends them off so that she can be alone with William, and the narrator comments,

> They seek the baths for fun and sport,
> Which they may find of many a sort
> Therein are chambers fair and neat
> From which Alice and Marguerite
> When they come forth, may be in truth
> No longer maids. . . .

Lovers bathe in a story in *The Decameron*, which furnishes as idyllic a description of a bathhouse, or *bagnio* as it was called in Italy, as any in literature. Invited to join a wealthy woman named Madama Biancofiore in a private apartment at the baths, a Florentine named Salabaetto finds two of her slave girls bearing a large mattress and a basket laden with gear. They set the mattress on a bedstead in the apartment and make it up with fine sheets, pillows and a counterpane. Then the slaves strip, enter the bath, and sweep and clean it. When Madama Biancofiore arrives, she and Salabaetto proceed to the bath: "Without letting any else lay a finger on him, she with her own hands washed Salabaetto all wonder-well with musk and clove-scented soap; after which she let herself be washed and rubbed of the slave-girls." Wrapped in rose-scented sheets, the bathers are carried to bed, to sweat for a while. Then they lie about in the nude, enjoying wine and sweetmeats while the slave girls sprinkle them with waters perfumed with rose, jessamine, orange and citron flower. Finally, Madama Biancofiore dismisses the servants, and the two make love. When it comes time to leave, they dress, enjoy more wine and sweetmeats, wash their hands and faces with fragrant waters and leave this earthly paradise.

From these private indiscretions, it was no great leap to professional sexual services. Reports that prostitutes plied their trade in the places where respectable people, including children, went to wash surfaced almost as soon as the bathhouses reappeared. In addition to hot water and steam, customers could often command food, wine and compliant serving maids. The term "stew" or "stewhouse," which originally referred to the moist warmth of the bathhouse, gradually came to mean a house of prostitution. So long as the baths' other customers did not feel inconvenienced or menaced, a quiet, well-regulated sideline in prostitution was not necessarily considered a problem. In fifteenth-century France, for example, there was no particular shame attached to patronizing prostitutes, and a bathhouse often became, in addition to its other functions, a bawdy house or *maison de tolérance* of a slightly better class than the brothels.

As time went by, stricter standards of morality and recurrent fears about crime and the spread of syphilis made the stews more worrisome. In the second half of the twelfth century, Henry II formally recognized the Southwark neighbourhood of London, where the bathhouses were concentrated, as a legal red-light district. But in 1417, wary of the disorder that attended them, London council banned the public baths, "except that households might have their own individual stews for cleanliness." The ban proved impossible to enforce, and a series of fifteenth-century laws attempted vainly to keep the stews respectable.

Emperor Wenzel (1378–1419) had the margins of his German translation of the Bible decorated with pictures of himself being bathed and his hair washed by comely bath attendants wearing transparent white dresses.

The popularity of public bathing inspired private baths for the prosperous. In earlier times, a guest who had made the arduous journey to a mansion or castle would be greeted with the customary offer of water for washing hands, face and feet. In the later Middle Ages, that hospitable custom extended to a full bath. The grandest of residences, such as the pope's at Avignon or that of the dukes of Brittany at Suscinio, might have a two-room bathing suite, heated by a hypocaust under the floor or in the wall. One room served as a steam bath, the other held a tub or tubs. Very occasionally, a private residence would be outfitted with a system of pumps and pipes that transported water from a distance. But most private baths depended on servants to carry the water from well

A Swiss bailiff's leisurely soak in a private tub is interrupted by an angry, uninvited guest—the husband of one of the women. From the *Schweizer Chronik* of 1586.

or river, as well as to heat it, fill and empty the tub and carry away the waste water. For that reason, the room with a two- or four-seater tub would often be just off the kitchen.

Around 1430, John Russell, who worked as steward to Humphrey, Duke of Gloucester, wrote his *Boke of Nurture*. Designed as a manual and etiquette book for pages and servants, it provides instructions about everything from touching food (only with the left hand) to picking the nose (do not). For the servant who attends his master in his bedroom, Russell's advice is detailed. In the morning he must comb his lord's hair with an ivory comb and provide warm water for him to wash his hands and face. The section titled "A bathe or stewe so called" gives step-by-step instructions for those times when the master wishes "his body to wasche clene."

The servant must enclose the tub by hanging sheets impregnated with sweet herbs and flowers from the ceiling, and bring sponges for the bather to lean or sit on in the bath, as well as a sheet to cover him while in the tub. Using a basinful of hot, fresh herbs, he washes his master with a soft sponge, then rinses him with warm rosewater. Finally, he wipes him dry and takes him to his bed, "his bales there to bete" (to cure his troubles). Although there is no mention of soap (which was used to wash clothing but rarely bodies in fifteenth-century England), this is a washing bath, as distinguished from a medicinal bath. When the latter is called for, the servant boils together what sounds like a vast herbal tea from

A fifteenth-century French miniature of a woman bathing outside while her husband bids her farewell. An embrace from a fully armoured knight looks uncomfortable, but no one seems embarrassed by the bather's nudity.

Calling you to bathe, Messire,
And steam yourself without delay.
Our water's hot and that's no lie.

hollyhock, mallow, veronica, scabious, heyriff, bresewort, wildflax and other herbs. The master sits in the resulting infusion, and Russell promises, "Let him bear it as hot as he can, and whatever disease he has will certainly be cured."

Even more than in the public baths, nudity among family and friends enjoyed a measure of toleration in the private bath. A story from late medieval Germany underlines this idea. When a servant arrived at a castle one autumn day with a message for the lord, he was told, "Go into the bath chamber, he is inside; the chamber is warm." Assuming that the lord was bathing, the servant removed his clothes and entered nude, to the dismay of the lord and his relatives. In fact, they were using the warm room as a sitting room, until winter fires would be laid in the usual reception room. But obviously, as the servant's behaviour shows, had the lord been in his bath, a nude messenger would have seemed perfectly normal.

As in Rome, however comfortable the bath chamber in a private mansion or castle, the public baths would outdo them when it came to the diversity of the accommodations and the sociability of the experience. In the sixteenth century, Count Froben Christof von Zimmern made a large claim for the bathhouses. It was their attractions, he noted scornfully, that had tempted the German aristocracy down from their isolated castles. "Our ancestors once lived on high mountains in their castles and

TUDOR RE-GIFTING

In 1539, after noticing that Philip of Bavaria picked his teeth with a pin, Lady Lisle sent him a tooth picker. She had owned and used it for seven years before passing it on to the Bavarian duke.

palaces," he wrote. "Back then loyalty and faith still existed among them. But today we are giving up our mountain fortresses and dwell in them no longer; instead we wish to live in the plains, so that we don't have to go far to the baths."

Although still tremendously popular, the bathhouses in the fifteenth and early sixteenth centuries were increasingly seen as places that disrupted the peace and encouraged bad behaviour. But, although an unsavoury reputation lost them a certain amount of goodwill, it was disease more than sin that did them in. The disease was the most catastrophic pandemic the world has yet known, the bubonic plague that killed at least one out of every three Europeans within a four-year period in the mid-fourteenth century. The Black Death, as it was called because of the characteristic dark, festering lumps in the groins, armpits and necks of its victims, originated in Asia and was transported to Europe by rats. Beginning in 1347 the Black Death invaded Italy, Spain, France, England, Germany, Austria and Hungary, sometimes travelling two and a half miles a day. By the time its first visitation had ended, twenty-five million people had died.

No one has described the plague's attack on individuals and society better than Boccaccio did shortly after it devastated Florence. *The Decameron*'s one hundred stories are so lighthearted and festive that it's easy to forget that their tellers have fled to the countryside near Florence in fear for their lives, and spin their tales to

Victims of the Black Death had buboes, dark, festering lumps in their groins, armpits and necks.

distract themselves from the surrounding horror. Before the stories—escapist literature in more ways than one—begin, Boccaccio gives a dispassionate, almost clinical account of the disease. In spite of prayers, processions and last-minute attempts at sanitation, it spread through Florence unchecked while doctors and priests stood helplessly by. Patients generally died on the third day after the appearance of the fatal lumps, some of which were as big as apples (they were swollen lymph nodes), and anyone who had so much as touched something handled by the sick person risked infection.

The plight of the sick was terrifying enough, but Boccaccio was even more confounded by the plague's effect on the able-bodied members of society. He watched as a panic-stricken populace rapidly sloughed off civility and something worse than barbarism took its place. Brothers fled from sick brothers, wives from their husbands and even mothers from their own children. The time-honoured mourning observances, in which women would lament in the house where the dead person was laid out, and men would congregate respectfully at the threshold of the house, were abandoned, and corpses were deposited in mass burial pits without ceremony or attendants.

Another Florentine observer, Marchionne di Coppo Stefani, chose an unforgettable image to describe the burials. Every morning, he wrote, when the burial pits held a fresh influx of newly dead bodies, the gravediggers shovelled more earth on them, to be followed the next morning with more corpses and then more earth, "just as one makes lasagne with layers of pasta and cheese." In Avignon, the land available for burial ran out, and the pope declared the river consecrated space so the dead could be tossed into the Rhône.

In 1348, Philippe VI of France asked the medical faculty of the University of Paris to investigate the origins of the plague. Their far-reaching *Opinion* began with a disastrous conjunction of Saturn, Jupiter and Mars that caused disease-infected vapours to rise out of the earth and waters and poison the air. Susceptible people breathed in the noxious air, became ill and died. Who was susceptible? Some of the risks had been recognized in Greek and Roman times: obesity, intemperance, an over-passionate spirit. Now the professors added a new one that struck

LETTER FROM FRANCE

"The women here are rather dirty, frequently with some itch on the hands and several other kinds of filth; but to make up for this, they have pretty faces, lovely flesh and are charming when they speak; besides they are very willing to be kissed, touched and embraced."

——From Guido Postumo to Isabella d'Este, 1511

fear into medieval hearts—hot baths, which had a dangerously moistening and relaxing effect on the body. Once heat and water created openings through the skin, the plague could easily invade the entire body.

For the next two hundred years, whenever the plague threatened, the cry went out: "Bathhouses and bathing, I beg you to shun them or you will die." Even so, some resisted the idea. In 1450, during an outbreak, when Jacques Des Pars, the physician to Charles VII, called for the closing of the Paris baths, he succeeded only in infuriating the bathhouse owners, and he fled to Tournai. But by the first half of the sixteenth century, it was understood that French baths would be closed during an eruption of the plague. "Steam-baths and bath-houses should be forbidden," the royal surgeon Ambroise Paré wrote in 1568, voicing a now common opinion, "because when one emerges, the flesh and the whole disposition of the body are softened and the pores open, and as a result, pestiferous vapour can rapidly enter the body and cause sudden death, as has frequently been observed." Sadly, the best medical advice of the day probably doomed many people, for the dirtier people were, the more likely they were to harbour *Pulex irritans*, the flea now believed to have carried the plague bacillus from rats to humans.

The alarming image of a body under siege had longlasting consequences. Even when a plague did not

A SAINT AT THE BATHHOUSE
The infant Thomas of Aquinas (ca. 1225–74) accompanied his mother to the baths in Naples, carried by his wet nurse. Unable to pry open the baby's clenched fist, the nurse was forced to bathe and dress him without loosening his fist. When they reached home, the mother forced his little hand open in spite of his tearful protest and discovered that the future saint was holding a prayer to the Blessed Virgin.

threaten, the porosity of the body made water a threat to the bather, who might contract syphilis or diseases as yet unknown and unnamed, or even become pregnant from sperm floating in the bathwater. Not only could bad things enter the body through water, but the all-important balance of the four humours could also be upset through pores opened by moisture. Worries about the body's vulnerability affected fashion as well as hygiene. Since the pores might be vulnerable even when dry and not heated, clothing should be smooth, tightly woven and fitted—taffeta and satin for the wealthy, oilcloth and jute or hemp sacking for the poor. Cotton and wool were too loosely woven, and fur offered too many places for poisons to lodge. As plagues recurred somewhere in Europe almost every year until the beginning of the eighteenth century, these fears about a too-permeable anatomy remained common currency for some 350 years.

François I closed the French bathhouses in 1538. In 1546, Henry VIII ordered the stews in Southwark closed. In 1566, the States General at Orléans closed the French bawdy houses, which by definition included any bathhouses still operating. "Twenty-five years ago, nothing was more fashionable in Brabant than public baths," Erasmus wrote in 1526; "today there are none, the new plague has taught us to avoid them." For roughly five hundred years, water had furnished comfort, pleasure, companionship, temptation—and cleanliness. Now, on much of the Continent, water was the enemy, to be avoided at all costs. The two centuries that followed Erasmus' lament would be among the dirtiest in the history of Europe.

FOUR

A PASSION FOR
CLEAN LINEN
1550–1750

ost middle-class North Americans wash their face at least once or twice a day, and it wouldn't occur to us to mention such a banal detail in a letter. But at the beginning of the eighteenth century, washing your face was no run-of-the-mill event. That is why we know that, on a hot August day in France in 1705, Elisabeth Charlotte, the Princess Palatine, was compelled to do something out of the ordinary.

The German-born princess was the widow of the Duc d'Orléans (the younger brother of Louis XIV) and the mother of three grown children. She had had a long journey on dusty roads to the royal château at Marly, and arrived covered in perspiration, her makeup a disaster. She dealt with her sweaty body not by washing it but by changing her chemise, or undergarment, and her dress. Her face, by contrast, had no article of clothing to cover it and was too far gone to ignore. She looked, she said, as if she were "wearing a grey mask." She was forced to do something so singular that she reported it: "I had to wash my face, it was so dusty," she wrote to a correspondent, announcing a newsworthy event. Marly's gardens were famous for their abundant fountains, but water was first and foremost a spectacle. "Water flowed in profusion in the gardens of Château de Marly," Georges Vigarello, the historian of French cleanliness, writes, "but liquid hardly touched the skin of those who lived there."

In 1576, the Italian musician Hieronymus Cardanus complained that men and women "swarmed with fleas and lice, some stank at the armpits, others had stinking feet and the majority were foul of breath."

While they avoided wetting the skin, except in an emergency such as the Princess Palatine's, the French court was devoted to a stylish facade. From the padded and covered-up styles of the sixteenth century to the nonchalance of eighteenth-century décolletage, it was a time of careful attention to appearances throughout Europe, of self-presentation as elegant as could possibly be afforded. Even so, the realities of the dirty body underneath threatened constantly to disrupt the graceful surface. Some were so common that they embarrassed no one.

The seventeenth-century Dutch painter Caspar Netscher painted a picture of a prosperous woman at home with her children. A maid waits in the background of the richly appointed room and the young woman at the centre of the picture, which is called *Mother's Care*, wears a brocade jacket and a satin skirt trimmed with brilliants. But she wields a comb in her dimpled hand: she is inspecting her small son's head for lice. It was a familiar theme in seventeenth-century painting, and no wonder, for children and adults, from the most privileged to the poorest, teemed with lice, nits and fleas.

Woman Catching a Flea, by Georges de la Tour, ca. 1638. The realities of the dirty body threatened constantly to disrupt the graceful surface.

Underneath the rich chiaroscuro of velvets and silks were bodies that went unwashed from one year to the next. At the French court, where the daily dressing of the monarch was a minutely choreographed ceremony, aristocrats perfumed themselves so as not to smell their neighbours. The sixteenth century had not been notably fastidious, even at the highest level: Elizabeth I of England bathed once a month, as she said, "whether I need it or not." But the seventeenth century raised the bar: it was spectacularly, even defiantly dirty. Elizabeth's successor, James I, reportedly washed only his fingers. The body odour of Henri IV of France (1553–1610) was notorious, as was that of his son Louis XIII. He boasted, "I take after my father, I smell of armpits."

The French essayist Michel de Montaigne, for one, regretted the demise of the bath, but he spoke of it, at the

Elizabeth I received a New Year's Day present from Mistress Twist, the court laundress: "four tooth-cloths [for rubbing the teeth clean] of coarse Holland wrought with black silk and edged with bone lace." Her Majesty was also given gold toothpicks, and she owned a gold ear-pick, decorated with rubies.

end of the sixteenth century, as a thoroughly dead practice. "In general I consider bathing healthful," he wrote, "and believe that we incur no slight disadvantages to our health for having lost this custom . . . of washing our body every day. And I cannot imagine that we are not much the worse for thus keeping our limbs encrusted and our pores stopped up with dirt." But encrusted limbs and clogged pores remained not just the norm, but the goal. The reigning medical authorities remained faithful to the medieval belief that blocked pores, in particular, sealed the body off from infection. And infection lay in wait all over Europe, as plagues recurred through the seventeenth and eighteenth centuries. One hundred thousand Londoners died in the Great Plague of 1665. A third of Stockholm's population perished in the plague of 1710–11, as did half the population of Marseilles in 1720–21.

Even when the plague was not imminent, the fear of water that dated from the late Middle Ages became more and more generalized. Doctors believed that baths threatened the body in various bewildering ways. "The bath, except for medical reasons when absolutely necessary, is not only superfluous, but very prejudicial to men," the French doctor Théophraste Renaudot warned in 1655. "Bathing fills the head with vapors. It is the enemy of the nerves and ligaments, which it loosens, in such a way that many a man never suffers from gout except after bathing."

Mindful of these dangers, the English philosopher and essayist Francis Bacon (1561–1626) designed a twenty-six-hour bath that would limit the penetration of the body by the bad, or "watery," part of the exercise while encouraging its "moistening heate and virtue." He achieved this delicate balance, or so he believed, first by sealing the body with oil and salves before immersion. Then the bather sat in the water for two hours. Emerging, he wrapped himself in a waxed cloth impregnated with resin, myrrh, pomander and saffron, which was intended to close the pores and harden the body, which had grown soft in the water. After twenty-four hours, the bather removed the cloth and applied a final coat of oil, salt and saffron.

In Bacon's extraordinary recipe, water is something to be used reluctantly and with elaborate precautions, but at least it does play a part. More often, particularly in the seventeenth century, water was avoided altogether, except for a cursory washing of hands. The mouth might be rinsed quickly, and the face wiped with a dry cloth. The head and hair should be washed "only with the greatest caution," according to Jean Liebault, the author of a popular French work about the beautification of the body first published in 1582 and reprinted in 1632. Instead of washing, he recommended that before bed the hair be rubbed with bran or powder, which would be removed in the morning with a comb.

ADVICE FOR THE PRIVY
Fair nasty nymph, be clean and kind
And all my joys restore
By using paper still behind
And spunges for before.
—"Song," John Wilmot, Earl of
Rochester, ca. 1680

What was visible needed attention, but only what was visible. Beginning in the sixteenth century, manuals of etiquette and health echoed the medieval handbooks' emphasis on washing the hands and face, but omitted their instructions for bathing the body. The modern scholar Daniel Roche studied a hundred French manuals of etiquette, called *civilités*, published from 1500 to 1839, and found instructions for cleaning only hands, face, head and hair until the mid-eighteenth century. At that point, feet are mentioned. Not until 1820 do the *civilités* begin to recommend that the rest of the iceberg—the body—be cleaned, in a bath.

Those were the prescriptions. How much did people heed them? The minimal, mainly dry hygiene recommended by authorities must have suited the vast majority, since washing water was still difficult to come by. We have only a few descriptions of routine washing at home, and those mostly come from the elite. Travel memoirs and correspondence are usually a good source of descriptions of daily life, at least of those aspects that a traveller finds unusual or interesting enough to note. But, given the general European inattention to hygiene at the time, memoirs of Continental journeys pay more attention to the state of the bed sheets and the presence of bedbugs than the availability of water for washing.

"I walk'd allmost all over the Town Yesterday, incognito, in my slippers without receiving one spot of Dirt, and you may see the Dutch maids washing the Pavement of the street with more application than ours do our bed chambers."

—Lady Mary Wortley Montagu, *Letters*, Rotterdam, 3 August 1716

When the English traveller Fynes Moryson toured Germany in 1592, he was amused when the servants at a village inn proffered some sheets they considered clean, since, as they assured him, no one had slept in them recently except for a ninety-year-old woman. On the other hand, the only places where Moryson was given water to wash his feet were in Lübeck and the Prussian towns of Danzig and Elbing. Travellers agreed in finding the streets and houses in the Netherlands and Switzerland the cleanest of all, but Dutch and Swiss bodies did not receive the same attention. The Dutch, for example, scandalized French visitors by eating without first washing their hands.

It was when they travelled to the Levant that Europeans encountered bathing customs so strange that they inspired accounts in fascinated, almost anthropological detail. A Swabian doctor, Leonhard Rauwulf, who visited Tripoli in the 1570s, describes the elaborate cleansing procedures he endured in the public bathhouse. After sweating, bathing and undergoing a strenuous massage that ended with the masseur standing on the prone Rauwulf's shoulder blades, he was taken in hand by an attendant. First, the attendant applied a depilatory concoction of arsenic, quicklime and water to Rauwulf's superfluous body hair. Then, using a rough cloth made of rope fibres, the attendant washed him all over with soap, finishing with his head. The final touch was the addition of *malun*, an ash-coloured dirt that cleaned the hair as well as encouraging its growth.

A DIVINE BATH
When an Englishman fell overboard one day, a Turk said, "Now God has washed you."

Rauwulf's comment on this remarkable experience distances him from the people who cleaned themselves so thoroughly. Muslims, he explains, have a religious obligation to bathe often, especially before going to the mosque, "to wash themselves clean from their manifold sins which they commit

Surprised in her bath, but not much is revealed. A fine lady's ablutions in the seventeenth century were limited to hands and occasionally feet.

daily." Either their religion is strangely scrupulous, he implies, or they are extraordinarily sinful—or both.

The Englishman Henry Blount, whose *Voyage into the Levant* was published in 1636, had a similar reaction to Turkish standards of cleanliness. The first thing the Turks did upon occupying a town, Blount reported, was to erect public baths, which they subsidized, so that any man or woman could wash there for less than twopence. Blount noted, as an unusual fact, "Hee or she who bathe not twice, or thrice a weeke are held nasty." After urinating or "other uncleane exercise of nature," these extremely particular people washed their genitals. If a dog touched their hand, they washed it; before they prayed, they washed face and hands, sometimes the head and genitals. Like Rauwulf, Blount rationalizes the Turks' hygiene as the result of special circumstances, commenting that cleanliness in "hot Countryes, and to men of grosse food" was necessary to prevent disease. Those from a more temperate climate, he implies, have less need of washing. Whether he considered the beef-laden English diet less "grosse" than the Turkish fare of lamb, rice and yogurt is not known.

For Europeans such as Blount and Rauwulf, a culture where people bathed several times a week and regularly washed their genitals was exotic and even bizarre. But European noses, however dulled, could still be offended by egregious smells. Everyone at the court of Louis XIV knew about the Sun King's halitosis. His mistress, Madame de Montespan, frequently complained to him about it and swathed herself in self-defensive clouds of heavy perfume. The king, in turn, detested her perfume. And at least one person, the same Princess Palatine who was forced to wash her face, found Madame de Montespan, in spite of her penchant for being rubbed with pomade and perfumes while lying naked, to be downright dirty.

The poor lacked the means to wash thoroughly, but the aristocrats' doctors forbade it. Since the most expensive medical opinion held that bodily secretions furnished a layer of protection, kings and queens bathed as infrequently as the poorest peasants. When the future Louis XIII of France was born, in 1601, the court physician kept notes on the child's washing history. It was not a lengthy account. At six weeks, his head was massaged. At seven weeks, his abundant cradle cap was rubbed with butter and almond oil. The baby's hair was not combed until he was nine months old. At the age of five, his legs were washed for the first time, in tepid water. He had his first bath at the ripe age of almost seven: "Bathed for the first time, put into the bath and Madame [his sister] with him."

Washing for royal adults was not much more thorough. When Louis XIV arose, the chief surgeon, the chief doctor and his nurse entered his room together. His nurse kissed him, according to the Duc de Saint-Simon, and the doctor and surgeon "rubbed and often changed his shirt, because he was in the habit of sweating a good deal." A valet sprinkled a little spirits of wine on his hands, and the king rinsed his mouth and wiped his face. That ended his ablutions. Nor was this a monarch who scorned physical exertion: after his morning devotions, Louis might vault, fence, dance or perform military exercises so energetically that he returned to his bedchamber perspiring freely. But the sweaty monarch did not wash; instead, he changed his clothes. It was by donning fresh clothes, and particularly a laundered shirt, that Louis XIV indicated to himself and others that he was "clean." He and his brother, Philippe, were considered particularly fastidious because they changed their shirts three times a day.

For the seventeenth century, clean linen was not a substitute for washing the body with water—it was *better* than that, safer, more reliable and based on scientific principles. White linen, learned men believed, attracted

> "It does not befit a modest, honorable man to prepare to relieve nature in the presence of other people, nor to do up his clothes afterward in their presence. Similarly, he will not wash his hands on returning to decent society from private places, as the reason for his washing will arouse disagreeable thoughts in people."
>
> —Giovanni Della Casa, *Galateo*, 1558

and absorbed sweat. As one wrote, with mystifying confidence, "We understand why linen removes the perspiration from our bodies, because the sweat is oleaginous or salty, it impregnates these dead plants [the flax from which linen was made]." In 1626, the Parisian architect Louis Savot considered adding bathrooms to his classically inspired châteaux and mansions but decided they were unnecessary. We can do without baths, he explained, "because of our usage of linen, which today serves to keep the body clean more conveniently than the baths and vapour baths of the ancients could do." According to Savot's reasoning, which he shared with his age, the Greeks and Romans needed baths because they failed to understand the cleansing properties of linen.

In the eighteenth century, Samuel Johnson defended a friend, the poet Christopher Smart, who was sent to a madhouse. One of the charges against Smart was, as Johnson put it, that "he did not love clean linen." To which Johnson, whose poor grooming was notorious, added that he himself "had no passion for it."

The middle and upper classes in the seventeenth century did have a passion for clean linen. Today we appreciate the appeal and the connotation of crisp white clothing and bed-linen—Estée Lauder's popular perfume White Linen, launched in 1978, was joined in 2006 by the even more impeccably named Pure White Linen, personified by Gwyneth Paltrow—but our ancestors took it far more seriously.

OF MADRID NIGHTS AND CHAMBER POTS

" At eleven at night every one empties those things in the street, and by ten the next day it is so dried up. . . . They say it's a thing prescribed by their physicians; for they hold the air to be so piercing and subtle, that this kind of corrupting it with these ill vapours keeps it in good temper."

—English courtier, 1623

On the basis of their "white and fine linen," Fynes Moryson singled out the women of Brabant as the cleanest in the Netherlands. When Marie Adelaide, the daughter of the Duc de Savoy, became engaged to the Duc de Bourgogne, she was sent to the French court to be educated. Madame de Maintenon, who was in charge of her care, measured the twelve-year-old's cleanliness by her need for linen. "They give her fresh underlinen every week," she wrote the girl's mother about Marie Adelaide's servants, "but she is cleaner and neater, by far, than the majority of children, and scarcely needs clean clothes."

The linen in question for both men and women was a smock-like shirt, or chemise, that reached to the knees. (Since Englishwomen did not wear underpants until the eighteenth century, the smock was their only underwear. Women on the Continent were wearing silk or linen under-breeches at least by the sixteenth century.) A story about a beautiful Renaissance aristocrat, Mary of Cleves, is a telling glimpse into a time that saw fresh linen as the route to cleanliness and that savoured at least some bodily odours. At her wedding to the Prince de Condé, the sixteen-year-old princess danced long and hard. Repairing to a cloakroom to freshen up, she changed her chemise. As usual, there is no mention of applying water, much less soap, to her perspiring upper body, simply the change of linen. At the same time, the Duc d'Anjou (later Henri III) entered the cloakroom to brush his hair

A young man courting an Austrian peasant girl hid his handkerchief in his armpit during a dance. When the object of his affection became flushed with exertion, he gallantly wiped her face with his handkerchief. His perspiration succeeded where all else had failed, and she was instantly smitten.

and mistook the princess's damp and discarded chemise for a towel. Wiping his face with it, he fell instantly in love with its pheromone-laced smell and the woman who produced it.

As linen became ever more the emblem of cleanliness and hence gentility, the man's shirt and the woman's chemise became increasingly visible. After being hidden under wool or fur in the Middle Ages, a thin edge peeks out at the collar in the last decades of the fifteenth century. In Hans Holbein's portraits of Elizabethan men and women, a broader expanse of linen sees the light of day, under a V-necked or round-necked overgarment. In the seventeenth century, the shirt comes into its own—for men, flaunting falling bands or cravat at the neck, gaping through slashed sleeves, ballooning out from the bottom of the doublet; for women, sporting ruffles at the plunging neck, with full sleeves that extended well beyond the dress sleeves.

The linen shirt begins to emerge, as seen in Hans Holbein's brother Ambrosius' sixteenth-century *Portrait of a Young Man*.

Even as fashions changed, it remained important to expose your linen. In 1711, the *Spectator* described an English beau who unbuttoned his chic silk waistcoat in several places "to let us see that he had a clean shirt on which was ruffled down to his middle." Inventories of wardrobes and wills show that people owned more shirts than any other article of clothing, and the number of shirts continued to grow through the eighteenth century. At the end of that century, Casanova met a young Italian man of letters in England, who summed up a life of frugal self-sufficiency: "I work at literature, am all alone, earn enough for my wants. I live in furnished lodgings, I own twelve shirts and the clothes I stand up in, and I am perfectly contented." The twelve shirts are a crucial detail, proving that he has enough linen to present a gentlemanly appearance.

At a higher social level, Casanova describes a young man brought up in Paris: "He can ride, play the flute, fence, dance a minuet, reply politely, present himself gracefully, talk nonsense prettily, change his linen every day, and dress himself elegantly." A daily change of linen required servants, and one of the chief duties of chambermaids or manservants was the care of their employer's undergarments. A French household manual from 1691 emphasizes at length the maid's responsibility for her mistress's linen. As for the skin under the immaculate linen, the servant need only know how to draw a foot bath and make a paste to clean the hands.

Since washing the body happened so seldom, it ceased to be a subject for painters. In place of the medieval woodcuts and illuminated manuscripts that pictured warmly sensuous bathhouse scenes came painterly odes to linen. The seventeenth-century Dutch in particular favoured outdoor scenes of cloth lying in bleaching fields and interiors that celebrated pure white, precisely arranged stacks of linen. In 1663, Pieter de Hooch painted two women carefully depositing such a freshly laundered pile in the chest that stands prominently in the front hall.

The painting, called *The Linen Chest*, is full of right angles, suggestive of the orderly way of life espoused by the Dutch bourgeoisie—the tiled floor, windows, doors and, above all, the inlaid chest and its precious, squared-away contents. In contrast, the round laundry basket by the door, with the dirty linen flung untidily over its rim, symbolizes the squalor and mess that must be avoided.

Naturally, there were national variations and peculiarities that coexisted with the general European distaste for washing with water. In Spain, the early Christian concerns about the corrupting influence of bathing and the late medieval worries about the plague were compounded by the Moorish occupation. Because the Moor was clean, the Spanish decided that Christians should be dirty. Many of the Moorish baths were destroyed by orders of Ferdinand and Isabella after the conquest of Granada in 1492, but enough remained that Philip II definitively banned them in 1576. Moors who converted to Christianity were not allowed to take baths, and a damning piece of evidence at the Inquisition, levelled against both Moors and Jews, was that the accused "was known to bathe."

Spanish confessors were urged to question their female penitents minutely about private washing and not to absolve those who washed regularly. Isabella, the daughter of Philip II, became a national heroine when she vowed, in 1601, not to change

"To cure the goat-like stench of armpits, it is useful to press and rub the skin with a compound of roses."
—sixteenth-century French recipe

her shift until the siege of Ostend was over. It lasted three years, three months and thirteen days, by which time her white undergarment had turned tawny-coloured.

By contrast, the German-speaking countries, where public baths were a particularly cherished institution, were slower to close them than the Spanish, French and English. This was true of eastern European bathhouses in general, where, in the words of the historian Fernand Braudel, "a sort of medieval innocence was retained." The German, Austrian and Swiss bathhouse owners and their customers confronted the usual fears about contagion and the intermittent squalls of outrage at the sins of the flesh that were encouraged behind bathhouse doors. Just as AIDS sparked the belief among some religious groups that the disease was a punishment for sexual immorality, many people saw the plague as divine retribution for sinful behaviour, which included bathhouse behaviour. But in Germany, worries about the plague worked in favour of the baths as well as against them: bathing, sweat cures and bleeding, all of which took place in bathhouses, were popular therapies during epidemics. In some towns, separate areas in the bathhouses were established to treat those suffering from the "French disease" (syphilis) or other ills. Vienna, Frankfurt and Bamberg, as well as other towns, closed their baths during epidemics, but others remained open.

The Thirty Years' War (1618–48) forced the closing of many German baths, and some never reopened. But others did, like the bathhouse in Heidenheim, which rescued its equipment from the ruins of the war, rebuilt and opened its doors again in 1652. The dwindling supply of firewood was a more permanent problem. Bathhouses

were voracious consumers of wood, and until early in the sixteenth century the upper bathhouse in Winterthur used about 30 cubic metres a day from the municipal forest. Once the shortage of wood made it necessary for the baths to buy their fuel, the owners—who were not allowed by law to raise their entrance fees—were forced to close on certain days and to charge regular fees for children in order to stay in business. By 1557, in Gerolzhofen, parents had to pay even for babes in arms. The bathhouses in Basel illustrate the difficulty of surviving when firewood became scarce. In the fifteenth century, the city supported fourteen baths; by 1534, there were seven; at the beginning of the seventeenth century, six; and by 1805, only one remained. In spite of all these vicissitudes, many German bathhouses persisted, particularly in conservative mountain regions, where the peasants remained devoted to the baths as well as the traditional remedies associated with them.

Even outside the German-speaking countries, people did not avoid water altogether. Men of all classes swam or waded in rivers and lakes when the weather permitted, as did some women. Swimming in rivers was a favourite pastime of the Spanish. At a time when soap was a rare luxury, the same word was used for bathing and swimming in several European languages (in English, the terms swimming suit and bathing suit are still synonymous), and "bathing" in a natural body of water was as close as most people came to all-over washing. Many Europeans still heeded the superstition—a relic from pre-Christian beliefs about the summer solstice—that an open-air bath on the feast of St. John the Baptist (June 24) would protect them from numerous maladies in the coming year. When Thomas Platter, a Swiss studying medicine in Montpellier, went to see the crowds plunge into the sea on the eve of the feast, in 1596, he reported an "astounding" number of women among them. Although leery of indoor bathing, as we shall see, both Henri IV and Louis XIV were strong swimmers. Anne of Austria and her ladies-in-waiting spent hours each hot summer day in the Seine, modestly covered in loose gowns of coarse muslin that billowed out in the water. So many Parisians swam in the Seine that in 1688 an enterprising couple named Villain marked likely spots with ropes and posts, and rented out canvas-covered changing rooms, shifts and towels.

But cool water had never been considered as dangerous as hot water. To immerse yourself in hot water, you had to be foolhardy, German—or ill. Recommending that sick people plunge themselves into a substance considered unwise for healthy people sounds paradoxical, but it was a case of desperate remedies. Because water could infiltrate a healthy body and disturb the balance of its humours, doctors and patients hoped that a carefully designed and monitored bath might also restore the humours' equilibrium in a diseased body. The emphasis in such a hazardous undertaking was on professional supervision, which is why the seventeenth-century French doctor Guy Patin discussed baths in his medical texts but not in his general works on health.

On a spring day in 1610, King Henri IV sent an emissary to the Paris house of the Duc de Sully, the superintendent of finances, requesting his presence at the Louvre. To everyone's consternation, Sully was taking a bath. He prepared at once to obey the royal summons, but his attendants begged him not to risk his health by going outside. Even the messenger was against it, saying, "Monsieur, do not quit your bath, since I fear that the king cares so much for your health, and so depends on it, that if he had known that you were in such a situation, he would have come here himself." "Such a situation"—a man taking a bath in his house—required the messenger to return to the Louvre to explain the complication to the king. Not inclined to treat this predicament lightly, the king, in his turn, consulted his own doctor, André Du Laurens. The doctor pronounced that the man would be vulnerable for several days after his bath. Sully was told, "Monsieur, the king commands you to complete your bath, and forbids you to go out today, since M. Du Laurens has advised him that this would endanger your health. He orders you to expect him tomorrow in your nightshirt, your leggings, your slippers and your nightcap, so that you come to no harm as a result of your recent bath." Normally, His Majesty did not travel to his ministers' houses, nor did he order them to receive him in their nightclothes—but a bath was no normal occurrence.

When Louis XIV suffered fits, starts and convulsive movements, followed by a rash on his chest, the royal doctors bled him eight times. During his convalescence, wishing to adjust the humours in his depleted body, the doctors decided to bathe him—but not before they ordered numerous safeguards, including a purge and enema the day before the bath, as well as extra rest. Even so, the king developed a headache, and "with the

CLEANING UP VERSAILLES
Shortly before Louis XIV died in 1715, a
new ordinance decreed that feces left in
the corridors of Versailles would be
removed once a week.

whole demeanor of his body quite changed from what it had been in the preceding days," Guy-Crescent Fagon, the king's personal doctor, aborted the treatment. In the following year, for the second and last time in the king's life, Fagon prescribed a bath, again without success. Laconically, he summed up the experiment: "The king was never pleased to become accustomed to bathing in his chamber."

Since bathing at home was so worrisome, an alternative was the spa. (Places with mineral springs had been called spas in honour of the famous hot springs of Spa, near Liège in Belgium, since the seventeenth century or before.) Belief in the curative powers of mineral springs dated at least from the Greeks. The Romans had positioned their baths whenever possible to take advantage of mineral springs, as advised by their medical writers, and medieval mineral baths at Bourbon-l'Archambault and Baden, among many others, were renowned as places of healing as well as recreation. But in the Renaissance, as the spontaneous, populist life of the old public bath-houses became troubling if not impossible, a new attitude arose in Italy about mineral baths. Rather than let amateurs do as they wished, doctors wanted to recover Greek and Roman teachings about therapeutic baths and to claim them as a professional responsibility. They insisted that bath lore, or balneology, as they called it, was a science with its own rationale and methodology.

As the Italian doctors noted, spas in the late sixteenth and early seventeenth centuries were far from places of order and discipline. A Swiss writer complained that visitors to Baden paid no attention to the rules, eating in the baths and remaining in the water day and night, "like unto ducks." When Fynes Moryson travelled to Baden in 1592, he reported that the brimstone in the water worked wonders on barren women, as well as those who suffered from "a cold braine, and a stomacke charged with rhume." But Baden was not all therapeutic: the scene Moryson describes, of men and women, monks and nuns, sitting together in water, nominally parted by a board that permitted conversation, card games and touching, was in essence the spectacle that had so scandalized the Florentine Poggio in the fifteenth century.

"Monsieur Leibnitz must have a very high degree of intelligence to make him such an agreeable companion. It is seldom that scholars are clean and do not smell bad, and that they have a sense of humour."
—Elisabeth Charlotte, Princess Palatine, 1705

It was not that Renaissance baths lacked rules and regimes, but that bath-goers felt free to ignore them. Michel de Montaigne was skeptical about doctors but hopeful that mineral waters would lessen or cure his kidney stones. Searching for relief in French, Italian and Swiss spas in the 1580s, he enjoyed defying medical orders. In Plombières-les-Bains, he ignored the prescribed purgative, drank nine glasses of the water each morning instead of the recommended one or two, and bathed every other day, rather than two or three times a day, as advised. In La Villa, near Florence, he insisted on bathing and drinking the water on the same day, rather than on alternate days, and on bathing his head while in the waters, contrary to approved practice.

In spite of balky spa-goers like Montaigne, the Italian doctors' campaign was successful, in that Italian and French spas became increasingly medicalized. Deliberately ascetic when it came to diet and social life, they became lucrative sources of income for attendant doctors. Merchants, lawyers, priests and nuns flocked to the spas, and the ailing poor occasionally made their way through alms and individual acts of charity, but spas most suited a wealthy, leisured class. A cure could require three to six weeks and often involved annual visits. In France, where the spa came into its own in the seventeenth century, royal patronage assured its success. It was popularly believed that the waters of Forges were responsible for the birth of Louis XIV (although his parents, Louis XIII and Anne of Austria, visited the spa in 1633 for infertility, and their son was not born until 1638). Louis XIV's mistress Madame de Montespan made regular pilgrimages to Bourbon-l'Archambault, and almost every member of his court (except the king himself) visited one of France's main spas—Bourbon, Vichy or Forges.

THE SPA TREATMENT
FOR INFERTILITY
"If you want your wife to conceive, send her to the baths, and stay at home yourself."
—Italian proverb

Madame de Sévigné, the aristocrat whose vivid letters to her daughter bring seventeenth-century France to life, was a typical spa-goer, hoping for a remedy for a specific malady and thoroughly obedient to medical authorities. In 1676, troubled by rheumatism, she travelled eight arduous days in her personal coach to Vichy. The regime, standard throughout France and inspired by Italian practice, involved drinking Vichy's sulphurous water, bathing in it and subjecting oneself to the shower, or pump. Madame de Sévigné reported her rheumatism much improved, and returned to Vichy in the next year for a follow-up. Ten years later, when she was over sixty, she travelled to Bourbon-l'Archambault. This time, her doctor forbade the showers (too hard on her nerves) and limited her to baths, drinking the water, and a strict diet that, sadly, allowed no sauces or ragouts. One look at the "lame and the halt, the half-dead who seek relief in the boiling heat of these springs," convinced her that she was one of the healthiest people there.

In the 1680s, about the same time that Madame de Sévigné was obeying orders in Vichy and Bourbon, the indefatigable Englishwoman Celia Fiennes was touring England, including its spas. Unlike the French and Italian spas, England's watering holes, like those in the German-speaking countries and Belgium, were designed for pleasure as much as therapy. Some visitors to English spas—which included Tunbridge Wells, Scarborough and Epsom—looked for a cure, but others courted, promenaded, danced, played cards, bowled and gambled.

Montaigne sought relief for his kidney stones in Swiss, French and Italian spas.

The premier spot to take the waters in England was Bath, a health retreat since pre-Roman times that was

"I began the operation of the pump today," Madame de Sévigné wrote her daughter on 2 May 1676.

It is no bad rehearsal of purgatory. The patient is naked in a little subterraneous apartment, where there is a tube of hot water, which a woman directs wherever you choose. This state of nature, in which you wear scarcely a fig-leaf of clothing, is very humiliating. I wished my two women to be with me, that I might see someone I knew. Behind a curtain a person is stationed to support your courage for half an hour; a physician of Gannet fell to my lot. . . . Think of a spout of boiling water pouring upon one or other of your poor limbs! It is at first applied to every part of the body, in order to rouse the animal spirits, and then to the joints affected; but when it comes to the nape of the neck, the heat creates a surprise which it is impossible to describe. This, however, is the main point. It is necessary to suffer, and we do suffer; we are not quite scalded to death, and are then put into a warm bed, where we sweat profusely, and this is the cure.

Less drastic but also uncomfortable, the treatment included drinking the sulphurous, near-boiling water at six o'clock each morning. The patients (and no one went to Vichy without a malady, the regime was too unpleasant) then walked to and fro, to encourage the evacuation of the water, talking all the while of the success of their efforts. The doctor who kept Madame de Sévigné company behind a curtain while she endured the pump also came to read to her during the two difficult daily hours of sweating, and she chose a course of Descartes for their edification.

The baths at Vichy, 1569. Mineral baths were places to flirt, cavort and sometimes get well.

known in the Middle Ages as Akemancastra (Sick Man Town). Like many visitors to Bath, Celia Fiennes was hoping for diversion, not a cure. Her immersion, as she recorded it in her diary, reads like an exquisitely measured baroque dance. Ladies descended into the various pools led by two male escorts who cleared the way and accompanied by a woman guide or two, "for the water is so strong it will quickly tumble you down." Half a century earlier at Bath, bathers of both sexes would have been naked, but by the 1680s a gentlewoman wore a large gown of stiff yellow canvas. Gentlemen wore trousers and waistcoats made of the same material. After walking a bit while holding on to rings affixed to the walls, socializing with acquaintances and peering at the ill being showered with scalding water (those who were lame were showered on their legs, the palsied on their heads), the bather would make a slow-motion exit. Going through a door into a private stairway, still in the water, Fiennes allowed her canvas gown to drop off just as her maids, above her on the staircase, flung a flannel nightgown over her head. Modestly and warmly attired, she was deposited in a Bath chair and carried to her lodgings.

Living in a world that regarded water as the source of illness, Montaigne, Madame de Sévigné and Celia Fiennes seemed to enter a separate planet when they

THE KING'S MISTRESS AND MADAME DE SÉVIGNÉ COMPARE SPAS

"Mme de Montespan talked to me about her trip to Bourbon, and asked me to tell her about Vichy, and how I liked it. She had gone to Bourbon, she said, in hopes of a cure for a pain in the knee, but had come back instead with a toothache. . . . I found her quite flat again in the rear end . . . but seriously speaking, her beauty is breathtaking."

—Madame de Sévigné, 1676

journeyed to La Villa, Vichy and Bath. None expressed any anxiety about plunging their bodies into warm water, even when it was sullied by dirt, blood and diseased peo-

ple. In the case of Montaigne and Madame de Sévigné, the hope of physical relief and the blessing of medical authority (however much Montaigne disdained it in the details) were decisive. English spa-goers such as Fiennes had proceeded a step further, in that they could take to the waters for pleasure alone.

Montaigne, Madame de Sévigné and Celia Fiennes were not bathing for the sake of cleanliness. Even as water became less frightening, it appeared that, except for hands and more rarely the face, Europeans had forgotten the link between water and hygiene. But the spa, which enjoyed both medical approval and social cachet, played a part in legitimizing water. The sophisticated, prominent clientele who took the waters saw them as health-giving, not threatening. That shift, along with the end of the plague and changing intellectual currents that glorified nature and the simple life, ushered in a new era in the history of cleanliness.

FIVE

THE RETURN OF WATER

1750–1815

One day early in the eighteenth century, a visitor arrived incognito at the women's Turkish baths in Sophia. Lady Mary Wortley Montagu, the young wife of the English ambassador to Constantinople, must have been an outlandish sight to the two hundred or so women in the bathhouse. She wore the strictly tailored riding habit in which she travelled, while the Turkish women were all, as Lady Mary wrote, "in the state of nature, that is, in plain English, stark naked." When they pressed their visitor to undress and bathe, she had difficulty refusing. Finally, one lifted the Englishwoman's dress, exposing her corset with its bone stays. The Turkish woman "ran back quite frightened," Lady Mary wrote, "and told her companion, 'that the husbands in England were much worse than in the East, for that they tied up their wives in little boxes, of the shape of their bodies.' . . . They all agreed that 'twas one of the greatest barbarities of the world, and pitied the poor women for being such slaves in Europe."

Lady Mary enjoyed the irony of the Turkish women's mistaken sympathy, but she was sincerely charmed by their hospitality and graciousness, as well as their beauty. She described the scene, with its marble benches, cushions, carpets and abundance of gleaming flesh, in such detail in her letters that the French painter Ingres copied several passages into a notebook. They inspired his 1863 painting *Le bain turc*. Lady Mary herself looked at the baths with an artist's eye and wished that a fashionable London portrait painter, Charles Jervas, could have been smuggled in:

> I fancy it would have very much improv'd his art to see so many fine Women naked in different postures, some in conversation, some working, others drinking Coffee or sherbet, and many negligently lying on their Cushions while their slaves (generally pritty Girls of 17 or 18) were employ'd in braiding their hair in several pritty manners. In short, tis the Women's coffee house, where all the news of the Town is told, Scandal invented, etc. They generally take this Diversion once a week, and stay there at least 4 or 5 hours.

But, open-minded and admiring as Lady Mary was, the Turkish way was not the English way. Although she attributed the Turkish women's smooth white skin to their cleanliness, she herself, at least by middle age, was notoriously grubby. The story goes that someone commented to her at the opera, "How dirty your hands are, my lady!" She answered, carelessly, "What would you say if you saw my feet?" In 1740, Horace Walpole complained that her filthy mobcap did not cover her greasy hair; twenty years later he noted that she was as grimy as ever.

Lady Mary's dirtiness was remarked upon, no doubt because she was an aristocrat, but in many ways it suited the England of her day. Women wore leather or bone stays, sometimes for decades, without washing them. Their quilted underskirts, also never washed, served until they were reduced to filthy, greasy tatters. Thomas Turner, a Sussex grocer in mid-century, held that a man should bathe regularly each spring—once— in connection with the annual bloodletting. His was not an extraordinary view. Travelling up the social scale, as Lady Mary's reputation makes clear, did not guarantee an increase in cleanliness. James Boswell, an educated member of the Scottish landed gentry and Samuel Johnson's biographer, washed so rarely that his odour was infamous. The Duke of Norfolk's servants seized the opportunity to bathe him when he was

UNPEELING AN UNDERSHIRT

"[The Marquis d'Argens] had worn a flannel under-waistcoat four years and durst not take it off for fear of catching cold. The King [of Prussia] drove out one fear by another, and told him that if he persisted to wear that waistcoat, his perspiration would be entirely stopped, and he must inevitably die. The Marquis agreed to quit his waistcoat. But it had so fixed itself upon him that pieces of his skin came away with it."

—James Boswell, 1764

insensible from drink. In his right mind, he never washed more than hands and face.

Rich and poor, men and women lived in close connection with each other's dirt, excrement and bad smells. The traditional departure of the ladies from the dining room after dinner in smart English houses enabled the gentlemen to open a door in the Chippendale sideboard, or a sliding panel in the wall, extract a chamber pot and relieve themselves without interrupting the conversation. Lord Chesterfield knew a man who ripped a few pages from his copy of Horace's poems when he went to the privy and read them while defecating. When he had finished, he wiped himself with the poems. The fact that he wiped at all meant that he was more fastidious than many of his contemporaries.

And yet change was in the air, wafting down from the top of the social ladder. Long-standing habits of mind and body were being unsettled—at least for some aristocrats, gentry and members of the enlightened middle class— and the centuries-old aversion to water was weakening. The causes, as large as Romanticism and as small as the popularity of cotton clothes, are various, and the English love of the cold bath is as good a place to start as any.

One of the first important post-classical recommendations for this daunting practice appears in John Locke's 1693 treatise on the rearing of a boy, called *Some Thoughts Concerning Education*. In it, he recommends washing the boy's feet every day in cold water and putting him in shoes so thin that they would leak and let in more water. "It is recommendable for its cleanliness," Locke writes of his idea, "but that which I aim at in it is health." He claimed that immersing the boy's legs and feet in increasingly cold water would harden and strengthen him. Although Locke was a doctor as well as a philosopher, his theory had more to do with wishful thinking than sound physiology. Also, his classical education had familiarized him with the ancient effeminate-warm-water versus virile-cold-water debate, and he emphatically sided with such hardy cold-bathers as Horace and Seneca.

In 1701, another doctor, Sir John Floyer, published *The History of Cold Bathing*, which made much more extravagant claims for immersion in cold water. The history consisted mostly of stories about the Greeks, Romans and unlettered northern peoples who bathed in cold water, followed by a catalogue of wondrous cures. Floyer's physiology does not inspire much more confidence than Locke's. Explaining how the simple act of bathing in cold water could restore health to the lame, the consumptive and the palsied, Floyer attributes it to the "Terror and Surprize" of an immersion: it "excites the drowsy Spirits to contract all their Tubes and membranous Vessels, by which all sensation is more lively, and all Actions of the Body more strong, and the Stupid Mind is powerfully excited."

BATHING, RUSSIAN STYLE
Catherine the Great (1729–1796) forbade mixed bathing, so no men were allowed in the women's bath, "except the necessary attendants, or painters or physicians, who came there to prosecute their studies. Accordingly, an amateur assumes one or other of these titles to obtain admission."

In addition to exciting the stupid mind, there was something patriotic and bracingly northern about bathing in frigid water. "A cold regimen suits cold countries," Floyer writes, connecting the practice with the longevity and energy of northern cultures. The Briton

In the second part of *Cold Bathing*, Floyer's colleague Dr. Edward Baynard noted that when two boys ran a race, if the loser was dipped in cold water and the race rerun, the loser would invariably win. Although cold baths were a traditional remedy for lust, honesty compelled Baynard to admit that they frequently had the opposite effect. One such bather whose passions had been reignited was inspired to versify:

> Cold Bathing has this Good alone,
> It makes Old John to hug Old Joan.
> And gives a sort of Resurrection
> To buried Joys, through lost Erection.
> And do's fresh Kindness's entail
> On a Wife Tastless, Old, and Stale.

who shunned southern imports, such as wine, coffee, tea, spices and tobacco, and plunged into cold water was living as nature intended.

The History of Cold Bathing was addressed to an audience that could cope with learned allusions and the odd Latin quotation. John Wesley, the founder of Methodism, pitched his *Primitive Physick: or, an Easy and Natural Method of Curing Most Diseases* at the folk level. His manual went through twenty-one editions in four decades after its publication in 1747 and was always on sale in Methodist chapels. For Wesley, as for other pre-Romantic champions of the simple and natural,

"Mrs. Watts, by using the Cold Bath two and twenty Times in a Month, was entirely cured of an Hysterick Cholic, Fits, and convulsive Motions, continual Sweatings and Vomiting, wandering Pains in her Limbs and Head, with total loss of appetite."

—John Wesley, *Primitive Physick*

"primitive" was good, and his home remedies ranged from a paste of honey and onions to cure baldness to tiny pieces of wine-soaked bread inserted in the nostrils to moderate a greedy appetite. Cold bathing was a key prescription, and he filled a page in listing the conditions, including blindness and leprosy, it had been known to cure.

In a sermon he delivered in 1791, Wesley adapted a Hebrew proverb into an English phrase that became a standard of mothers and schoolteachers: "Cleanliness is next to godliness." Although now used mostly as a prod for children who need to shower or clean their fingernails, the cleanliness Wesley referred to was that of dress. Similarly, *Primitive Physick* rarely concerns itself with personal hygiene. Houses, clothes and furniture should be "as clean and sweet as possible," but for bodies, he recommended only frequent shaving and foot washing. Babies should be dipped in cold water every morning until the age of eight or nine months, to prevent "Rickets, Tenderness and Weakness," but after that only their hands and feet needed to be immersed.

The cold baths Wesley recommended were in plain water, as were most of Floyer's. But Floyer also endorsed sea bathing, particularly for paralytics. That was bizarre advice in the early eighteenth century, when people regarded the sea with dread and entered it only as a last, futile measure after being bitten by a mad dog. People waded and swam in rivers and lakes but not in the sea. For hundreds of years, it had been terrifying—vast, unpredictable and the supposed home of horrific monsters. As the eighteenth century progressed, a different attitude emerged. It owed much to a new sensibility, voiced with particular eloquence in Edmund Burke's

The Romantic view of the sea meant that young ladies seeing it for the first time were expected to break down. When Charlotte Brontë travelled to Bridlington, where she caught her first glimpse of the sea, "she could not speak till she had shed some tears."

1756 treatise *Origin of Our Ideas of the Sublime and Beautiful*, which glorified what was dark and alarming. At least since the Renaissance, people had found the sea ugly because it frightened them. Now people began to find the sea sublime, for the same reason— because it frightened them. Gingerly at first, they began to visit seaside villages, peering at the fishermen, their boats and their gear while they worked up the stomach to gaze at the sea. Where the fishermen's houses had turned their backs on the water, now prosperous people started to build residences that looked out on it. Seascapes, formerly a rather despised genre, began to look intriguing and would soon be crowding out the landscapes at painting exhibitions.

CRY ME AN OCEAN

Even royal insanity (which was in fact porphyria) might be helped by a salt-water bath. In 1789, after his first episode of madness, George III, his wife and his daughters travelled to Weymouth. The entire village was decorated with signs saying "God Save the King," and the bathing women (in charge of escorting, unwrapping and wrapping the bathers) wore the slogan around their waists and tucked into their bonnets. A band stood by, and when the regal head was submerged, they struck up "God save Great George our King." When his health allowed, the king returned to Weymouth annually.

In 1750, Dr. Richard Russell published a Latin tome entitled *A Dissertation on the Use of Sea-water in the Diseases of the Glands.* In it, he described hundreds of glandular problems in lurid detail, almost all of them cured or improved through the use of seawater. Unexpectedly, this compendium of secular miracles became a runaway bestseller in a pirated English version that went into five printings in its first decade. The historian Jules Michelet praised Russell as "the inventor of the sea"—

an overstatement with more than a germ of truth. Russell had proved to the eighteenth century's satisfaction that the sea was not only sublime but also healthful. He built a grand house overlooking the English Channel in Brighton, up until then a disregarded place that blossomed under his influence into one of England's greatest resorts. His patients were instructed to bathe in the sea, preferably at five in the morning in the winter, and drink seawater. Some were massaged with seaweed and showered with heated seawater.

In her unfinished novel *Sanditon,* which takes place at the seaside, Jane Austen mocked the myriad, contradictory claims made for salt water and sea air. Together, she wrote, they were "nearly infallible, one or the other of them being a match for every Disorder, of the Stomach, the Lungs or the Blood; They were antispasmodic, anti-pulmonary, anti-septic, anti-bilious and anti-rheumatic. . . . They were healing, softing, relaxing, fortifying and bracing, seemingly just as was wanted, sometimes one, sometimes the other." Much the same could have been said of the grandiose claims for plain cold water.

But, although their promises were dubious, Floyer, Wesley, Russell and the other cold-water advocates were influential figures in the return of water. The popularity of mineral water spas in the seventeenth century had begun its rehabilitation, but mostly for the upper classes and the aristocracy. Now, in the eighteenth century, the revival grew, as doctors assured people from all classes that plain water from the nearest well or river or sea was healthy—the stark opposite of its reputation for the past four hundred years. Getting into water to improve your health was the thin end of a wedge that would culminate in bathing for the sake of cleanliness.

In Tobias Smollett's satirical novel *The Expedition of Humphry Clinker,* a family treks through the spas and bathing places of Britain. Although hot-water spas were flourishing when Smollett wrote in 1771, the head of the fictional family, Matthew Bramble, is revolted by their unsavoury conditions. At one, ghostly-looking patients in the last stages of consumption linger round the hot well. When Bramble enters the water at Bath, he meets a child covered with scrofulous ulcers, and he frets, "Suppose the matter of these ulcers, floating on the water, comes in contact with my skin, when the pores are all open, I would ask you what must be the consequence?"

"They may say what they will, but it does one ten times more good to leave Bath than to go to it."

—Horace Walpole, in a letter to the naturalist George Montagu

Fortunately for Bramble, there is a healthier alternative at Scarborough, where Britons under doctors' orders plunge into the North Sea. Even in July, Bramble cannot help "sobbing and bawling out" from its briny cold, but it is a punishment he prefers to the disease-laden waters of the mineral spas. Smollett paints a graphic genre picture of ladies and gentlemen entering Scarborough's bathing machines, aquatic coaches where the men strip and the ladies change into flannel bathing costumes while being carried to a depth that accommodates their modesty. After their bath, they return to the confines of the machine and disembark, dressed, on the beach. Of this "noble bath," Bramble's nephew writes, "You cannot conceive what a flow of spirits it gives, and how it braces every sinew of the human frame."

Cranky, hypochondriacal Matthew Bramble resembled his creator in several ways. As a doctor, patient and writer, Smollett was a lifelong devotee of cold, clear water. Born in Dumbartonshire, in the west of Scotland, he grew up swimming in the Leven River. After apprenticing in surgery, he moved to London and built a literary life that included fiction, history and journalism. In 1752, in *An Essay on the External Use of Water*, he took issue with the unhealthy conditions at Bath. His description of the filthy water was bad enough, but that had often been noted. What dismayed Bath's promoters more, because it was a relatively novel idea—and voiced by a doctor—was Smollett's conviction that the vaunted minerals in the spa's water did little beyond blocking the pores and producing a crust on the skin. This marks an important shift in scientific thinking, away from the centuries-old conviction that plugged pores preserved the crucial balance of the humours and prevented the entry of disease. Now, with the doctrine of the humours falling from favour and a new appreciation of the role of perspiration, Smollett's contemporaries increasingly believed that pores should be open. Ultimately, that "new" idea would lead to the promotion of regular washing.

Smollett insisted that it was ordinary water, "the Element itself," without minerals, that improved a host of disorders. In his forties and fifties, haggard and ill, suffering from asthma and what may have been the beginnings of tuberculosis, he had frequent occasion to test his belief. He spent two years, from 1764 to 1766, living on the Continent. Although he took an interest in the remnants of Roman baths—reporting with disgust that grimy-looking women were washing clothes in the baths at Nîmes—warm water struck him as a suspicious, self-indulgent element. People who lived in hot countries, he admitted, needed cleansing baths, "especially before the use of linen was known." But how much better it would have been for the Romans if they had plunged into the Tiber rather than their warm baths, "which became altogether a point of luxury borrowed from the effeminate Asiatics, and tended to debilitate the fibres already too much relaxed by the heat of the climate."

"Is it for the sake of your health, or is it by choice that you take baths, and were you born under the sign of the fishes?"

—writer Julie de Lespinasse, 1769, when the Marquis de Condorcet told her that he bathed occasionally

Smollett was made of sterner stuff. At Boulogne, in northern France, he swam in the sea daily for fifty days. It produced a head cold, but the fever and stitches in the chest from which he suffered disappeared and his strength and spirits increased. In Nice, where he stayed for ten months, Smollett swam regularly in the Mediterranean, beginning in early May. The local people stared astonished at the tall, thin Briton: "They thought it very strange, that a man seemingly consumptive should plunge into the sea, especially when the weather was so cold; and some of the doctors prognosticated immediate death." Although he continued to lose weight, Smollett was sure that his bathing regime justified the risks. "I have breathed more freely than for some years," he wrote from Nice, "and my spirits have been more alert."

Watching Smollett bathe, some Swiss officers stationed at Nice followed his example, then a few other inhabitants. Smollett's 1766 account of his odyssey, *Travels through France and Italy*, in which he described Nice's climate and sea bathing in glowing terms, did much to popularize the town among English people. The Hôtel d'Angleterre became the centre of a lively expatriate scene, and a visitor to Nice in 1786 complained, "The whole neighbourhood has the air of an English watering-place." The French regarded this misguided sea bathing as yet another instance of English eccentricity, and only began venturing into the water around the 1830s, some sixty years after the English invasion.

Although Smollett praised cold water for its curative qualities, he also took a fascinated interest in cleanliness. Italian and French standards of hygiene struck him as laughably inadequate. He remarked, as did many travellers, that the apartments at Versailles were "dark, ill-furnished, dirty, and unprincely," and that the French "have not even the implements of cleanliness." Some enlightened French, Smollett admitted, were beginning to imitate the English—but only in those points where English superiority was undeniable. His list of "superiorities" is interesting, including the penny post and a new informality in dressing. In addition, there was talk in Paris of supplying houses with water piped in from the Seine, as English towns were increasingly doing with their rivers. "They have even adopted our practice of the cold bath," Smollett wrote, "which is taken very conveniently, in wooden houses, erected on the side of the river. " These new-style bathhouses had low entrance fees and separate, comfortable rooms for men and women.

(Another English innovation was the indoor toilet, as opposed to an outdoor privy. Beginning about 1770, such an accommodation was known in France as the "*lieu à l'anglaise*," or "the English place." French attempts to duplicate English toilets were not always successful, judging by one Smollett saw at Nîmes. The mistress of the inn had installed it for the convenience of English travellers, but the French, "instead of using the seat, left their offerings on the floor," which had to be cleaned three or four times a day. This was a "degree of beastliness," Smollett wrote, even worse than that seen at Edinburgh, a city renowned for its uncleanliness.)

In spite of Nice's glorious climate, two years abroad was enough for Smollett. "I am attached to my country," he wrote as he prepared to return to England, "because it is the land of liberty, cleanliness, and convenience." Smollett's loyalty to his adopted country aside, England did look like that to many Europeans. Its constitutional freedoms and the presence of a sizeable middle class struck them as uncommonly enlightened. The cleanliness and convenience seemed to go hand in hand with the liberty, for the English citizenry demanded running water, indoor toilets, washable cotton clothing and a degree of everyday comfort that was unheard of on the Continent. In the second half of the eighteenth century, all things British were *à la mode* on the Continent, especially in France—the self-confident ways of the English; their tailored but relatively easygoing clothing, especially for women; their informal country gardens. The English cachet that accompanied cold bathing undoubtedly helped its spread across the Channel.

The English word loo for toilet may come from (1) *lieu à l'anglaise*, the French term for toilet, or (2) *Gardez l'eau!* (Watch out for the water!), called to alert passersby that chamber pots were being emptied from upper-story windows into the street.

Although Louis XIV's Versailles included an impressive *appartement des bains* with a massive marble tub, the Sun King, as we have seen, was not fond of bathing. But his heir, Louis XV (1715–74), was, and his private rooms always included a bathroom with two tubs, one for soaping, the other for rinsing. By his time, the bathing suite had changed its name and nature: unlike the *appartement des bains*, the new *cabinet des bains* was intimate, panelled in light-coloured carved wood, with a portable copper tub, easily moved from window to fireplace as the bather wished. Gloomy grandeur, designed to imitate the ancients' style but not their practice, had given way to informal charm. In 1751, when Louis XV's mistress, Madame de Pompadour, designed a *bijou* house for herself called Bellevue, it included a boudoir, an intimate room next to her bedroom that contained a toilet and a bidet. A wing that bordered the courtyard held a sumptuous bathing apartment for the king and Pompadour, decorated with François Boucher's nude paintings *Toilet of Venus* and *Bath of Venus.*

For the English, cold water and cleanliness were associated with vigour and northern virility. The French were nurturing a more hesitant interest in the same things, to which they added a Romantic attraction to the natural. Their guiding light in this was Jean-Jacques Rousseau. Rousseau's name runs through the period like a piece of homespun thread, often sturdy and thick, at other times thin to the point of invisibility, but always present in the fabric of the time. Championing simplicity over artifice, freedom over constraint, the country over the city, Rousseau became particularly influential after *Emile,* his treatise on education, was published in 1762. Although progressive voices had been speaking out for decades against restraining babies in swaddling clothes and sending them away from their mothers to be wet-nursed by strangers, it was *Emile* that caused a significant part of the educated middle classes and the aristocracy to rethink those practices. Even Marie Antoinette became a disciple of Rousseau, who inspired her desire to nurse her first child and her passion for her make-believe farm.

We know only a little about Rousseau's own cleanliness, and what we know suggests that he was a child of his times, still relying at least partially on fresh linen rather than water. As a young man, he gave up gilt, white gloves and his sword, sold his watch and resolved to live simply. But his wardrobe of fine linen shirts outlasted his reformation, at least temporarily. He had acquired them in Venice and become very attached to them. As he put it, what had begun as an object of cleanliness had become a luxury. He

was unable to renounce them, but on Christmas Eve, 1751, someone freed him from his "servitude," as he called it, by stealing the lot. Because a large washing had just been done, no fewer than forty-five shirts were spread out in the attic to dry when the thief entered. "This adventure cured me of the passion for fine linen," Rousseau wrote, "and since then I have had only very common material, more suited to the rest of my outfit."

Rousseau's other intimate habits were not particularly delicate. When a urinary complaint made it necessary to void frequently and urgently, he wrote to a friend about his difficulties. When in public, he had to wait to excuse himself until some fine lady stopped talking. Then, after he had repaired to a staircase, hoping to relieve himself there, as was customary in both France and Italy at the time, he would find more ladies. Finally, he would seek out a courtyard, which would turn out to be full of maids and teasing lackeys. "I do not find a single wall or wretched little corner that is suitable for my purpose," he complained. "In short, I can urinate only in full view of everybody and on some noble white-stockinged leg."

Although Rousseau wrote little that was specific about cleanliness, he commended it warmly when he encountered it and deplored its absence. Again and again in *The Confessions,* he praises the "charming cleanliness" of a house or a person. Embarrassed about his taste for young ladies as opposed to the daughters of the poor, he admits that their personal cleanliness and delicacy are powerful attractions. Rousseau, who grew up in Geneva, never overcame his first impression of Paris's "filthy and stinking little streets" and its "air of dirtiness." For him, cleanliness was part and parcel of the purity and naturalness he associated with the countryside. (Those more intimately acquainted with an eighteenth-century farm than Rousseau ever was might have challenged his image of the clean rural life.)

His most extended discussion of cleanliness comes in the early pages of *Emile.* Praising Thetis, who plunged her son in the waters of the Styx so that he would become invulnerable, Rousseau urges the same course—symbolically and literally—on modern parents. Follow nature, he commands, who hardens children by all sorts of troubles. Rather than bathing the newborn in warm water with a little wine, as was the

French practice, one should return the child gradually to his natural strength.

> Wash your children often, their dirty ways show the need of this. If they are only wiped their skin is injured; but as they grow stronger gradually reduce the heat of the water, till at last you bathe them winter and summer in cold, even in ice-cold water. To avoid risk this change must be slow, gradual, and imperceptible, so you may use the thermometer for exact measurements.
>
> This habit of the bath, once established, should never be broken off, it must be kept up all through life. I value it not only on grounds of cleanliness and present health, but also as a wholesome means of making the muscles supple, and accustoming them to bear without risk or effort extremes of heat and cold.

There is no need for doctors, Rousseau insists: "Hygiene is the only useful part of medicine, and hygiene is rather a virtue than a science."

When Emile grows up and chooses a partner, Sophy, cleanliness is one of her chief virtues. What some might consider over-fastidious—Sophy dislikes cooking because "things are never clean enough for her" and gardening because she imagines the manure heap smells disagreeable—Rousseau sees as a sign of her natural refinement. Sophy learned hygiene at her mother's knee:

> According to her, cleanliness is one of the most necessary of a woman's duties, a special duty, of

the highest importance and a duty imposed by nature. Nothing could be more revolting than a dirty woman, and a husband who tires of her is not to blame. She insisted so strongly on this duty when Sophy was little, she required such absolute cleanliness in her person, clothing, room, work, and toilet, that use has become habit, till it absorbs one half of her time and controls the other; so that she thinks less of how to do a thing than of how to do it without getting dirty.

Sophy sounds uncannily like the germ- and dirt-phobic modern people shaped and preyed upon by advertisers, but Rousseau denies that there is anything either affected or exaggerated in her attitude. "Nothing but clean water enters her room; she knows no perfumes but the scent of flowers, and her husband will never find anything sweeter than her breath. . . . Sophy is more than clean, she is pure." Sophy is, in short, like nature itself— or at least like the idealized, sweetly smelling nature glorified by Rousseau.

For much of the seventeenth and eighteenth centuries, the court at Versailles had tried to distance itself as much as possible from nature. They devised a parody of freshness, using wigs, rouge, powder and oils. They tried to mask the pervasive smell of sweat with heavy perfumes based on civet, ambergris and musk. Unwashable brocades, velvets and satins were cut and padded to conceal and distort the body's natural shape.

But by the last third of the eighteenth century, even those closest to the king had been inching toward something different. In 1775, Jean-Baptiste Gautier d'Agoty painted Marie Antoinette. Her powdered hair was built up to a giddy height and threaded with pearls, ribbons, diamonds and feathers; her real arms, waist and hips were impossible to discern under the scaffolding of court dress. Only eight years later, she sat for another portrait. This one, by Louise Vigée Le Brun, was startling in its informality: her loose hair only lightly powdered, the queen wears a simple white muslin dress and a straw hat *à l'anglaise*. It was an outfit that suited her

A detail from *Marie Antoinette Wearing Court Dress*, 1775. The court at Versailles hid the real body behind rouge, wigs and a carapace of brocade and satin robes.

hamlet at Le Petit Trianon, a cluster of rustic buildings complete with a herd of Swiss cows, where Marie Antoinette played at living the simple life. One of her last improvements was a water mill she had installed there in 1789. She was said to be sitting beside it when a messenger came to tell her that the mob was closing in on Versailles.

The queen's attraction to Rousseau's ideals could not save her, but his spirit proved impressively resilient. He died in 1778, before the French Revolution, but with the downfall of the monarchy, his beliefs became even more attractive. Now the artifice of the *ancien régime* was worse than outmoded: it was associated with oblivious, arrogant tyranny. There was a brief period, particularly intense during the Terror, when it seemed revolutionary, and hence virtuous, to be dirty. Helen Maria Williams, an Englishwoman living in France, wrote in 1793 that the old term *muscadin*, meaning "a scented fop," had been revived, "and every man who had the boldness to appear in a clean shirt was branded with that appellation." But it did not last. In the new world that was dawning, clean hair and shining faces looked more spontaneous and progressive than the old style of grimy splendour.

Even perfumes became lighter and floral, more suggestive of springtime meadows than the animal-based scents that had epitomized seventeenth-century taste. The late-century vogue for cotton—chintzes, calicos and muslins—and simpler silhouettes made clean clothes more possible and unwashed bodies more noticeable. Later, when the clinging, short-sleeved Empire dress swept into fashion at the beginning of the nineteenth century, even more was revealed, and the Duchesse d'Abrantes claimed, "An elegant woman does not pass two days without bathing."

As the French say, *"L'appétit vient en mangeant,"* appetite comes from eating. A certain amount of fashionable cleanliness awakened a desire for more. In the letters and diaries of the second half of the eighteenth century, the writers comment frequently on other people's cleanliness or lack of it, especially on the bad smells that accompanied inadequate hygiene. It was as if noses, desensitized for centuries when no one washed, were being invigorated by the presence of the relatively few who smelled clean. In her memoirs, the Margravine of Bayreuth complained that Elisabeth von Braunschweig-Bevern, her sister-in-law and the consort of Frederick II, "smelt terribly strong." The

Murder in the bath, *à la française*. In 1793, the revolutionary leader Jean Paul Marat was sitting in his *sabot*, or slipper bath, to calm his persistent skin irritation when Charlotte Corday stabbed him to death.

Holy Roman Emperor Joseph II wrote of his prospective brother-in-law, King Ferdinand IV of Naples, that, although ugly, he was not downright repulsive: "He is clean, except for his hands; and, at least, he does not stink."

When Princess Josephine of Savoy was about to marry Louis XVI's brother, the Duc de Provence, the Savoyard ambassador to France insisted that she take better care of her hair and teeth. "It is embarrassing for me to discuss such things," he wrote to the princess's father, "but these mere details to us are vital matters in this country." Similarly, when a German princess, Caroline of Brunswick, travelled to England to make what turned out to be a disastrous marriage to the Prince of Wales, her escort, Lord Malmesbury, reported that she neglected

"Baths for reasons of health, or for voluptuousness, or cleanliness, are hardly ever taken in winter. Spring and summer are the most suitable seasons."

—*Le médecin des dames*, 1771

her *toilette* so much that she "offended the nostrils by this negligence." He despaired of getting her to wash and change her underwear often enough to meet English court standards.

At the same time, more people were washing more regularly and teaching the young to attend to their cleanliness. When Lord Chesterfield's letters to his illegitimate son were published posthumously in 1774, Samuel Johnson belittled his advice as teaching "the morals of a whore, and the manners of a dancing master." But the late eighteenth century considered the *Letters* such pearls of wisdom that, in addition to numerous editions, they alphabetized Chesterfield's maxims and printed them as etiquette books. Lord Chesterfield hectored his son repetitively on the subject of cleanliness. His particular concern was the care of the mouth and teeth, since he himself was toothless at fifty-three. If he did not wash his mouth each morning and after every meal, he warned

"Wash your ears well every morning, and blow your nose in your handkerchief whenever you have occasion; but, by the way, without looking at it afterwards."

—Lord Chesterfield, *Letters*

his teenaged son, "it will not only be apt to smell, which is very disgusting and indecent, but your teeth will decay and ache, which is both a great loss and a great pain." The whole body had to be washed, too, for the same reasons. "A thorough cleanliness in your person is as necessary for your own health, as it is not to be offensive to other people," he wrote in 1749. "Washing yourself, and rubbing your body and limbs frequently with a flesh-brush, will conduce as much to health as to cleanliness."

Authorities might canonize water—*Le Tableau de Paris* intoned, "What gives a woman real style: cleanliness, cleanliness, cleanliness"—but their effect on most people's lives is hard to measure. One marker is the number of public bathhouses in Paris. At the beginning of Louis XIV's reign, in 1643, there were two, mostly used for erotic assignations, hair removal and curative steam baths. By 1773, there were nine public baths, and by 1830 their numbers had grown to seventy-eight. But opinion remained divided about when and even if one should bathe—and whether in hot or cold water. Compared with the English and Germans, the French were slow to welcome the return of water. The Germans, who had never relinquished their liking for warm water, now took up cold-water baths enthusiastically. In general, the Spaniards and Italians kept aloof from cold baths.

Even so, the hygienic horizons for educated and well-travelled people in western Europe widened. All this change came slowly and was probably often more theoretical than actual. Baths and bidets existed, rather as Jacuzzis and saunas do now in North America: they were options, more easily available to the comfortable middle classes on up. The important thing was that they existed, and a growing body of public opinion valued them.

Immersing oneself in water while naked still seemed strange to many women, if not men. One solution to the modesty problem was to cloud the bathwater. In 1772 the handbook *Le médecin des dames, ou l'art de les conserver en santé* advised dissolving powdered almond paste, bran, flour or resin in spirits of wine, then casting them into the bath. More often, female bathers would wear a bathing robe or, failing that, underwear. When Elizabeth Montagu finally succeeded in locating a bathing tub in the ducal house of Bulstrode, where she was staying in 1741, she wrote to her mother, "Pray look for my bathing dress, till then I must go in in chemise and jupon!"

Marie Antoinette had a bath most mornings, usually in a slipper bath rolled into her bedroom. Wearing a long-sleeved chemise made of English flannel while in the tub, the queen breakfasted there, her tray resting on the bath's rigid cover. "Her modesty, in every particular of her private toilet, was extreme," her lady-in-waiting Henriette Campan wrote. When her two bathing women assisted her out of the tub, "she required one of them to hold a cloth before her, raised so that her attendants might not see her."

In the last years of the 1780s, a young Englishman named Arthur Young went travelling in France and Italy. Like other wanderers of the day, he paid close attention to local standards of hygiene and personal decorum. The Continental habit of spitting inside a house and the sorry state of the "necessary houses," or toilets, scandalized him, as did the shamelessness with which men and women relieved themselves in public. In spite of these bad habits, Young decided, "the French are cleaner in their persons, and the English in their houses." This was a minority view, since most eighteenth-century observers, English or not, judged both English people and houses to be cleaner than the French. Young based his judgment, at least in part, on a small piece of furniture he claimed was universal in every French dwelling, modest or grand: the bidet. He was quite wrong about that, for bidets remained unusual until the twentieth century and were seen only in the most luxurious establishments in the eighteenth century. But he was right to note the "chair of cleanliness," as it was sometimes called, as a significant piece of furniture.

Although most people associate bidets with France, and the French word is used in English, Spanish and Italian, it was the Italians who invented an oblong vessel, set on a frame or cabinet, designed to wash the genital and anal area of men and women. Bidets first appeared in France in the sixteenth century but were rare until the middle years of the eighteenth century. At that point, they are increasingly noted in cabinetmakers' account books and the inventories of great houses. Usually, although the bowl was still earthenware or tin, they were luxurious pieces of cabinetmaking used by the aristocracy and their mistresses.

NICKNAMES FOR THE BIDET
- the hygienic little horse (Italy)
- the hygienic guitar (Spain)
- the violin case (France)
- *le petit indiscret* (France)

As twenty-first-century movie stars are showered with shoes, purses and clothes by ambitious designers, the king's mistresses received gifts of jewellery, bibelots and bidets. In 1751, Madame de Pompadour was given a bidet made of rosewood veneer, with fittings of gilded bronze, by the cabinetmaker Duvaux. Pierre de Migeon, another prestigious furniture maker, presented her with a walnut bidet equipped with crystal flasks; its lid and back were covered in red leather with gold nails. A later mistress of Louis XV, Madame du Barry, had a silver bidet.

"A knight of the bidet"—slang term for a French pimp, from about 1880.

An eighteenth-century woman astride her bidet, in Louis-Léopold Boilly's engraving.

When fifteen-year-old Marie Antoinette travelled from Vienna to France to marry the dauphin in 1760, the modern conveniences in her coach included a bidet trimmed with red velvet, embroidered in gold. Men used them as well as women, and cabinetmakers designed ever more ingenious examples, such as a back-to-back double bidet, a double bidet arranged like a loveseat, and one that converted into a chair.

The bidet remained recherché, and mainly French. An English writer in 1752 referred to it as the "machine which the French ladies use when they perform their ablutions," and a persistent Anglo-Saxon suspicion that clean genitals might lead to lascivious behaviour (even oral sex) kept the chair of cleanliness mostly on the other side of the Channel. But its popularity, however limited, indicated a new under-

In August 1785, Samuel Kempton, tinsmith, coppersmith and ironsmith, offered to supply New Yorkers with "those truly useful Machines, called Bidets, so much used in England and France," especially effective for barrenness, imbecility and the "renovating of constitutions injured by luxurious excesses."

standing that particular parts of the body, not just hands and face, needed cleaning, and that water was an ideal medium for that purpose. *Le médecin des dames* advised daily washing of a woman's "natural parts," with aromatic plants or spirits added to the water. *Le conservateur de la santé*, in 1763, was even more explicit about areas that needed vigilant washing:

> If perspiration or sweat remain on these parts (the armpits, the groin, the pubic area, the genitals, the perineum, between the buttocks or "the furrow") the warmth inflames them, and, apart from the unpleasant smell which results and is spread about, part of these exhalations, and of the substance of which they are formed, is taken up by the absorbent vessels and carried into the circulation where it can only do harm by disposing the humours to putrefaction.

Here the old beliefs in the permeability of the body and the importance of the humours remain—the danger is that sweat will re-enter the body and upset or putrefy the humours—but now they are combined with a new faith in the ability of water to prevent harm.

Nothing illustrates the new importance of water and washing better than its role in the lives of Napoleon and Josephine. Both commoners from the outskirts of the French world—he from Corsica, she from Martinique—they adored hot, fragrant baths. Their establishments always had a bathroom, which was a relative rarity in 1795, when they first set up housekeeping in a small, neo-Greek pavilion at 6 rue Chantereine, near the Tuileries. Josephine decorated their bathrooms like salons, with mounting ostentation, until the end of their marriage. She began the day with a long soak, accompanied with oils and carefully chosen perfumes.

Napoleon owned several bidets, one in silver gilt, equipped with crystal bottles and a silver-gilt box for sponges. But his real love was a steaming bath, where he generally spent two hours each morning while an aide read him newspapers and telegrams. During tense times, his bath lengthened: while the Peace of Amiens was collapsing in 1803, it stretched to six hours. A century earlier, Louis XIV had avoided water. Now the monarch of France could not begin the day without a prolonged immersion.

Lord Byron said that his times were distinguished by three great men: himself, Napoleon, and the finest of all—Beau Brummell. It is a provocative list, in which two are men of achievement, and the third a dandy whose gambling debts led to exile and ruin. Typical of their age, all three men loved water. Byron was a swimmer, Napoleon a devotee of bathing and Brummell, in the words of another admirer, "a great reformer who dared to be cleanly in the dirtiest of times."

We will probably never know what made young George Bryan Brummell a zealot for cleanliness, any more than we can understand why he took the Prince of Wales and London society by storm. The grandson of a shopkeeper and the son of an upwardly mobile clerk, Brummell, who was born in 1778, was an unlikely champion of washing and sober dress. In the late-eighteenth-century aristocratic society to which he aspired, men of dubious cleanliness wore gaudy colours and showy fabrics, and newspapers reported on men's fashions at least as enthusiastically as they did on women's. By about 1810, when the plainly dressed Brummell had become the standard of elegance, fashionable men were competing to wear the most unostentatious blue coats, black trousers and white shirts. Without peacock colours and extravagant trim to distract the eye from their dirt, they took up soap, water and brushes.

Little of this could have been predicted when "Buck" Brummell, as he was then called, was entertaining his classmates at Eton with his dry wit. In later years, they recalled his white stock, the stateliness of his walk and the dismay that dirty streets on a rainy day caused him. Other than that, he seemed an unremarkable young man, who left Oxford after a few months at age sixteen and joined the Tenth Hussars, commanded by the Prince of Wales. Brummell was neither particularly handsome nor obviously talented at anything. But

"His clothes seemed to melt into each other with the perfection of their cut and the quiet harmony of their colour. . . . He was the personification of freshness and cleanliness and order."

—Virginia Woolf, "Beau Brummell"

somehow his nonchalance, his graceful deportment and his undefinable charisma captivated the sophisticated thirty-six-year-old prince.

Brummell described his aesthetic—apparently born fully matured—in a few famous phrases. Of his revolutionary restraint in dress, he said, "If John Bull turns around to look at you, you are not well-dressed, but either too stiff, too tight, or too fashionable." Of his consummately neat looks, he explained, "No perfumes, but very fine linen, plenty of it, and country washing." The country washing referred to his linen, not his body, but a scrupulously clean body was the ground upon which Brummell built his elegance. In a daily three-hour operation, he began by washing every part of himself. After shaving, he abraded himself with a "flesh-brush" made of pig's bristles—a Regency strigil, in effect—until he looked as if he had scarlet fever. Then, taking up a dentist's mirror and a tweezers, he removed every extraneous hair from his face. In his simple but perfectly tailored coat and pants, with starched white linen, which he changed at least three times a day, there was nothing extraordinary about Beau Brummell except his extraordinary neatness and cleanness.

While stylish London did its best to imitate him, legends circulated about Brummell's devotion to cleanliness. He travelled everywhere with his own chamber pot, having once suffered the horror of seeing a cobweb in one in a country house he was visiting. (Such a pot, in a folding mahogany case with a carpet cover, was listed in the sale catalogue of his effects.) He is said to have objected to the admission of country gentlemen to Watier's supper club, certain that their boots would smell of horse manure and cheap blacking. A story was told about his stay at Belvoir Castle, where, in the gallery reserved for bedrooms, a great bell hung, to be pulled only in case of fire. About half an hour after the household and their guests had retired for the night, the bell began to ring loudly enough to rouse not only the entire castle but the neighbouring houses. Confusion ensued and everyone rushed into the hall in their night-clothes, but no fire could be found. Finally, Brummell advanced in his deliberate way, saying complacently, "Really, my good people, I regret having disturbed you, but the fact is my valet forgot to bring me my hot water."

Obviously there were neurotic elements to Brummell's attachment to hygiene, as well as a certain ironic burnishing of his own mystique. At the same time, he owed something to the new climate of ideas that found dirt repugnant. Lord Chesterfield's emphasis on cleanliness paved the way for Brummell, although the aristocrat would have scorned him as excessive and not entirely *comme il faut*. Even Rousseau's exaltation of hygiene found an echo in the dandy who shared at least some of his values—Brummell and Rousseau's Sophy would have enjoyed commiserating about the difficulty of staying perfectly clean.

Although the Prince of Wales and Brummell had a falling out in 1812, probably because Brummell's tart tongue ran away with him, it was his gambling debts that made life in England impossible. In 1816, he escaped his creditors by fleeing to Calais. His life in exile makes sad reading. He continued his cleansing rituals, even when taken to debtors' prison in Caen in 1835.

The loss of his freedom did not worry him as much as the absence of his dentist's mirror, tweezers, ewer and basin, shaving and spitting dish, soaps, pomades and eau de Cologne. Their arrival in prison raised Brummell's spirits considerably, and an astounded Frenchman described the care with which he washed all the parts of his body every day, using twelve to fifteen litres of water and two of milk. Between two and four in the afternoon, he would appear in the prison courtyard, perfectly coiffed and in immaculate linen.

After he was released, his debts mounted while his health declined. Sixteen months before he died of tertiary syphilis, which had probably plagued him for years, his intestines became paralyzed and he lost control of his bowels. The man who dreaded dying of "filthiness," as he said when he was separated from his elaborate toilet kit, was now unable to keep himself clean. Luckily, his mental state had deteriorated so much that he seemed unaware of his condition. Cared for by the Sisters of Charity in an institution for the mentally ill, he died at sixty-two in 1840.

Brummell's most tangible legacy, the starched white cravat, barely survived him. His wit, so admired in his London days, has neither the sting nor the complexity of Oscar Wilde's epigrams. His name endures as a byword for a male fashion plate, but his real achievement was the connection he forged between gentlemanliness and cleanliness. At the beginning of Brummell's career, according to his nineteenth-century biographer William Jesse, combs, hairbrushes and nail brushes "were not in general and indiscriminate use amongst the members of the clubs in St. James's Street." In 1886, when Jesse wrote

Brummell's biography, they were to be found in the dressing rooms of every London club. Clean and dirty had exchanged places: now the latter, not the former, was considered eccentric.

SIX

BATHS AND HOW
TO TAKE THEM
EUROPE, 1815–1900

*C*harles Dickens was born to be clean. Finicky, fastidious, with a dandy's taste in flashy waistcoats, he regularly inspected his children's bedrooms for the slightest evidence of untidiness. He was also a champion of progress, which is where people placed cleanliness in the nineteenth century. In the summer of 1849, the novelist and his family rented a house on the Isle of Wight. Dickens crowed to friends that they had driven a local carpenter and "all visitors in search of the Picturesque" mad by erecting an immense wooden caravan on the beach, which shut in a waterfall and converted it into "A Shower Bath! . . . Which we take, every morning, to the unbounded astonishment of the aboriginal inhabitants." Dickens sat under the shower in a big tub that was perforated at the sides and bottom. Although he took a daily cold bath in London—still a minority activity—his improvised shower struck him as even better.

As a result, when he bought a London house just off Tavistock Square in 1851, Dickens had an expensive, state-of-the-art bathroom built that included both a bathtub and a cold shower. Sending his architect a sketch of a curiously modern-looking tub and shower, framed in wood and shielded by waterproof curtains, Dickens italicized the most important thing in the room: "*a Cold Shower of the best quality, always charged to an unlimited extent.*" A tepid shower did not interest him, he wrote, but a cold one "has become a positive necessary of life to me. And without any disparagement to the Warm Bath, this, in perfection, it is my first object to secure."

When Dickens designed false bookcases and books to disguise the door from the drawing room to his study, he invented a seven-volume series facetiously called "The Wisdom of Our Ancestors." In addition to volumes called *Superstition*, *The Block*, *Ignorance*, *The Rack*, *Disease* and *The Stake* was one simply titled *Dirt*.

The water closet, or toilet, also in the bathroom, would be partitioned off. "I think (as a matter of sentiment)," he wrote the architect, "the Bather would be happier and easier in mind, if the W.C. did not demonstrate itself obtrusively. . . . I have not sufficient confidence in my strength of mind, to think that I could begin the business of every day, with the enforced contemplation of the outside of that box. I believe it would affect my bowels."

Dickens got his first-class shower, whose strength was such that it was known in the family as "The Demon," but not without more expense. Within a month of the family moving in, the water in the bathroom failed twice. Dickens wrote an indignant note to the Water Works, and an inspector arrived with remarkable speed and pronounced that an additional cistern, capable of holding 300 to 400 gallons, was needed. Describing himself half-jokingly as "helpless and affrighted," Dickens ordered the second cistern immediately.

Letting cold water pour down on one's head was still controversial enough that the heiress Angela Burdett Coutts, Dickens' friend and collaborator in charitable projects, expressed concern about its safety. Thanking her for her solicitude, he responded, "But I do sincerely believe that it

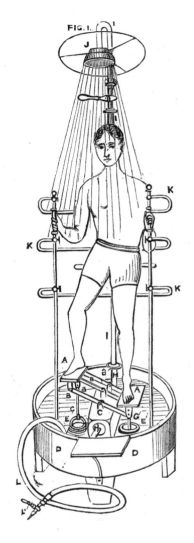

Bozerian's Shower Bath, 1878. Exercise as well as hygiene: in this British invention, the showerer activates the water by pedalling.

does me unspeakable service. I take but a very small part of the shock, on the head; and I have quite a remarkable power of enduring fatigue for which I believe I am very much indebted to this treatment. . . . I think it is of service to me as a Refresher—not as a taker out, but as a putter in of energy. . . . You have not seen the dreadful instrument yet, as it is set up here!"

Not everyone shared Dickens' enthusiasm for "the dreadful instrument" or for thorough washing in general, but more and more were experimenting with immersion. While they waited for the requisite pluck or plumbing to enter a shower or bathtub, people continued to clean themselves piecemeal, using a basin and pitcher for a stand-up wash, or a small, low tub in which they sat for a sponge bath. Ultimately, a full bath or a shower became the gold standard of cleanliness, but this did not happen for the majority of Europeans until the twentieth century. Submerging the body in water while washing it was a lost practice, and people recovered it gropingly and tentatively. That a doctor would write an article in 1861 called "Baths and How to Take Them" may seem slightly comical to us, but her audience was grateful for professional guidance through unfamiliar territory.

Hygiene manifestos and manuals multiplied in the first half of the century, as scientists ventured into a new world where cleanliness and health overlapped more than they had for centuries. The reigning doctrine of infection since the Middle Ages, the miasmatic theory, held that disease spread through bad smells, stuffy air and rotting material. Cleanliness obviously limited the spread of miasmas, but now there was an additional reason to keep clean. Beginning in the 1830s, the idea of the skin's respiratory

THE GREAT DIVIDE

"Are you a bath person or a shower person? It is impossible to exaggerate the character-revealing difference between the two."

—Michel Tournier, *Le miroir des idées*, 1994

function captured the attention of scientists on both sides of the Atlantic. If the pores were plugged with dirt, the theory went, carbon dioxide could not exit through the skin, and experiments on animals suggested that the consequences could be dire. Horses whose hides were shaved and then tarred slowly asphyxiated. If glue was added to the tar, death came more swiftly. Other unfortunate animals were coated with varnish, and also died.

Although we now know that such deaths were caused more by loss of thermal control than by respiratory problems, the nineteenth-century physiologists who did the experiments convinced the hygienists that cleansing the pores regularly with warm water was crucial to health and even to life. When Francis Bacon bathed in the seventeenth century, he took remarkable precautions to keep the pores as tightly closed as possible, to minimize the water that entered the body. Now doctors urged the opposite course. To them, a dirty skin, which was still seen by the peasantry as protective and strengthening, interfered with the proper functioning of the body.

On a visit to England in the 1860s, the Frenchman Hippolyte Taine found its houses deficient in taste. On the outside, they veered from bland to overly picturesque, "like toys made of painted cardboard." Inside, they lacked the French attention to matching colours and styles of furniture. But what they lacked in appearance, they made up for in comfort and service, especially in their bedrooms. On his dressing table in a country house, Taine found a large jug, a small jug, a medium one for hot water, two basins, a toothbrush dish, two soap dishes and a water bottle with tumbler. On the shelf underneath was a shallow zinc tub for the morning sponge bath; nearby

Bathing for health as well as cleanliness, at home or in a hotel—all possible with the folding bath cabinet.

was a towel horse with four different kinds of towels, one very thick. In the morning, a servant brought a jug of hot water and a linen mat to stand on while washing; the water was replenished before luncheon and dinner. Taine begged pardon for these "trifling details," but they showed the degree of luxury demanded by the English: "It has been laughingly said that they also spend one-fifth of their lives at a wash-basin."

Taine's view was shared by many of his compatriots, who had regarded England since the end of the eighteenth century as the land of modern conveniences and hygiene. But the French overestimated the extent of British cleanliness. In 1812, London's Common Council refused to supply the Lord Mayor with a shower bath in his residence because "the want thereof has never been complained of." The master of a Cambridge college had a different reason for saying no when it was suggested that baths be built for the students: there was no need, he responded, since "these young men are with us only for eight weeks at a time." Even Queen Victoria, when she took up residence in Buckingham Palace in 1837, had no bathroom. She used part of her allowance for clothing and personal items to have hot water piped into her bedroom, where she bathed in a portable tub.

Piped-in water on every floor and multiple water closets and baths had been feasible since the mid-eighteenth century, but few people, even prosperous ones, took advantage of the technology until a century later. When personal daintiness was not particularly desirable and servants could carry the water, why disrupt the household by installing a complicated system of pipes, boiler and cisterns? Hot piped water did begin to appear upstairs in expensive English houses around the 1840s, but the old ways still suited many people for decades to come. Even for people who went in for modern improvements, the situation was not perfect. The geyser, a small tank attached to the bathtub where piped-in cold water could be heated when a bath was wanted, became popular in the 1860s. Usually powered by gas, it was loud and dangerous, exploding every so often.

SPANISH ABLUTIONS

"The Duke of Frias, when a few years ago on a fortnight's visit to an English lady, never once troubled his basins and jugs; he simply rubbed his face occasionally with the white of an egg, which, as Madame Daunoy records, was the only ablution of Spanish ladies in the time of Philip IV."

—Richard Ford, English Hispanophile and essayist, 1845

Nor was a bath in one of the stately homes of England guaranteed to be pleasant, at least as Lord Ernest Hamilton remembered his boyhood in the 1860s and '70s. Immersed in a large iron tank that was shrouded on the outside in mahogany, the bather consulted a brass dial and chose Hot, Cold or Waste. When cold water was wanted, a clean, colourless flow appeared from a circle of perforations at the bottom of the bath.

A call on the hot water supply, however, did not meet with an effusive or even a warm response. A succession of sepulchral rumblings was succeeded by the appearance of a small geyser of rust-coloured water, heavily charged with dead earwigs and bluebottles. This continued for a couple of minutes or so and then entirely ceased. The only perceptible difference between the hot water and the cold lay in its colour and the cargo of defunct life which the former bore on its bosom. Both were stone cold.

Small wonder that these tubs "were not popular as instruments of cleanliness." Lord Ernest and his brother used theirs instead as a lake for toy boats and as an occasional aquarium.

Luckily for the Briton who was intent on cleanliness, there were various ways to achieve it, each described in a book published in 1860, *The Habits of Good Society: A Handbook for Ladies and Gentlemen*. A warm bath of 96 to 100 degrees would clean best, according to the anonymous author, but left the bather powerless and prostrate. A cold bath "cleanses less, but invigourates more." It was a perilous venture even a day after eating a heavy meal, and "persons of full temperament" should avoid it altogether. As for the shower, which was dangerous for general use, the less said the better.

The Habits of Good Society goes into considerable detail about materials and technique for the bath it

In 1849, at Miss Browning's Academy at Blackheath, parents paid extra for their daughters to take a weekly hot bath. Two sisters who did so were called "the bathing Garretts."

considers safest, the daily sponge bath. A flat metal basin, about four feet in diameter, should be filled with cold water. The ideal sponge, as coarse as possible, is a hefty one foot in length and six inches across. When completely filled with water, it should first attack the stomach: "It is there that the most heat has collected during the night, and the application of cold water quickens the circulation at once." To soap or not to soap the body is debatable, but the writer prefers a rough towel or hair glove, without soap. After a man's bath, the author recommends exercise, with or without dumb-bells: "The best plan of all is, to choose some object in your bedroom on which to vent your hatred, and box at it violently for some ten minutes, till the perspiration covers you. The sponge must then be again applied to the whole body. It is very desirable to remain without clothing as long as possible, and I should therefore recommend that every part of the toilet which can conveniently be performed without dressing, should be so."

The people wielding sponges and boxing at lampshades were almost invariably from the middle and upper classes. The working class still lacked the means for thorough and frequent washing, a fact that was making the English increasingly uncomfortable. Somewhere around the beginning of the nineteenth century, people started becoming aware that the poor were dirtier than the well-off. Although that sounds like an obvious and ancient idea, it was in fact relatively new. When the middle and upper classes feared water, roughly from the Renaissance to the end of the eighteenth century, they washed as little as peasants or the urban poor. In fact, since the royal body was the most precious body in the kingdom, and hence deserved the greatest protection from the dangerous assault of water, it is possible that James I of England and Philip V of Spain were dirtier than some of their subjects. Great wealth or status had not made the Duke of Norfolk or Lady Mary Wortley Montagu cleaner or sweeter-smelling than the average Briton.

Englishwomen "wash every other part of the body, but, unhappily for their own comfort as well as that of their husbands, they seem averse to let clean water reach the vagina."

—Dr. William Acton, 1841

Now that rough equality between the classes was dying out. In 1804, Lady Buckingham celebrated her birthday with a dance for the tenant farmers on her estate. "We all danced with the tenants," one of her house guests reported. "I laughed a great deal to see the different mixture of people. We could hardly breathe it was so hot and the smell was beyond anything." The fact that the poor smelled unpleasant was only noticeable once Lady Buckingham and her house guests washed more and hence smelled better. When William Makepeace Thackeray coined the term "the Great Unwashed" in 1849, in his novel *Pendennis,* he was naming a new kind of class divide.

The threat of disease made this particular chasm not just disagreeable but frightening, and nowhere more so than in Britain, where the Industrial Revolution had been born and was mushrooming most quickly. Spurred on by the belief that unventilated rooms, foul odours and decomposing garbage made them sick, the middle classes in mid-century were taking steps to clean themselves and their houses. But the filthy conditions of the urban poor were more difficult to correct, and dangerous not only to themselves but to the larger population. Again and again in his novels, Dickens uses the fear of contagion to symbolize the interconnectedness of society on all levels. The smallpox that spreads from the wretched hovel of Jo the crossing-sweeper to the comfortable home of Lady Dedlock's daughter in *Bleak House* (1853), for example, is a forceful reminder that the neglect of its weakest members makes society as a whole vulnerable.

At the same time, the squalor of the industrial cities was worsening. The potato famine in Ireland sent tens of thousands of poor people to England, especially to Liverpool. In 1841, the twenty-seven houses of Church Lane, in the St. Giles district of London, held 655 people. Only six years later, the same houses held 1,095 people. Unclean water and filthy housing allowed typhoid, typhus, diphtheria and other infectious illnesses to flourish as a matter of course. But it was the appearance of cholera—an acute, often fatal disease native to China and India—in the 1830s that finally terrified Britons into action. Out of self-interest, if not benevolence, England needed to clean its meanest slums and most desperate people.

In the summer of 1842, after three years' work, Edwin Chadwick presented his *Report on the Sanitary Condition of the Labouring Population of Great Britain* to the House of Lords. Aided by dozens of local observers, Chadwick, the secretary to the Poor Law Commission, painted a horrific picture of life without ventilation, functioning privies, clean water or privacy. Entire families—parents and children from babies to adolescents—slept in one bed. Chadwick quoted a doctor who was asked about the

"HARD WORK AND COLD WATER":
THE WATER BABIES

One of the nineteenth century's most popular works for children, Charles Kingsley's *The Water Babies* appeared in 1863 and was reprinted nearly a hundred times. Behind the adventure story lies the Victorian conviction that cold water would transform a filthy ragamuffin into a model citizen. It centres on Tom, a young chimney sweep whose physical, spiritual and intellectual darknesses are closely intertwined: "He could not read nor write, and did not care to do either; and he never washed himself, for there was no water up in the court where he lived. He had never been taught to say his prayers."

One day, cleaning a great house, Tom loses his way in its endless chimneys and exits into a lady's bedroom. There he finds a big bath filled with water and a sleeping girl with golden hair and white skin. Stunned, Tom wonders, "And are all people like that when they are washed?" and tries to rub some of the soot off his wrist. Then he catches sight of himself in a mirror— "a little ugly, black, ragged figure, with bleared eyes and grinning white teeth. He turned on it angrily. What did such a little black ape want in that sweet young lady's room?"

Tom's conversion begins at that minute, with the realization that he is filthy. He falls into a delirium, saying over and over, "I must be clean, I must be clean." Only after dying and finding a new life as an amphibious water baby can Tom be reborn as a human who appreciates "hard work and cold water." Kingsley, an Anglican minister and keen sanitary reformer, ends by admonishing his young readers: "Meanwhile, do you learn your lessons, and thank God that you have plenty of cold water to wash in; and wash in it too, like a true Englishman."

hygiene of the workers in his district. He answered: "Generally extremely filthy. I have said that I could almost smell from what street a man came who came to my surgery: I do not think the poor themselves are conscious of it, but the smell to other persons must be extremely offensive. I certainly think that the want of personal cleanliness, and of cleanliness in their rooms, and the prevalence of fever, stand in the relation of cause and effect."

Another doctor, from Chipping Norton, described a husband, wife and five children all ill with smallpox in one bedroom with two beds. The walls, the sheets and the patients were black; "two of the children were absolutely sticking together." Disarmingly, the doctor adds that he has enjoyed many a biscuit and glass of wine in a dissecting room holding ten bodies under dissection, but he completely lost his appetite during his visit to the smallpox cases: "The smell on entering the apartments was exceedingly nauseous, and the room would not admit of free ventilation."

The poor themselves could be equally disarming about their personal habits. One man, when told that he had to be washed on admittance to a workhouse, protested that this was equivalent "to robbing him of a greatcoat which he had had for some years." A collier in Lancashire, asked how often the drawers (those who transport coals) washed their bodies, answered, "None of the drawers ever wash their bodies. I never wash my body; I let my shirt rub the dirt off; my shirt will show

> "I do not blame the working man because he stinks, but stink he does. It makes social intercourse difficult to persons of sensitive nostril. The matutinal tub divides the classes more effectually than birth, wealth or education."
> —Somerset Maugham, On a Chinese Screen, 1922

that. I wash my neck and ears, and face, of course." Of the young women working in the colliery, he said, "I do not think it is usual for the lasses to wash their bodies; my sisters never wash themselves, and seeing is believing; they wash their faces, necks and ears." His standard of cleanliness was that of the seventeenth century: you washed what showed ("seeing is believing") and let your linen do the rest. When the interviewer mentioned the collier's traditional full-dress outfit of white stockings and starched, ruffled shirt, the worker assured him that the whiteness covered a wilderness of dirt: "Their legs and bodies are as black as your hat."

In the wake of Chadwick's report, England faced the cumbersome business of improving sanitation for the poor. Repairing, enlarging, ventilating and plumbing antiquated slums would be the work of decades, even generations. Building bathhouses was easier. Since the closing of most of London's public bathhouses in the sixteenth century, the city had usually supported a few baths, which as in Paris were used as much for assignations and barbering as for bathing. Toward the end of the eighteenth century, as washing became more fashionable, some commercial bathhouses—with a more single-minded focus on bathing—opened, but with fees and facilities designed for the middle and upper classes.

Bathing accommodations for the poor appeared in fits and starts. In the aftermath of the cholera epidemic of

CASANOVA IN 18TH-CENTURY LONDON

"In the evening I frequented the most select bagnios where a man of quality can sup, bathe, and meet well-bred women of easy virtue. There are plenty of this sort in London. The entertainment only costs about six guineas, and with economy one can do it for four; but economy was never one of my failings."

1832, a Liverpool labourer's wife named Kitty Wilkinson strung up a clothesline in her backyard and lent out her copper basin to any woman who wanted to wash her family's clothes. That was the germ of the public laundry, an immediately popular idea. The city of Liverpool took up Wilkinson's idea, added hot and cold baths to the laundry facilities, and opened the Frederick Street Baths in 1842. It was Britain's first public washhouse and bathhouse, and more than forty thousand baths were taken there during its first three years.

Laundries and baths made a natural combination, and in 1846, the Baths and Washhouses Act authorized boroughs and parishes to build and maintain these facilities. The act stipulated that a customer in the lowest-class bath could not be asked to pay more than twopence for clean water and a clean towel (more middle-class establishments charged two shillings), and at least two-thirds of the baths had to be in the cheapest category. Bathhouses built as a result of the act usually had one or two plunge pools or larger pools meant for swimming, a number of private bath compartments and a laundry. Within six years, Birmingham, Hull, Liverpool, Bristol, Nottingham, Tynemouth and Preston had built baths. London had thirteen, including a model bathhouse at Whitechapel, visited by Belgian and French delegations eager to import the English innovation to the Continent.

In the first few decades after the 1846 act, bath building in England progressed slowly. There were financial disappointments. Free baths were considered insulting to the poor, and the nominal charge was intended to be a first step on the ladder of self-reliance. Unfortunately, the low fees rarely stretched to cover maintenance, and boroughs and municipalities were reluctant to add to their financial burden with more baths. But the bath builders and health reformers had a more fundamental problem: the majority of the poor did not crave baths. When even prosperous people had to learn the point of bathing, the poor had a much less lively sense of its value. The most up-to-date facilities for the poor held little appeal and numerous worries for them. Many older people still believed that taking a bath was a risky, strenuous affair. One woman told investigators that "baths were fine for them as do have the needful strength." Both young and old thought they could catch colds or infections from bathing. More men than women used the baths, partly because their work made them dirtier, partly because men had fewer domestic responsibilities added on to their workday, and partly because many working-class women felt that going to a public bathhouse was not respectable.

The poor were not the only ones who found bathing suspect. Earnest and self-denying, the middle class and the more religious circles of the upper class distrusted the self-indulgence of immersion in warm water and preferred the cold bath, especially for men. Beyond religious affiliation, the English gentry looked askance at modern plumbing. Because the middle classes and the *nouveaux riches* welcomed gas, water closets and piped-in water, the upper classes drew back. Many a denizen of a sprawling, stony-cold country estate looked on "mod cons" as slightly uncouth, overeager and—worst of all—middle-class.

Lady Diana Cooper, the daughter of the eighth Duke of Rutland, was born in 1892, but her memories of turn-of-the-century life at Belvoir Castle, in Leicestershire, have a medieval ring. It was the same castle where Beau Brummell had frightened the household by pulling the fire bell, and nothing had been modernized in the century that followed. The broad hallways were completely unheated, and candles and oil lamps furnished the only light. "Gas was despised," Lady Diana wrote. "I forget why—vulgar, I think." Most primeval of all were the water-men.

> The water-men are difficult to believe in to-day. They seemed to me to belong to another clay. They were the biggest people I had ever seen. . . . On their shoulders they carried a wooden yoke from which hung two gigantic cans of water. They moved on a perpetual round. Above the ground floor there was not a drop of hot water and not one bath, so their job was to keep all jugs, cans and kettles full in the bedrooms, and morning or evening to bring the hot water for the hip-baths. We were always a little frightened of the water-men. They seemed of another element and never spoke but one word, "Water-man," to account for themselves.

Only after 1906, when Lady Diana's grandfather died and her father inherited Belvoir, did it begin to emerge into modern times. "Bathrooms were carved out of the deep walls, rooms and passages were warm without the coal-man's knock, the water-men faded away into the elements."

Of course, the owners of country houses and large town establishments could maintain the old ways because their servants took care of the drudgery. Even when there was a bathroom on each floor, women often preferred to wash in the privacy of their bedroom or dressing room, with or without a full-size tub. Trotting down drafty corridors in a dressing gown was not as nice as slipping into a warm bath prepared before the fire in one's room. As late as the 1920s, Lady Fry thought "bathrooms were only for servants."

When it came to public baths, as with the Industrial Revolution in general, England led and the Continent followed. Between 1800 and 1850, the industrial cities in Germany and France doubled in population. Antiquated water supplies, sewers and street-cleaning practices were modernized first, but that was not enough. As Oscar Lassar, a Berlin doctor and one of Germany's leading sanitary reformers, asked, "What is the use of all the care with which our cities are cleaned, drainage and trash removal regulated, and ventilation increased, when the person himself must dispense with the most basic cleanliness?"

In Germany, the beloved bathhouse tradition that dated from the Middle Ages had dwindled to near-extinction, surviving mostly in small, remote places. But the Romantic infatuation with cold water and swimming helped the return of public baths: swimming became part

Be clean on the outside and clean within
Pure your speech and pure your thoughts.
—Inscribed on the walls of
a Stuttgart bathhouse

of basic training for the Prussian army in 1817, and public beaches and outdoor baths multiplied around the country in the first half of the nineteenth century. In 1855, a group of Hamburg businessmen built the first bathhouse inspired by English example, with Berlin following suit later in the year. By the end of the century almost every German city had erected at least one large-scale public bathhouse. Unlike English ones, these new baths were not exclusively or even primarily for the working class. An *Armenbad*, or poor bath, was considered condescending. Poor and prosperous should bathe together, "united in the cause of health," as a Bonn architect put it. Less idealistically, the middle classes wanted bathing facilities, too. In 1881, fewer than 4 per cent of houses in Cologne had bathrooms. More significant, the great majority of mansions springing up on the city's showy new boulevard, the Ringstrasse, also did not include a bathroom. While the English upper-middle classes were content to spread their oilcloth on the bedroom floor and wash in a portable tub, the Germans, like latter-day Romans or their own medieval ancestors, preferred going out to bathe.

And there was something reminiscent of a Roman bath—not the full-blown Imperial version, but the well-equipped colonial type—in the new German bathhouses. (Stuttgart's bathhouse went one better than the Romans, including among its lavish facilities a bath for dogs.) Also like its Roman predecessor, the nineteenth-century German bath became an emblem of civic pride, an important part of a city's boast that it fulfilled the physical and spiritual needs of its citizens.

Cologne's Hohenstaufenbad, which opened in 1885, was typical. Built on the Ringstrasse, close to the Opera

House and other examples of local prowess, the bath was designed in the elaborate Renaissance Revival style, rich with murals, decorative glass and verses painted on the walls that celebrated cleanliness, progress and the continuity with Roman bathing. The Hohenstaufenbad offered separate swimming pools for men, women and workers, a restaurant, a barbershop and three different classes of bathtubs. The Volksschwimmbad, or people's swimming pool, was located at the back of the building, with a separate entrance not on the Ringstrasse.

But building civic temples where the well-to-do bathed in style while the poor entered—literally—at the back door did not succeed in bringing sanitation to the masses. The poor felt ill at ease in such sumptuous surroundings, and swimming pools and private baths did not serve their needs particularly well. Swimming pools were expensive to maintain and recreational rather than cleansing. A bath was necessary before a swim, but bathtubs and grimy workingmen made a bad combination, because the worker was soon sitting in his

own dirty water. The statistics were not encouraging: one turn-of-the-century survey suggested that the average German took five baths in a year. Although the lavish bathhouses were not self-supporting, municipalities persisted in building them—they were too prestigious and too much enjoyed by the bourgeoisie to discontinue.

In 1883, Dr. Lassar proposed a new and affordable way of cleaning the working class. At the Berlin Public Health Exhibition, he displayed a model bathhouse that consisted only of individual stalls with nozzles mounted high on the wall—simple showers. The shower, more or less rudimentary, had been known to the ancient Greeks as well as to Montaigne and Madame de Sévigné, but the popular mind connected them with prisoners, soldiers and horridly cold water. Although Lassar was influenced by the Prussian army showers, the "People's Bath" he exhibited in Berlin sprayed warm water. A corrugated-iron building, it held five shower cubicles for men and five for women. Probably inspired by the new public urinals of Paris, the showers were also intended for the street. At the exhibition, tens of thousands of adventurous visitors paid ten pfennigs for a shower that included the use of soap and a towel.

Calculating that one mark paid for the water for 33 baths or 666 showers, Lassar claimed that his innovation would save more than 66 million marks a year. An American sanitary engineer agreed. The "rain bath," as the shower was called, was

> the simplest, quickest, cheapest, cleanest and withal best bath for people's bath houses; the one which requires the least space, the least time, the least amount of water, the least fuel for warming water, the least attendance, the least cost of maintenance. Standing under such an inclined spray the bather can soap and rub his body, rinse it with more clean warm water, which falls down in a gentle yet invigorating rain of fine jets from the neck downward. . . . The rain bath has, for all these reasons, become the modern favourite method, and is destined to be the bath of the future for people's baths.

The unappealing streetside shower-houses never caught on, for obvious reasons. But Vienna, Frankfurt and several other German cities soon added rows of showers to their public bathhouses, usually at a cost of ten pfennigs per shower. By 1904, 101 of 137 German public baths included showers, usually in combination with baths. Although clearly more economical, showers did not become as well used as Lassar had hoped. Perhaps they never entirely outgrew their institutional, slightly menacing image. Perhaps even a timed and regulated bath in a bathhouse promised more comfort than standing, naked and vulnerable, waiting for a spray whose heat and power could be unreliable. Whatever the reason, the shower never won mass approval in Germany or England.

The struggle between dirty and clean proceeded somewhat differently in France. As in England, the scientific and medical establishment had a new interest in cleanliness, buoyed up in France by the establishment of a chair of hygiene at the University of Paris's Faculty of Medicine in the early 1790s. And there was no question that Parisians, for example, were cleaner in the nineteenth century than they had been in the *ancien régime*. "Rancid pomade and dirty powder no longer hide handsome black or silver-blonde hair," a doctor wrote in 1804. "The people change their underwear more often, fre-

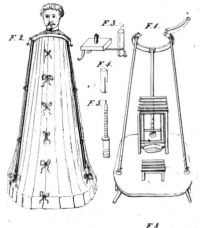
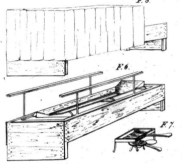

Yet more ways to steam oneself: these elaborate contraptions were available from the 1830s.

quent public baths more often, and prefer simple and comfortable clothes."

But beyond the mode for natural, revealing coiffures and gowns, French practices did not dramatically change. Apartments and houses remained ill-equipped with water, more from lack of interest than from an inability to install running water. In the 1830s, when a third of London houses had hidden pipes that delivered and removed water, the chief water engineer for Paris was still insisting that such an endeavour would be too costly and dangerous—the damp introduced into houses by the pipes would stay forever.

Monuments were a greater priority than plumbing, as the sharp-eyed Englishwoman Frances Trollope noted when she visited Paris in 1835. After seeing the city's newest pride, the Church of the Madeleine, she wrote, "I think it would have been more useful, for the town of Paris, to have saved the sums it cost to build for the construction and laying of pipes to distribute water to private houses." For that to happen, attitudes would have to shift.

According to Dr. J. A. Goullin, the traditional washing schedule has much to recommend it: *Saepe manus, raro pedes, nunquam caput*: "Hands often, the feet rarely, the head never."

—*La mode sous le point de vue hygiénique*, 1846

Charles François Mallet admitted as much in his 1830 book about water distribution in Paris: "It is a question here of changing our habits, of exchanging the niggardly manner with which we now use water in favour of a generous use of this element essential to life and domestic health, and in favour of the habits of washing which are so beneficial to health, and which will eventually be introduced into France as has for long been the case with our neighbours across the sea." The mention of Britain's superiority in these matters was almost automatic. Although the French exaggerated the English devotion to hygiene, they were right in seeing that objections to cleanliness were less deeply rooted there than in France, and that reformers and sanitarians were more influential.

Washing thoroughly at home remained, at least until the 1870s, almost as difficult as it had been in the seventeenth century. When the water for a bath had

Bébé montre qu'il ne craint pas l'eau froide.

S'il veut qu'on l'embrasse, il faut que Bébé prépare la place.

Des pieds à la tête, Bébé sera l'enfant frais et rose que tout le monde veut embrasser.

Seul, comme un grand homme, Bébé procède chaque jour à sa toilette.

Bébé learns to wash. In spite of the ringlets and nightdress, this is a little French boy mastering the elements of good hygiene, from braving cold water to cleaning his face to make it more kissable.

BATHS AND HOW TO TAKE THEM   185

been laboriously prepared, a Parisian apartment often had no better place for a filled tub than the hallway. One day, in the dim light of a friend's hall, the poet Stéphane Mallarmé witnessed the drowning of the painter Edouard Manet's overcoat. When Manet politely folded it and laid it down on what he thought was an opalescent marble-topped table, it turned out to be a full bathtub. Even when an apartment had a room dedicated to washing, it did not necessarily have a bathtub. When Hector Berlioz died in 1869, the inventory of his apartment included two washing rooms, but no tub. Washing without a tub proceeded bit by bit, as the writer Edmée Renaudin remembered:

> A small jug of water was brought. "What shall we wash today?"—"Well," replied our Alsatian maid hesitantly, "your face, your neck?—Ah, no, you washed your neck yesterday!—Well then, your arms, up to your elbows, and make sure you roll up your sleeves!" Personal hygiene was attended to while squatting over a bowl. We took it in turns on alternate days.

Public baths were more convenient—at least in theory. A few, such as the Chinese Baths on the boulevard des Italiens in Paris, were opulent, supplying heated robes, rest rooms, reading rooms and abundant servants. Their fee was correspondingly high, from five to twenty francs at mid-century, when a worker's daily wage was two and a half francs. Most bathhouses were significantly less costly, but did not attract more than a small percentage of the population. In 1819 the public baths in Paris provided 600,000 baths for a population of

700,000—a little under one bath a year for each Parisian. Thirty years later, the numbers indicated that the average Parisian patronized the baths twice a year. In fact, the bathhouses were largely located in wealthy and bourgeois neighbourhoods, so that prosperous people bathed more than the average, and poorer people less. Beginning in the 1860s, piped-in water began to flow in the luxurious quarters of Paris's Right Bank, and then on the Left Bank. By the 1880s, solidly middle-class apartments often had running water. But old hesitations remained, which some French reformers connected to their Catholicism. One of the English advantages when it came to hygiene, they theorized, was their religion:

BATHS TO GO, OR THE CARRY-IN BATH

In 1819, a Monsieur Villette introduced Paris to a German innovation that allowed people to bathe at home in privacy and safety. A service, called a *bain à domicile*, delivered to the client's house or apartment, even on the top floor, all the necessities of a bath—a tub, a robe and sheet, and hot, cold or tepid water as ordered. When the bath was over, everything was whisked away, including the water, which was usually removed by a hose that ran from the tub to the gutter on the street. The *bain à domicile*, a titillating combination of intimacy and commercialism, inspired comic songs, stories and a popular practical joke, in which mischief-makers ordered several baths to be delivered in the middle of a friend's dinner party. But however much people enjoyed talking about the *bains à domicile*, only a thousand were ordered in 1838, in a city of more than a million inhabitants.

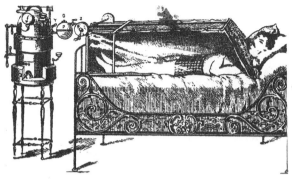

The owner of this French apparatus could have a steam bath in his own bed.

since Protestants (in their view) did not share their Catholic prudery about nudity, washing the body could be more straightforward and more thorough. In her treatise for French women, *On Politeness and Good Taste, or the Duties of a Christian Woman in the World*, published in 1860, the Countess Drohojowska advised: "Never take more than one bath a month. There is in the taste for sitting down in a bathtub a certain indolence and softness that ill suits a woman." The Countess de Pange recalled, "No-one in my family took a bath!" They washed in a tub filled with two inches of water or sponged themselves, rather than sinking into water up to their necks, which seemed "pagan, even sinful."

The women who were known to bathe more often and more magnificently than the average were the most exclusive courtesans as well as actresses and dancers, who were often the mistresses of rich men. Mademoiselle Moisset, of the Opéra Comique, decorated her bathroom with engraved mirrors and panels in the fashionable Oriental style, and had a bathtub in silvered copper set into a richly carved wooden surround. Mademoiselle Devise, who danced at the opera, had a copper tub encased in wickerwork. La Paiva, a celebrated late-century prostitute, covered the walls of her Moorish bathroom with onyx. Her tub, also set in onyx, was silver, ornamented with a copper frieze. The oils and unguents, the precious pots and bottles, and the long, languid hours these women spent soaking and anointing themselves were as legendary as the bathrooms themselves.

The connection between opulent bathing and women of ill repute was suspicious enough. But even without the example of actresses and mistresses, the idea of a woman or girl immersing herself, nude, in warm water had an unsavoury tinge. Many convent-educated girls were ordered to bathe in a shirt or shift, but boys and men also had to be protected from "the moral dangers of spending an hour naked in the bath-tub." A *Manual of Hygiene,* published in 1844, urged that "certain parts of the body" (which are never named) should be washed only once a day. Noting that some people, especially women, washed these parts more than once a day, the author wrote, vaguely but ominously, "We do not advise this. We wish to respect the mystery of clean-liness. We will content our-selves with observing that everything which goes be-yond the boundaries of a

An early French theme bathroom, a Gothic *salle de bain.*

healthy and necessary hygiene leads imperceptibly to unfortunate results."

Prudery in the name of religion or propriety may partly have been the socially acceptable face of an age-old disinclination to wash all over. Whatever its source, it was real enough that several French women in the second half of the century tried to convince their readers that cleanliness and morality went hand in hand. One was the Baroness Staffe, who published *Le cabinet de toilette* in 1893. Taking a leaf from the luxurious retreats of the *demi-monde*, respectable bourgeois and aristocratic women had set up their own *cabinets de toilette*, ultra-feminine refuges in an alcove in the bedroom or next door, where the serious work of grooming was done in private. The baroness favoured these womanly sanctuaries, as sumptuous as could be afforded.

She sketches such a *salle de bain*, where the walls are covered in onyx and marble, the shower stands hidden behind a silk curtain in a corner, and "*le* tub"—she uses the English word when describing a low, portable basin—sits in the other corner, ready when a sponge bath is called for. The bathtub proper has taps for hot, cold and tepid water, and marble shelves nearby hold the necessary perfumes and oils. On a chaise longue covered with a white bearskin, the bather "rests from the fatigues of immersion and hydrotherapy." She wears an elegant garment with a new name— the *robe de bain*, or bathrobe,

CHACUN À SON GOÛT

The French woman's *cabinet de toilette* was devoted more to ideas of luxury, femininity and secrecy than efficient, thorough hygiene. When French visitors to the 1900 Exhibition of Hygiene in Paris beheld the American bathroom, with streamlined, fixed appliances and a complete absence of frills, they disdained it as a "laboratory" and a "factory for washing."

has replaced the *peignoir*, the robe in which you combed your hair.

The baroness's bathing advice was typical of enlightened opinion in her day. To keep the pores open, which is essential for good health, everyone must wash every day. That can be done in a full tub if one is available and the doctor permits a *"grand bain,"* or with a sponge bath if not. One must be very strong to endure a cold bath, and only under doctor's orders. Hot baths can be useful for those who are troubled with excessive blood to the brain. But for most people, the lukewarm bath is best, and for no more than half an hour. Wait three to four hours after a full meal before bathing, the baroness advises, and don't bathe in someone else's water, no matter how healthy that person. ("Mothers who take their children into the bath with them ignore the fact that this habit is very dangerous to these little beings whose delicate skin can absorb unfavourable, even dangerous exhalations.") She recommends friction with a brush or a rough towel. Soap, which should not be used every day, should be white, very pure and either lightly perfumed or completely unperfumed.

The baroness is most eloquent when discussing, not how to bathe, but why to bathe. To those who find cleanliness irreligious, she writes that the real impiety is neglect of the body. And yet girls leave convent schools and boarding schools with little understanding of hygiene—a subject their mothers "often acquired themselves, little by little, sometimes not without humiliations." Too many of these

"Instead of the tub, which freezes your feet, ridiculous with its noisy theatrical thunderclaps, a wooden bucket, a vat, that's it! A good wooden vat of Montigny wood, hooped beech, in which I can sit cross-legged in the hot water, and which scrapes the behind in an agreeable fashion."

—Colette, *Claudine in Paris*, 1901

mothers perpetuate the problem by remaining silent about their daughters' cleanliness. Doctors, who should preach the purity of the body as the doctors of the soul preach the purity of the spirit, are also failing them. Cleanliness, the baroness insists, takes us close to the angels of light, while dirtiness drags us down into the primordial sludge.

Many French people, even the wealthiest, resisted the call of the angels. In the thirteen châteaux that the architect Edouard Dainville built or renovated in Anjou between 1856 and 1881, he designed a grand total of two bathrooms. In the other eleven châteaux, owners, guests and servants made do with a basin and ewer, or perhaps a sponge bath, which was called in France "the English wash." (In England, such a bath is still occasionally called "the French bath.") Things began to improve by the end of the nineteenth century, when water closets and baths in grand houses seemed less remarkable. In the 1880s, when the Rothschilds enlarged their Château d'Armainvilliers, the new wing had seven en suite bathrooms on the bedroom floor. But plenty of aristocratic holdouts still balked at modern plumbing. In the 1960s, when the English wife of the Vicomte de Baritault inspected his château, Roquetaillade—which had been elaborately rehabilitated in the nineteenth century by the restoration architect Eugène Viollet-Le-Duc—she counted sixty chamber pots, no toilets and one bathroom.

Before 1850, the Parisian poor could bathe in the Seine in the summer, either in the crowded, roughly enclosed *bains à quatre sous* (four-penny baths) or more surreptitiously,

French soldiers enduring showers and baths at Vichy.

and without paying any fee, in a secluded stretch of the river. Hospitals and poorhouses provided indoor baths—though not many and never inviting—in all seasons. In France, as in England some years earlier, the coming of cholera in 1849 gave a new urgency to the question of hygiene for the poor. Public bathhouses were erected, although fewer than in England, and initially the French were predictably unenthusiastic. The poor found them unappealing, and the middle classes fretted about the morality of the poor. "Excessively prolonged baths produce in working-class girls and women of the people a troublesome susceptibility," warned Bourgeois d'Orvanne, and everyone knew what that susceptibility was.

Prudery was only part of the problem. Behind it lay a deeper French indifference to cleanliness, according to a report commissioned by the Ministry of Public Education in 1884. Charged with an investigation of school hygiene, the committee began with a sweeping statement:

"The women I paint are simple, decent persons, totally absorbed in the care of their bodies."

—Edgar Degas, on his paintings of women washing themselves

It must be admitted first of all that, of all the civilized nations, ours is one of those which cares least about cleanliness. . . . The most superficial enquiry is sufficient to prove that, even among the well-to-do classes, strict bodily cleanliness does not always extend beyond the visible parts of the body. . . . Habits are even worse among rural populations. One has only to practise medicine in the country to know the terror that the recommendation of a bath inspires in most peasants.

The committee put its finger on at least one undeniable fact: France's large peasant population feared washing and glorified dirt. Proverbs underscored the belief that dirt was protective: "People who take baths die young." "Dirt nourishes the hair." "If you want to reach old age, don't take the oil off your skin." A powerful body odour promised a robust sexuality: "The more the ram stinks, the more the ewe loves him." Peasants obeyed an age-old intuition that washing, if done at all, should accord with the seasons. After the winter hibernation, a spring dip in the river might be called for. But for people who were washed thoroughly only at birth and after death, a bath was a fearsome rite of passage that often signified the end of life. When a peasant, upon arriving at a hospital, was bathed in a full-size tub and never recovered, it was routine to blame the bath. "It was the big baths that killed her off," peasants said. Or "he died in the big baths."

French reformers tried to counter these folkloric notions with a wide-ranging public education campaign. Booklets on hygiene, public health columns in the newspapers and hygiene classes in the schools were pitched at levels that excluded almost no one. In his *Encyclopédie de la santé, cours d'hygiène populaire,* published in 1855, J. Massé describes a bath in painstaking detail, taking nothing for granted, beginning with the equipment—a small tub, a dish half full of cold water, a kettle of hot water, a large piece of flannel and two large sponges of the kind used to clean floors (but no soap). First the bather rubs his body all over with the cloth. Then, dipping his two sponges into water, one in each hand, he begins the work of washing. "Do not leave off for a moment," he is instructed, "use your water in such a way that you have enough to operate for at least one minute; and as soon as you have finished, step out of the tub and quickly take a towel to dry yourself."

THE MINER'S WIFE
WASHES HER HUSBAND

"She had gone down from his back to his buttocks and, warming up to the job, she pushed ahead into the cracks and did not leave a single part of his body untouched, making it shine like her three saucepans on spring-cleaning Sundays. . . . The bath always ended up like this—she made him excited by rubbing so hard and then towelling him everywhere, tickling the hairs on his arms and chest. It was the time when all the chaps in the village took their fun and more children were planted than anyone wanted."

—Emile Zola, *Germinal*, 1885

Hygiene in the school curriculum, launched in 1882 by Jules Ferry, the minister of education, began with the youngest children and proceeded through the grades. Personal hygiene infiltrated the whole curriculum, appearing not just in health and science classes, but also in dictations, assigned readings and recitations. A dictation for children in the early grades reads, "Louise does not like cold water. This morning she thought she had washed herself because she gently passed the flannel across the end of her nose. Her face stayed dirty and her hands black. Her mother does not want to kiss her in that state."

Another dictation, about a studious but dirty little boy, continues with questions: "Why do people not like this little boy? ... Does he look after his hair?" The lesson concludes, "Conjugate: I know my duty. I wash my hands. I wipe and polish the brasswork."

But the cleanliness preached in the schools focused on the visible, especially hands and face. No one expected the textbooks to mention the anal or genital areas, but almost the only part of the body other than hands and head that was recommended for washing was the feet. Even a minimal schedule of washing was honoured more in the breach than in the observance in French boarding schools. Bathing once a month in the winter, as ordered by the committees on hygiene, was rarely possible in large parts of the country. In a late-nineteenth-century survey of *lycées* throughout France, fewer than half had bathing accommodations for boarding students, and infrequent visits to the municipal bathhouse were considered sufficient. In some schools, only students who were ill took full baths.

Public bathhouses, which began so haltingly in nineteenth-century France, won a slow, partial approval. One of the successes in France was the laundry side of the bathhouse, which was always more patronized than the baths—a priority given to clean clothes rather than bodies that recalls the France of Louis XIV. When it came to the washing of bodies, the situation improved with the importation of the German shower around the beginning of the twentieth century. Traditional reservations persisted—a newspaper cartoon showed a maid helping her mistress into her portable home bath, while asking if it was true that she, the maid, would have to wash in public. Her friend had read that in the paper: "But that would be indecent!" In spite of those qualms, municipal showers were popular almost immediately and they attracted many more women than in Britain. In 1908, half of the municipal showers' 150,000 customers were women. One of the traditional features of working-class districts, public showers continued to be built in poor French neighbourhoods and in villages until the late 1930s. The French, especially those in cities and towns, had taken some long strides toward cleanliness in the course of the nineteenth century. But at the same time they, and Europeans in general, were being far outdistanced by a country they thought of as a rough pioneer upstart—America.

SEVEN

WET ALL OVER AT ONCE

AMERICA, 1815–1900

At the end of the eighteenth century, Elizabeth Drinker did something brave. The Drinkers were prosperous Philadelphia Quakers, and Henry Drinker had installed a primitive shower in their backyard in 1798. For the first summer his wife hesitated, watching her daughters and women servants entering the upright box and pulling a chain that released the water stored in an overhead container. The women showered in gowns and oilcloth caps. Elizabeth did not submit herself to the new contraption until 1 July 1799. "I bore it better than I expected," she reported in her diary, "not having been wett all over at once, for 28 years past."

Before the Civil War, Americans were as dirty as Europeans. As in Europe, the odd wealthy maverick nourished a craving for cleanliness, but at the beginning of the century, most Americans, like their British cousins, regarded unwashed bodies as inevitable and unworrying if not positively healthful. By the 1880s, however, something happened that no one could have predicted. The United States—rising, pushing and still raw in many ways—had become the Western country that most embraced the gospel of hygiene. And by the end of the century, urban Americans, at least, routinely distinguished between filthy Europeans and their own "clean" ways.

Charles Dickens, in Philadelphia in 1842, wrote admiringly that the city "is most bountifully provided with fresh water, which is showered and jerked about, and turned on, and poured off, everywhere."

Why did Americans take the lead? One answer is, because they could. Water mains and sewers were installed in new cities more easily than in ancient ones. With abundant, cheap land, houses with ample space for bathrooms became the domestic norm, in contrast to Europe's old, crowded apartments. Because servants were always in short supply in democratic America, labour-saving devices were prized. High on the list was plumbing, and from the 1870s American plumbing outstripped that of every other country.

But to say "because they could" only pushes the question further back. America's physical and technological advantages were important but not definitive. More widespread cleanliness, although difficult, would have been possible in Europe sooner if people had wanted it more, since plumbing technology existed long before there was a popular demand for it. Why did Americans, apparently more than Germans, Spaniards, French and English people, want to be clean? They feared disease, and had repeated outbreaks of typhoid and cholera, but no more so than the Europeans. They were influenced by the same scientific theories—from the mistaken belief in the dangers of miasma to Pasteur's germ theory, which became widely accepted only at the beginning of the twentieth century.

There was no one overriding reason why America became the standard-bearer of personal cleanliness, but rather a confluence of several reasons. Americans prided themselves on their penchant for innovation, from the remarkable invention of New World democracy to the Yankee ingenuity that produced a better apple-corer. Scrupulous personal cleanliness and the means to achieve it—piped-in hot water, toilet soap, even the advertising that alerted people to the benefits of hygiene—were new. Without an inherited caste system, Americans were looking for more egalitarian ways to define civility and mark status, and cleanliness, which was increasingly within the grasp of most Americans, turned out to be a good way to do that. Their success during the Civil War in controlling disease through hygiene led them to see it as progressive and civic-minded. They loved what was religious and patriotic, and by the last decades of the century, cleanliness had become firmly linked not only to godliness but also to the American way.

In addition, Americans prided themselves on their open-mindedness, a quality that could strike others as a susceptibility to fads and crank theories. An early craze

A devotee of Vincenz Priessnitz's hydropathy takes an outdoor shower in Silesia.
Nineteenth-century Americans took up his cold-water cure enthusiastically.

that inclined them to think well of water and cleanliness was hydropathy, which seized the country in mid-century. Hydropathy, or the water cure, came to America from Silesia, the mountainous corner of central Europe shared by Germany, Poland and Czechoslovakia. There a farmer named Vincenz Priessnitz claimed to have healed a feverish cow and his own sprained wrist and crushed ribs with cold water and wet bandages. When he opened a treatment centre called Grafenburg in 1826, forty-nine people came seeking help. Fifteen years later, the patients numbered from 1,500 to 1,700 annually, and Priessnitz had earned the equivalent of $150,000. His clientele included princes and princesses, counts and countesses, generals and priests. It was not unusual at Grafenburg to find titled Austrian women standing naked in the pine woods under a wooden pipe that spouted spring water.

Priessnitz's reported success at curing a wide variety of illnesses moved doctors to cut open his sponges, looking for the medicine hidden in them, but there was none. He believed that disease left the body through the skin, so he concentrated on cleaning and opening the pores and encouraging circulation with plain, cold water. If the problem was localized, there were baths for the afflicted part. For more general complaints, Priessnitz developed the wet sheet, which could envelop the patient for several hours.

Although the majority of his patients came from Central Europe, some were Americans, including Elizabeth Blackwell, the first woman to graduate from an American medical school. Back home, the Americans spread the water-cure doctrine to an audience that took it up enthusiastically. Perhaps because they lacked Europe's established spas and because hydropathy suited their liking for pragmatism, economy and self-reliance, Americans welcomed it with particular fervour. Although one of the attractions of hydropathy was that it could be practised at home, there were more than two hundred water-cure centres, stretching from Maine to San Francisco. In the 1850s, the *Water-Cure Journal,* which appeared twice a month, counted 100,000 subscribers. Hydropathy remained popular from the 1840s

MATRIMONIAL CORRESPONDENCE

"I am nineteen years old; and a strong believer in the Water-Cure system, Temperance and Woman's Rights. I am in part vegetarian, eat flesh-meat occasionally, but care nothing about it. I drink cold water entirely, and bathe twice a day."

—A letter in the *Water-Cure Journal*, 1854, from a woman who called herself "Crazy Sabe" to 1900, but its greatest days were over by the beginning of the Civil War.

Although hydropathic procedures can sound like summer camp pranks, water-cure enthusiasts were often intellectuals and reformers whose influence extended beyond the sphere of health cures. They included Harriet Beecher Stowe, the author of *Uncle Tom's Cabin*. In 1846 she was exhausted by poverty, overwork and the births of five children in ten years of marriage. Her husband was a clergyman, and his congregation sent her to the Brattleboro (Vermont) Cure, where she stayed ten months. "I have gone before breakfast to the wave-bath," she wrote of her schedule, "and let all the waves and billows roll over me until every limb ached with cold and my hands would scarcely have feeling enough to dress me. . . . At eleven comes my douche [shower] . . . and after it a walk. . . . After dinner I roll ninepins or walk till four, then sitz-bath, and another walk until six."

Stowe recovered, and the water cure's lessons of exercise, plain food and, above all, the importance of water stayed with her. Water was too valuable an element, she decided, to be restricted to the sick. Everyone must have the means to open their pores, let out noxious matter and stay healthy. Almost twenty years after she visited Brattleboro, Stowe wrote an article called "Our Houses—What Is Required to Make Them Healthful" in the *Water-Cure Journal*. A "great vital element" in every house, she insisted, was "'water water everywhere'; it must be plentiful, it must be easy to get at, it must be pure. . . . There should be a bath room to every two or three inmates, and the hot and cold water should circulate to every chamber." In the 1860s, a bathroom with hot water for every two or three inhabitants was beyond utopian, but within a century Stowe's vision had become reality in the majority of American houses.

The national penchant for cleanliness was also spurred on by a more prosaic, entirely profit-driven corner of American life—the hotel. When the Duc de Doudeauville was asked if he intended to install bathrooms in La Gaudinière, the extraordinarily opulent château he was planning near Vendôme in the 1860s, the Frenchman answered haughtily, "I am not building a hotel." The duke may have disdained to follow the example of hoteliers, but there is no denying that when it came to bathrooms, hotels, especially in the United States, were trailblazers.

American hotels differed from European ones in that they were big, new and designed for a population willing and able to pay for luxuries once limited to the gentry. In 1829, when Boston's Tremont House opened its Greek Revival doors, the hotel world changed forever. Its innovations included individual patent locks on each of the 170 rooms, French cooking, gaslight in the public rooms and a substantial chunk of hard, yellow soap to go with the ewer and bowl in each bedroom. Most important for the history of cleanliness, the hotel advertised the presence of eight basement "bathing rooms where guests could wash themselves all over." Plumbing in those days

THE BATH OF THE FUTURE

" 'There is always a bath prepared in the hotel, and I do not even have to bother to leave my room in order to take it. If I just press this switch the bath will start moving, and you will see it appear all by itself with water at a temperature of 37 C.' Francis pressed the switch. There was a muffled noise which swelled in volume. . . . Then one of the doors opened and the bath appeared, sliding on its rails."

—Day in the Life of an American Journalist in 2889, Jules Verne, 1889 extended no further than the basement or first floor, so the location was a given. Baths made sense for travellers, who journeyed on muddy roads or in stuffy coaches, and public bathing establishments occasionally rented space in hotel basements or set up near hotels. But the Tremont House, which charged a princely two dollars per day, was the first hotel to provide bathrooms for the exclusive use of its guests.

Seven years later, in 1836, John Jacob Astor launched the Astor House in New York City. Even more lavish than the Tremont, it had, astonishingly, a bathroom and water closets on each floor, supplied with water from a roof tank with a steam pump. After that, each new luxury hotel tried to top the Tremont and the Astor. "Jonathan," the mocking English name for an American, was already beginning to amaze Britons with his appetite for all-over washing. In 1853, the *Illustrated London News* greeted the opening of the Mount Vernon hotel in Cape May, New Jersey, with a mixture of wonder and ironic condescension. Noting the 125 miles of gas and water pipes, and baths with taps constantly ready to spew out hot as well as cold water, the reporter wrote, poker-faced, "Jonathan is as great in hotels as he is in everything else."

In the decades before the Civil War, when few Americans had hot-water pipes above the first floor, a stay in a hotel (and Americans, by European standards, were keen travellers) introduced many of them to the comfort of a hot bath in convenient proximity to their bedroom. By the end of the century, various hotels were vying to be the first that could boast "every room with bath." The probable winner was the

Hotel Statler in Buffalo, the first in the chain founded by Ellsworth Statler. In 1908, the new hotel advertised "A Room and a Bath for a Dollar and a Half."

Where hotels led, private houses followed, although more slowly. Thousands of homeowners and builders looked for inspiration in the pattern books, complete with floor plans, written by the influential American architect Andrew Jackson Downing. In 1842, in a design for a cottage "in the Old English style," Downing positioned an eight- by ten-foot room with a bathtub on the second floor, directly above the kitchen so that its pipes connected to the kitchen boiler. At the end of the passage, separate from this early "bath-room," as Downing spelled it, was a compartment with a toilet. In general, English architects preferred to divorce bathtubs and water closets, but by mid-century Americans were tending to put all the plumbing in the same room. Many people continued to use wash-basins in their bedrooms until the final decades of the century, so the sink came last to the usual trinity of modern bathroom fixtures.

In the mid-nineteenth century, only the wealthiest Americans had a fixed bathtub in its own room, but Downing and another popular author of pattern books, Clement Vaux, inserted these novel rooms into fairly modest houses as well as more expensive ones. Their authority, and the wide dissemination of their pattern books, inclined many Americans to think that owning a bathroom someday would be a fine thing. Another champion of the bathtub was Sarah Josepha Hale, the editor of America's foremost women's magazine, *Godey's Lady's Book,* who is credited with the spread of the Saturday night bath. Of twelve model houses she presented in the magazine in 1861, seven had second-floor bathrooms with piped-in water. (The ones without had been constructed in the 1850s or were cheaper houses.)

If hotels had convinced Americans that cleanliness could be delightful, and hydropathy that it was healthy, the Civil War persuaded them that it was moral and socially enlightened. Although it would probably not have been decisive in isolation, combined with the other elements at work in mid-century, the war was pivotal when it came to American thinking about cleanliness. Even before Fort Sumter was attacked in 1861, Americans were mulling over the lessons of the Crimean War, particularly Florence Nightingale's success in limiting deaths through sanitation. As her biographer, Lytton Strachey, wrote, she had based her work "upon the wash-tub, and all the wash-tub stood for." By scouring hospital walls and floors, laundering bed and personal linen and washing patients, Nightingale revolutionized hospital conditions and became an international cult figure, particularly among American women. One of her American disciples was the same Dr. Elizabeth Blackwell who had championed hydropathy. After visiting Nightingale in London, she declared that "sanitation is the supreme goal of medicine."

Nightingale had focused attention on the fact that deaths from disease and infection in wartime outnumbered those from gunshot wounds and that cleanliness could reduce those deaths. Inspired by her example, in 1861 the Union government established the United States Sanitary Commission, an agency devoted to preventive hygiene for the volunteer army. Headed by Frederick Law Olmsted, the architect of Central Park, the commission was at first condescended to, in the words of one of its founders, as "a respectable body of supposed fanatics and philanthropists, backed by a large class of anxious and sympathetic women." But the commission pressed on, preaching the extraordinary gospel that a man could not fight well unless he was clean. Olmsted ordered that each soldier be given clothes brush, shoe brush, toothbrush, comb and towel and be expected to account for them once a week. The nineteen-year-old soldier who wrote home to Wisconsin complaining that it took all his extra time to keep clean was not alone.

To the surprise of almost everyone, the commission was an outstanding success. Deaths in the Union Army from disease, although still higher than from battle, were significantly reduced, as seen in the contrast between the Civil War and the Mexican-American War of 1846–48. The Union Army had three deaths from disease for every two from gunshot wounds. In the Mexican-American War, six soldiers had died from disease for every one killed in battle. But the commission's triumph reached beyond the Civil War. By "wrapping cleanliness and order in the mantle of patriotism and victory," as the contemporary historian Suellen Hoy puts it, the commission forced Americans to think differently about hygiene. Doctors and government officials had new respect for simple, ordinary cleanliness. Veterans returned home impressed with the comforts of hot water, foot baths and even soap. And civilians, whose wives, mothers and sisters had volunteered in the thousands to further the work of "Sanitary," as the commission was known, became accustomed to constant discussions about "Sanitary." That was not trivial, for, as the writer and clergyman Edward

The war hospital at Fredericksburg, Virginia, May 1864. The Sanitary Commission of the Union Army taught Americans the virtues of soap and water.

Everett Hale wrote, "prominence given to a word gave, of necessity, prominence to an idea."

The newly prominent idea quickly became symbolic. Dirt was seen as primitive and chaotic, exactly what Americans did not want to be. Cleanliness, on the other hand, promised morality, good order and reform. Women were crucial in these wars against dirt, just as their volunteer work had been critical in the Civil War. The success of their war work, which was very similar to the cleaning, cooking and nursing they did at home, gave them confidence and a reputation for significant skills. While the model middle-class Englishwoman of the day, the so-called Angel in the House, had servants, her American counterpart was much more directly involved in the running of her household. Cleanliness—practising it and teaching it to her children—became an important and typically American part of the womanly arsenal.

After the war, flushed with confidence and a messianic sense of purpose, the sanitarians moved their campaign to the clean-up of the northern cities, which occupied them during the 1870s and '80s. Beginning in the 1880s, when a new wave of European immigrants threatened to unsettle the national equilibrium, they would focus on teaching them personal cleanliness. But first they faced four million freed slaves—not newcomers to America, but newcomers to self-reliance.

For Booker T. Washington, the century's most prominent African American, the key to that was cleanliness. Born into slavery on a Virginia plantation in 1856, Washington had been taught by a few demanding New Englanders who impressed him with the importance of neatness and hygiene. As a houseboy for a Vermont ex-schoolteacher, he acquired a lifelong inability to leave a scrap of paper on a floor or a yard. After that, in his late teens, he travelled to the Hampton Normal and Agricultural Institute in Virginia, hoping to be admitted. When the head teacher asked the young applicant to sweep a classroom, Washington swept it three times and then dusted it four times. His thoroughness won him admission.

Booker T. Washington taught African Americans self-reliance through "the gospel of the toothbrush."

Hampton had been founded by General Samuel Chapman Armstrong to educate freed slaves. The son of missionaries to Hawaii, Armstrong saw both Polynesians and African Americans as people "in the early stages of civilization" who needed fundamental skills. Armstrong's own cleanliness was legendary: while a student at Williams College, he took a cold sponge bath every morning, and during the Civil War, when he commanded a black regiment, he claimed that his camps were the cleanest in the brigade. Adopting Armstrong's belief in basic skills, Washington sighed at the spectacle of African Americans trying to learn Greek and Latin when they were barely literate in English. In his autobiography, *Up from Slavery*, he describes one of the saddest sights of his life—a young black man studying French with grease on his clothes, and filth all around him.

In 1881 Washington founded Tuskegee Institute in Alabama. There he oversaw an education for African Americans that included learning how to sleep between two sheets, wear a nightgown and bathe. "Absolute cleanliness of the body has been insisted upon from the first," Washington wrote. "Over and over again the students were reminded in those first years— and are reminded now—that people would excuse us for our poverty, for our lack of comforts and conveniences, but that they would not excuse us for dirt." Borrowing the idea from General Armstrong, he preached "the gospel of the tooth-

BOOKER T. WASHINGTON INSPECTS THE ROOMS AT TUSKEGEE

"We found one room that contained three girls who had recently arrived at the school. When I asked them if they had tooth-brushes, one of the girls replied, pointing to a brush: 'Yes, sir. That is our brush. We bought it together, yesterday.' It did not take them long to learn a different lesson."

brush," and this stratagem became so well known that students often arrived at Tuskegee carrying almost nothing but a toothbrush. Convinced that its use brought about "a higher degree of civilization," Washington noticed that when a student replaced a first or second toothbrush on his own initiative, he was rarely disappointed in that student's future.

Urban overcrowding and squalor had been a fact of American life since the 1840s, when more than a million Irish immigrants settled in the port cities of the Northeast. In the 1880s, hundreds of thousands of southern and eastern Europeans began arriving, and by 1900, 37 per cent of New York City's three and a half million people were immigrants. However disadvantaged, the poor in France were French, and the poor in Germany were Germans. The Americans faced a more complex situation in that the people they wanted to convert to cleanliness were foreigners who at first understood neither the English language nor American customs.

Like the ancient Romans setting out to civilize an empire with, among other things, baths, the Americans believed that a crucial way to Americanize the newcomers was to teach them how to wash. Only recently convinced of cleanliness themselves, they had the zeal of the newly converted, seeing hygiene as the antidote to most un-American attitudes and practices. The public bath, a confident Chicago reformer claimed, was the "greatest civilizing power that can be brought to bear on these uncivilized Europeans crowding into our cities."

The "uncivilized" newcomers, who were considered so dirty that Ellis Island was designed to shower eight thousand of them every day, posed the familiar threat to the health of all. Jacob Riis, the reforming chronicler of New York's tenement houses, sketched a terrifying picture of the "filth diseases" that could spread through the city from the garment workers who finished pieces of clothing in their tenement apartments. In *How the Other Half Lives*, published in 1890, he wrote,

"The only water the Irish use is holy water."
—Nineteenth-century American saying

> It has happened more than once that a child recovering from small-pox, and in the most contagious stage of the disease, has been found crawling among heaps of half-finished clothing that the next day would be offered for sale on the counter of a Broadway store; or that a typhus fever patient has been discovered in a room whence perhaps a hundred coats had been sent home that week, each one with the wearer's death-warrant, unseen and unsuspected, basted in the lining.

As for the vaguer menace, the immorality that flourished in the slums, cleanliness would remedy that, too. When New York opened a public bathhouse, Riis breathed a sigh of relief, for now "godliness will have a chance to move in with cleanliness. The two are neighbours everywhere, but in the slum the last must come first."

(Sanitarians in Europe as well as America believed firmly in the connection between cleanliness and morality, and a paper published in *Science* in 2006 seems to con-

Jacob Riis's photograph of New York newsboys washing up in their lodging-house was published in his 1890 book, *How the Other Half Lives.*

firm the link, but not in the direction they intended. Behavioural researchers found that when subjects were asked to imagine they had done something unethical, they filled in the blanks of incomplete words, such as W–H and SH–ER, making WASH and SHOWER. Subjects who had imagined doing ethical acts returned various words, such as WISH and SHAKER. Half the subjects who had imagined unethical acts were given the chance to wash their hands. Then all the subjects who had imagined the doing of unethical acts, unwashed and washed, were asked to volunteer to help researchers who needed unpaid subjects. Those with washed hands were about 50 per cent less likely to volunteer—suggesting that the cleansed felt absolved enough, and had no need to do a good deed.)

One of the main places where newcomers learned to think and act like Americans was the big-city public school. A Jewish immigrant to New York City named Sol Meyerowitz remembered:

> The teacher would start the day with a reading from the Old Testament, then she would inspect our hair, turn our hands around, look at our ears, examine my neck to see if it was dirty. One day she sent me home because I had a dirty neck. And she actually rubbed my skin to see if it was dirty.
>
> We were just a bunch of sad kids, you know, snotty little sad kids: always poorly dressed. We were dirty, dirty. You had a bath maybe once a week, and you wore your underwear all week.

Teachers demonstrated the use of the washing bowl and soap, and one complained to Riis of a new student, "He took hold of the soap as if it were some animal, and wiped three fingers across his face. He called that washing." A public school principal in New York City ordered that the teachers ask the children every day, "What must I do to be healthy?" The children were to chorus in answer:

> I must keep my skin clean
> Wear clean clothes
> Breathe pure air
> And live in the sunlight.

Jacob Riis's famous photograph appeared in his 1902 book, *The Battle with the Slum*. He captioned it "The Only Bath-tub in the Block: It Hangs in the Air Shaft." The two-acre block he referred to, on New York's Lower East Side, held thirty-nine tenements and 2,781 people, including 466 children under the age of five.

Schools were useful for training future parents and citizens, but worsening conditions demanded quicker solutions. A cholera epidemic in 1849 intensified calls for public baths, but America's municipal governments had other priorities—water and sewage systems, fire and police departments. The country's first bathhouse designed for the poor opened its doors on Mott Street in New York City's Lower East Side in 1852, but it survived less than a decade. Its fees of five to ten cents per bath were probably too high for a poor family.

NOT IN MY NEIGHBOURHOOD
When a public bathhouse was proposed in the late nineteenth century near Tompkins Square in New York City, the German and Irish inhabitants protested that they weren't so poor as to need one. They petitioned that it be built instead in the Jewish and Italian neighbourhood.

After the Mott Street failure, America dragged its feet for forty years, while the country struggled with the Civil War, labour unrest, depressions and yet more immigrants.

By the early 1890s, most European countries had public bathhouses, some almost fifty years old. Ironically, although it was committed to a hygienic society, America had none, while fewer than 3 per cent of tenement dwellers in New York and Chicago had bathrooms. In that decade, America found a bathhouse hero in Simon Baruch, a doctor and the father of the financier Bernard Baruch. On a visit to his native Germany, the senior Baruch was inspired by the country's municipal baths, and he determined to import them to America. A prolific author of medical articles, an expert on hydrotherapy and the surgeon who reportedly performed America's first appendectomy, Baruch wrote, "I consider that I have done more to save life and prevent the spread of disease in my work for public baths than in all my work as a physician." His first success, in 1891, was the opening of the People's Baths on the Lower East Side. Wesley's proverb, "Cleanliness Next to Godliness," greeted bath-goers and passersby from above the door. Equipped with twenty-three showers, three bathtubs and an initial gift of eighty pounds of soap from the Colgate Company, the baths were welcomed as the herald of a clean, progressive future.

The national turning point came four years later, in 1895, when the New York State legislature ordered that medium-sized and large cities build municipal baths. Within six years, seven cities in the state had opened baths. By 1904, there were thirty-nine municipally run baths in the country, as far west as Chicago and Milwaukee. New York City alone had twenty-six baths by 1915. American bathhouses were designed only for the poor, because by the end of the nineteenth century, most urban middle-class Americans had baths in their houses. The Americans followed the German model, providing showers instead of baths. (Baruch thought tub baths were "dangerously relaxing," and the architect responsible for New York's West Sixtieth Street Baths disallowed tubs because they were "a source of jealousy and confusion.") And, true to the national temper, they were speedy. Once an American patron picked up his two-inch bar of soap and towel, he had twenty minutes for undressing, showering and dressing, in contrast to the European standard of half an hour.

But whether they were modest neighbourhood bathhouses, as in Chicago, or lavishly equipped complexes, as in New York and Boston, the American public baths suffered the same fate as many of their European counterparts. They were underused, except during the hottest days of summer. In America, they came too late. After hesitating for half a century, Americans began building bathhouses just as private bathtubs were becoming common. New York's Model Tenement House Reform Law of 1901 required that each floor of a new apartment be furnished with water; a later expansion of the law ordered that water be available in every apartment. Other large cities followed with similar laws. In practice, since the builders had to install plumbing, a tub was usually added at the same time. Of the tenement apartments built in the first decade of the twentieth century, 86 per cent had bathtubs. Once a tub became the norm in new tenements, older ones had to install bathrooms to stay competitive. The building of American public bathhouses ended by the First World War, and by the mid-1930s, 89 per cent of New York City's apartments had baths or showers.

> Compared with 10 years ago, "rags and dirt are now the exception. . . . Perhaps the statement is a trifle strong as to the dirt. . . . Soap and water have worked a visible cure already that goes more than skin-deep. They are moral agents of the first value in the slum."
>
> —Jacob Riis, *The Battle with the Slum*, 1902

Even for the middle classes, the cleansing of America continued for decades. Since 1841, when she published her *Treatise on Domestic Economy*, Catharine Beecher had been the country's reigning expert in the blossoming fields of household science and hygiene. In 1869, with her younger sister, Harriet Beecher Stowe— famous since the Civil War as, in Abraham Lincoln's words, "the little woman who wrote the book that started this great war"—she wrote *The American Woman's Home*. Their model house had running water that came from an attic reservoir, a forcing pump in the basement and a second-floor bathroom conveniently close to the bedrooms. It was not quite the ratio Harriet had called for in the *Water-Cure Journal* of one bathroom for every two or three inhabitants, but it was headed in the right direction.

The chapter on cleanliness in *The American Woman's Home* begins with a lengthy scientific discussion of the skin, supplemented with detailed drawings of perspiration tubes and lymphatic vessels. When the pores are blocked, according to the Beechers, the waste is carried to the lungs, liver and other organs, and this results in disease and "the gradual decay of vital powers." To prevent this, the entire body needs to be washed every day. For the same reason, clothes (which can press the noxious matter into the pores and reintroduce it into the body) need to be changed frequently, and the Beechers recommend against sleeping in the garment that was next to the body during the day.

"The popular maxim, that 'dirt is healthy,' has probably arisen from the fact, that playing in the open air is very beneficial to the health of children, who thus get dirt on their persons and clothes. But, it is the fresh air and exercise, and not the dirt, which promotes the health."

—Catharine Beecher, 1841

For those with a full-size tub, a tepid bath should last no more than thirty minutes. Afterward, the body should be rubbed with a brush or rough towel, "to remove the light scales of scarf-skin, which adhere to it, and also to promote a healthful excitement." In spite of the bathroom in their model house, the authors dispute the growing idea that a full-size bathtub is necessary for a thorough cleansing. Nor do they mention soap. The important thing is friction: "A wet towel, applied every morning, to the skin, followed by friction in pure air, is all that is absolutely needed."

Nineteenth-century sanitary reformers frequently compared human health and cleanliness with that of animals, usually to the humans' disadvantage. To illustrate what friction can achieve, the Beechers describe an experiment done on pigs, whose skin, they say, resembles that of humans. Six pigs were curry-combed regularly for six weeks, while other pigs were untouched. Because friction encourages all the organs to work more efficiently, the curried pigs gained thirty-three more pounds than the un-curried pigs, while eating five fewer bushels of feed. A man who took care of his skin in this way, the authors conclude, would save over thirty-one dollars in food annually.

In fact, the people who were best placed to heed the Beechers' progressive ideas lived in cities and towns. In 1877, according to a study of bathing habits done by the Michigan Board of Health, most people in that rural state "were very little accustomed to the general ablution of the body—in other words, not clean." Almost by definition, hygiene was most difficult on the frontier, where conditions remained primitive throughout the nineteenth century and well into the twentieth. In the 1830s, an Englishwoman, Susanna Moodie, and her family homesteaded in southern Ontario. When their farmhand would not sit down to eat after a day in the fields without first washing his face and hands, the Irish maid-of-all-work thought that was ridiculous. "Och! My dear heart, yer too particular intirely; we've no time in the woods to be clane," she told him when he asked for soap and a towel. Soap was so much trouble to make that it was saved for laundry, "without yer wastin' it in makin' yer purty skin as white as a leddy's." And if he wanted water, he should go down to the lake: "That basin is big enough, anyhow."

The women in Upper Canada were "cleanly in everything that [related] to their houses, but negligent of their persons unless when dizened out for visiting."

—John Howison, an English traveller in 1822

Eighty years later, in 1911, another Englishwoman, Ella Sykes, spent six months working as a "home-help" in the western Canadian provinces. If it was not quite a case of "we've no time in the woods to be clane," it was not far from it. Sykes sometimes wondered "whether the farmer class ever 'washed' at all, as I understood the word." They made do with an enamel basin in the kitchen, where they cleaned their hands and faces and dried them on a grimy towel. Sykes saw no other evidence of washing. She alone insisted on a jug and basin in her room, which she supplemented with a folding india-rubber bath. But even the Canadian farmers were cleaner than the European immigrants, as Sykes discovered when she met a schoolteacher in Alberta. Proposing to sew a top button onto a Galician child's shirt—it was fastened with a nail—the teacher discovered that the child's mother had sewn him into it for the winter.

Five out of six Americans were still washing with a pail and a sponge in 1880. Before the bathtub could spread beyond the most prosperous urban circles, it had to get better and cheaper. In mid-century, the craftsman-built tub of tin or copper encased in a wooden surround was a luxury, for which its owners paid a surcharge on top of their normal municipal water bill. Cast iron tubs, plain, galvanized or enamelled, and without cabinetry, began to be made in factories in the 1870s, followed by vitreous china and solid porcelain models in the 1890s. Better production techniques meant that in 1900 the average worker produced ten tubs a day, compared with 1870, when an enterprise that might involve several workers usually turned out one tub a day. The Sears catalogue is a good index of the spread of bathtubs and indoor plumbing. In 1897, wash-basins, sinks and urinals fitted for plumbing could be bought from Sears, but not bathtubs or toilets. By 1908, the consumer had a choice of three complete "bathrooms"—tub, sink and toilet—ready to be connected to plumbing. Depending on the style and finish, either enamelled sheet steel or the more expensive enamelled cast iron, the prices for the set ranged from $33.90 to $51.10.

Along with the plumbing and fixtures came changing expectations and perceptions. Unwashed, odoriferous

FOR THOSE WHO HAVE
SMELLY FEET

"In very hot weather they should be washed both morning and evening, and the stockings should be changed twice a week in winter, and three times in summer"

—*The Lady's Guide to Perfect Gentility*, 1859

During the sixteenth, seventeenth and most of the eighteenth centuries, when people avoided water and believed that a clean linen shirt extracted dirt, there was little or no demand for toilet soap. The rich women who used it, mostly on face and hands, thought of it as more a cosmetic or perfume than a cleanser. In the nineteenth century, as people groped their way back to the lost practice of immersing their bodies in water, they began to debate the pros and cons of using soap to clean themselves. Many authorities discouraged it as unnecessary or irritating, but by the end of the nineteenth century toilet soap had triumphed.

A few technical developments helped make that possible. The invention of processes, beginning in the late eighteenth century, that produced soda ash from salt rather than wood ash also reduced the price of soap and made a product that was harder and milder, unlike the gelatinous and irritating soap made from wood ash. Animal fats, which came from goats, cattle, sheep and—most pungent of all—whales and seals, and produced harsh, unappetizing soap in shades of white, grey and black, had to be replaced. Better transportation made the importation of olive oil soaps more affordable, and soap manufacturers on both sides of the Atlantic experimented with various formulas involving cottonseed oil, coconut oil and palm oil. Ivory soap and Palmolive (named for its blend of palm and olive oils) were early successes.

people, who had been an unremarkable part of the landscape for as long as anyone could remember, were increasingly seen as obnoxious. Emily Thornwell sounds this note surprisingly early, in *The Lady's Guide to Perfect*

Gentility, which was published in 1859. "Now what must we think of those genteel people who never use the bath, or only once or twice a year wash themselves all over, though they change their linen daily?" she asks. "Why, that, in plain English, they are nothing more or less than very filthy gentry."

Not only are they dirty, but they smell bad. When their perspiration is stimulated by exercise, "they have a something about them which lavender water and bergamot do not entirely conceal." There is a range in the strength of the odour, Thornwell admits, but everyone who does not wash frequently will smell unpleasant, as the fluid that leaves the body becomes "rancid" from lack of soap and water. Here, Thornwell is not writing about bathing for the sake of health; rather, she is advising her readers how not to "offend"—a verb that will become ever-present in twentieth-century soap and deodorant advertising. This concern, which Europeans would later see as peculiarly American, probably surfaces only when thorough cleanliness becomes a possibility. Then Thornwell voices her most menacing warning: *those who trouble others by their body odour often have no idea that they are doing so.* This fact, "above all things, should put ladies on their guard."

The possibility that you could offend without being aware of it produced an anxiety that advertisers would successfully exploit, again and again, in the century to come. The potent

THE CARE OF BLACKHEADS
"When [the blackhead] is pressed between the points of the fingers, the curdy matter is forced out, in appearance much resembling a small white worm with a black head. In fact, ignorant persons suppose them to be worms, but a magnifying glass shows what they really are."

—*The Lady's Guide to Perfect Gentility*, 1859

marriage of soap and advertising became one of the major hygienic themes of the first half of the twentieth century, a union that raised standards of cleanliness to unheard-of heights.

EIGHT

SOAP OPERA

1900–1950

liza Doolittle, the Cockney flower seller in George Bernard Shaw's 1912 play *Pygmalion*, needs a bath. That is not her decision but comes from the man who proposes to teach her to speak English properly. Professor Higgins sends her off to the bathroom with his housekeeper, Mrs. Pearce. Eliza expects to go to the scullery, but to her surprise, she's taken to the third floor, where she mistakes the bathtub for a clothes-washing copper. When Mrs. Pearce tells her that she's going to get in the tub and be washed, she reacts with horror: "You expect me to get into that and wet myself all over! Not me. I should catch my death.

I knew a woman did it every Saturday night; and she died of it."

Not deterred, Mrs. Pearce tells her that Professor Higgins bathes in cold water in the gentlemen's bathroom every morning. If she is to sit with him and learn to speak English like a lady, she will have to wash herself: "They won't like the smell of you if you don't." Eliza sobs that it isn't "natural," that she has never had a proper bath in her life. Mrs. Pearce insists, "You know you can't be a nice girl inside if you're a dirty slut outside." (In 1912, slut could still mean simply dirty, not necessarily immoral.)

Things go from bad to worse when Eliza realizes that she is expected to take off all her clothes, something else she has never done before, since she sleeps in her clothes.

Eliza Doolittle might have bathed in a bathroom like this one, from an upper-middle-class English house at the start of the twentieth century.

"It's not right: it's not decent, " she protests. Mrs. Pearce answers that she can change from "a frowsy slut to a clean respectable girl" or return to selling flowers, and Eliza cries, "Oh, if only I'd a known what a dreadful thing it is to be clean I'd never have come. I didn't know when I was well off."

Mrs. Pearce pays no attention. As if preparing to do surgery, she puts on a pair of white rubber sleeves, fills the bath with hot and cold water, tests its temperature with a thermometer, and adds bath salts and a fistful of mustard. Finally she takes up an intimidating long-handled scrubbing brush and lathers it with a soap-ball. Eliza, by now "a piteous spectacle of abject terror," enters the tub and Mrs. Pearce snatches away her bath gown and sets to work. The stage direction reads, "Eliza's screams are heartrending."

Heartrending they may be, but Eliza learns to like her bath. When she returns to the drawing room, dressed in a kimono, and joins Professor Higgins and her father, Mr. Doolittle tries to take credit for how well she's cleaned up. She says,

> I tell you, it's easy to clean up here. Hot and cold water on tap, just as much as you like, there is. Woolly towels, there is; and a towel horse so hot, it burns your fingers. Soft brushes to scrub yourself, and a wooden bowl of soap smelling like primroses. Now I know why ladies is so clean. Washing's a treat for them. Wish they could see what it is for the likes of me!

Only one thing about the bathroom still displeases Eliza. Brought up to abhor nudity, she is appalled by the presence of the looking glass. She doesn't know where to look, considers breaking it and settles for throwing a towel over it. Some taboos die harder than others.

Eliza Doolittle came by her suspicions about the bath naturally. Age-old doubts about cleanliness lingered on well into the first third or half of the twentieth century in parts of Europe. A London social worker summarized the tepid attitude she found in the slums, around the time that Shaw wrote *Pygmalion*: "Generally speaking the people of the neighbourhood do not clamour for facilities for bathing and washing, but when such are there, the fashion for using them steadily increases." Getting accustomed to the public baths was only the beginning. The poor had to be convinced of the health benefits of washing thoroughly. Women had to be assured that the premises were clean, quiet and patronized by school-mistresses and other genteel women.

The baths at Dunfermline, Scotland, were unusually popular. In a survey carried out in 1913–14, half the bathers were women, an exceptionally high percentage. Accounting for the baths' success, the investigators noted excellent accommodations and a population of "superior factory hands" without baths in their homes, schools or factories. Equally important, the baths had an enthusiastic staff and the town had "a complete absence of any social stigma attached to the use of the baths." Even so, we would not consider Dunfermline a particularly well-washed town, at least judging by its bathhouse. A grand total of 36,510 baths were taken in a year in its thirty tubs. For a population of 28,000, that works out to one bath a year for two-thirds of the people, and two baths a year for the remaining third. Yet these figures were impressively high when compared with other places in Britain.

Perhaps a love of washing could be instilled more easily in young minds. Observers had noted the unwholesome air of slum schoolrooms, rank from dirty clothes and bodies. An international congress on school hygiene held in Paris in 1910 recommended that shower baths be built in all schools. Larger towns in Norway, Switzerland, Sweden and Germany already included showers as part of their school program, and Austria, France, Holland and Belgium were following their lead. Fifteen British school boards approved their use. It was a challenge for teachers, who had to overcome parental objections, learn to separate out and arrange for treatment of the verminous children (one in three), inspect underwear and supervise the showers, all the while promoting the idea that washing was fun. At least according to their own reports, they seem to have succeeded in the last objective. Children showered once a week, and some of the graduating girls told their teachers, "I shall miss my shower bath." They asked, "as a special favour, to be allowed to have two during the last week of their school life."

Claiming that "the bathing habit is distinctly on the increase," a 1918 report on British public baths allowed itself a note of muted triumph. Still, progress could hardly be described as galloping, since once-a-year attendance at big-city baths at the start of the First World War ranged from under 20 per cent to 80 per cent. The

"What separates two people most profoundly is a different sense of cleanliness. What avails all decency and mutual usefulness and good will toward each other—in the end the fact remains: 'They cannot stand each other's smell!' "

—Friedrich Nietzsche

habit of bathing publicly caught on most in London, where the Friday night visit to the neighbourhood bath-house became a working-class institution that lasted through the 1930s.

Social workers, public health experts and doctors were convinced that the poor would take even less advantage of a bath at home than they did of the public baths. Persistent reports in Britain and America—amounting to an urban legend—that the rare tub found in a working-class house or tenement was invariably used to store coal bolstered this prejudice. The authorities were wrong, and the working class took up frequent washing only when they had baths at home.

The poor found it hard to love the bathhouses. Hungary, with its rich tradition of Turkish-style baths, still tempts bathers out of their own bathrooms to soak in company. People with tubs at home continue to patronize the public baths in Morocco and Japan. But the bathhouses built to wash the great unwashed in Europe and America sorely lacked the camaraderie and pleasure that enliven these traditional baths. Intentionally or not, they were joyless, even reproving. Private compartments with a carefully calculated measure of time and warm

"The hygiene book made the not uncommon error of allowing one or two utterly impractical edicts to discredit much good sound common sense. It prescribed a nightly bath which everyone knew was silly. The teacher did not have one and neither the McFarlanes nor . . . the Robbs, where she boarded would have tolerated for a week a woman who required a wash-tub full of warm water before retiring."

—J. K. Galbraith on early-twentieth-century schooling in southern Ontario

A Frenchman in his makeshift shower. Fewer than one in ten French people had a bathroom in the first half of the twentieth century.

water could not compete with the ease of bathing at home, once that was possible, or with the familiar comfort of not bathing.

While the poor were resisting public baths and before most of them had their own bathrooms, a relatively new prejudice was thriving among the middle classes. It was a bias that people, especially on the left, were more reluctant to voice as the century advanced. But in 1937, in *The Road to Wigan Pier*, George Orwell dared to write "four frightful words which people nowadays are chary of uttering, but which were bandied about quite freely in my childhood." The words expressed what Orwell considered the secret heart of class differences in the West, and were: "*The lower classes smell.*"

Because of that visceral aversion, Orwell wrote, even the bourgeois European who thought of himself as a Communist found it difficult to see a working man as his equal: "Very early in life you acquired the idea that there was something subtly repulsive about a working-class body; you would not get nearer to it than you could help." Obviously, a "great sweaty navvy" or a tramp was beyond the pale, but even the skin and perspiration of fairly clean lower-class people, like servants, were considered unappetizingly different from those of the middle classes. "Everyone who has grown up pronouncing his aitches and in a house with a bathroom and one servant is likely to have grown up with these feelings," Orwell wrote, "hence the chasmic, impassable quality of class-distinctions in the West."

Orwell asks, do the working classes really smell? Certainly they are dirtier than more prosperous people, because their work is more physical, their workplaces are often unclean, and they lack the plumbing that makes cleanliness easy. "Besides, the habit of washing yourself all over every day is a very recent one in Europe, and the working classes are generally more conservative than the bourgeoisie." But more important than any actual smell is the fact that the middle class *believes* that the working class has a repellent odour, and that conviction begins early, when the bourgeois child "is taught almost simultaneously to wash his neck, to be ready to die for his country, and to despise the 'lower classes.'"

That particular class distinction could begin to die out only when workers could wash their own necks with ease. Louis Heren was born in 1919 in Shadwell, a slum district in the East End of London. Just as Orwell defined the middle classes as people who pronounced their h's and had a servant and a bathroom, Heren's passage from Cockney messenger boy to foreign editor of the London *Times* was marked by bathrooms, or the lack of them.

Heren's widowed mother ran a coffee shop, and the Shadwell house he grew up in had no bathroom. On Friday evenings, the three children bathed in a galvanized iron tub in front of the sitting room fire. His uncle Lou went to the local public baths, where he paid twopence for a tub with hot water, a fresh towel and soap. How and when his mother washed remained a mystery to the boy Heren; the adult Heren assumes she used the wash-basin in her bedroom. Each bedroom had a china basin, a jug of cold water, a bar of red Lifebuoy soap and a well-used chamber pot under the bed. (The house's one toilet was

"Dirt is matter in the wrong place."
—Henry J. Temple, Viscount Palmerston
(1784–1865)

too far away to use at night.) Within this late-blooming Victorian environment, "we were expected to be clean, and were never really dirty although I was then known in the family as Stinker."

In 1934, the fifteen-year-old Heren left school and began work as a messenger for the London *Times*. All *Times* employees were eligible for the Boxing Club, and Heren trained religiously despite a fatal deficiency: his eyes instinctively closed whenever he saw a straight right heading for his face. He remained a member of the Boxing Club for the exercise, he writes, "and because of the baths." For an adolescent, the tin tub in front of the sitting room fire was no longer an option. The public baths were crowded "and a bit mean."

> In comparison the baths at *The Times* were sheer luxury. There were rows of them, showers and long baths, glistening with white tile and stainless steel taps and rails, and with an unending supply of hot water, I would wallow in them with the tap trickling hot water to maintain an almost unbearable heat. Our mother would warn me about catching cold, but I must have been the cleanest boy in Shadwell. The baths in the gym were further proof of the superiority of *The Times*, and my good fortune.

When Heren was eighteen, in 1937, his mother moved the family to a dingy neighbourhood called Crofton Park—a definite step up, because the house included their first bathroom. And Heren too moved up, from wartime soldiering, where he learned the correct way to use a knife and fork at Sandhurst, to *Times* assignments as a correspondent on five continents, ending up in 1970 as the paper's foreign editor. Looking back on his life, he writes, "On balance I am glad that I was born a Cockney." But not wanting to fall into cozy nostalgia, he adds, "I do not see moral merit in poverty as such. It is not uplifting to live without a bathroom." It is telling but by no means unusual that when Heren sums up his journey from the slums to the most accomplished reaches of the middle class, his concrete example of the distance between the two is the new totem of bourgeois life, the bathroom.

Toilet soap and advertising grew up together. Both had existed in some form for centuries, but they emerged as mainstream, large-scale businesses at the end of the nineteenth century. In the case of soap, the new germ theory helped its popularity, although it took decades for the discovery of disease-causing microbes to percolate down to ordinary consumers. In fact, even sanitarians and public health experts were surprisingly reluctant to abandon the traditional belief that disease spread through decaying matter and bad smells. When the Viennese doctor Ignaz Semmelweis insisted that delivery room doctors and medical students wash their hands before attending their patients, he was ridiculed, even though the practice dramatically reduced death from puerperal sepsis. In 1865, when Semmelweis died, his simple but radical idea was still discounted. Only after Robert Koch in Germany and Louis Pasteur in France advanced the germ theory in the 1870s and '80s was the work of Semmelweis and other hygienic pioneers, such as Joseph Lister of Glasgow, taken seriously by scientists. Even so, many public health administrators, doctors and visiting nurses continued to preach the old miasma theory, which concentrated on garbage, drains and ventilation. By the beginning of the twentieth century, the germ or contagionism theory had triumphed—a revolutionary concept but, until sulfa and antibiotics were developed in the 1930s and '40s, a terrifying prospect. Almost the only way to fight microbes was by washing them off. As cleaning the body became more widespread and people began using soap as well as water, manufacturers on both sides of the Atlantic laboured to produced an affordable, gentle soap from vegetable oils.

HYGIENIC CRUELTY
In 1931, halitosis was cited as grounds for divorce.

Procter & Gamble, in Cincinnati, was typical, experimenting for years with various formulas involving palm oil, cottonseed oil and coconut oil. Finally, in 1878, the researchers had a recipe that pleased them, to be called P&G White Soap. Luckily for Procter & Gamble, Harley Procter, the company's sales manager, declared the new name stunningly unappealing. One Sunday, at Mount Auburn Episcopal Church, he listened to the minister read from Psalm 45: "All thy garments smell like myrrh, and aloes, and cassia, out of the ivory palaces, whereby they have made thee glad." Inspired, he christened the new hard white soap Ivory.

A year later, Procter & Gamble had another piece of good fortune, when a worker left the new soap's

By the beginning of the twentieth century, the middle-class American family living in a large town or city either had a modern bathroom or expected to have one soon. The house of Ida and David Eisenhower, in Abilene, Kansas, was typical. Built in 1887 with six rooms, it had no bathroom. The Eisenhowers and their six sons (the third was Dwight, the future president) bathed in a galvanized washtub in the kitchen, several sharing the same water. In 1908, Abilene introduced a municipal water system, and the Eisenhowers converted a small bedroom into a three-piece bathroom, although water for the bath still had to be heated on the kitchen stove. In 1919, the installation of a gas hot-water heater made that unnecessary.

steam-powered mixing machine unattended for too long. The overflowing lather that resulted was presumed to be useless, but when hardened and cut into cakes, not only did it clean, but it floated. Thus was born Ivory's enduring catchphrase, "It floats!" Together with its name and its other slogan, "99 and 44/100% pure," it promised an airy, immaculate product.

Harley Procter was unusual in his grasp of publicity and image, but soap makers and advertisers soon understood that they were natural allies. Since there was a high profit margin in soap but not a great deal to distinguish one brand from another, there was all the more reason to proclaim the superiority of individual brands. The newish business of advertising tried out new schemes and techniques on the newish commodity, toilet soap. By the end of the nineteenth century, soap and patent medicines

Inculcating the handwashing habit—an early Pears' soap ad.

had become advertising's biggest customers.

One of the first companies to buy full-page magazine ads was the British firm Pears' Soap. Some of its early ideas, such as a little black child who bathes with Pears' and emerges lily-white from the neck down, are worse than dated. But celebrity testimonials, which Pears' began using in the 1880s, proved one of the most successful ways to sell soap. Underneath a picture of a bathing beauty holding a sheet to her bosom while she selects a cake of Pears' was a commendation ("matchless for the hands and complexion") from Adelina Patti, the opera singer. The possibility that the pretty bather was Patti remained open. Lillie Langtry, the actress and the Prince of Wales' mistress, also recommended Pears'. Less titillating and designed for the religiously inclined American public was a testimonial from Henry Ward Beecher, a nationally known minister (and the brother of Catharine Beecher and Harriet Beecher Stowe), who endorsed Pears' and washing in general for their next-to-godliness qualities.

B. T. Babbitt, of Babbitt's Best Soap, had another idea—the premium. Customers who sent in twenty-five soap wrappers received illustrations, some of which were printed in the hundreds of thousands. Wool Soap, on the other hand, appealed to its customers' altruism by donating a penny to the Chicago temple of the Women's Christian Temperance Union for each wrapper returned by a customer. Members of Woodbury's "Facial Purity League" received club buttons, although it's hard to visualize many late-nineteenth-century women wearing them. Sapolio Soap invented a jolly town, "Spotless Town," and its chief personages, who were characterized by simple, memorable jingles. All these gambits—testimonials, premiums, prizes, catchy slogans and jingles, continuing characters—that were later refined and adapted in ad campaigns for a variety of products made their first appearance in advertisements for soap. Although advertisers stressed the germ-fighting powers of soap, especially in ads targeted at mothers, they were more likely to focus on its ability to make its users youthful, beautiful and above all sweet-smelling.

When it came to rendering the world as clean and odourless as possible, the 1920s were a watershed decade. As cities expanded, and people worked close to one another in crowded offices and factories, they grew unhappily aware of the smells produced by their own bodies and those of others. The arrival of women in the work world accelerated this new sensitivity. The fastidiousness that had first surfaced, tentatively, in late-eighteenth-century Europe was becoming an American

"Ultimately the drugstore became the symbol of the industrialized aura; it is the supermarket of mass-produced glamour and scents for a deodorized population. People who obsessively scrub away their auras can pick and choose a better one there."

—Ivan Illich, H_2O and the Waters of Forgetting

obsession. At the same time, prosperity was at an all-time high. People could afford the products that would enable them to live in a smell-less zone, a safe place where they would neither "offend" nor be "offended."

In the same decade, advertising was becoming ever more ingenious at satisfying existing wants and creating new wants. Sometimes, as with Listerine, it gave a new name to an old problem and achieved astounding success with an old product. A favourite case study in the annals of advertising, Listerine—a mixture of thymol, menthol, methyl salicylate and eucalyptol—had been invented in 1879 as a surgical antiseptic. Without changing the recipe, its owners, Lambert Pharmacal, began marketing it to dentists in the 1890s as an oral antiseptic and then, in 1914, to the general public as a mouthwash. Sales were mediocre, so in the early 1920s the president, Gerald Lambert, asked the company chemist to itemize Listerine's uses. An arcane word in the chemist's list—"halitosis," a condition supposedly remedied by Listerine—piqued Lambert's interest and prompted a new advertising campaign.

Americans were so unfamiliar with the term that Listerine's ads continued to define halitosis for at least five years. But people had noticed bad breath at least since the ancient Greeks. And Americans were not unfamiliar with romances that didn't materialize, marriages that didn't happen or mysteriously failed, and job offers or promotions that never came. The reason behind many of these everyday heartbreaks, Lambert Pharmacal assured the public in a series of compulsively readable ads, was unpleasant breath.

Take Edna, a charming flapper whose birthdays crept alarmingly toward "that tragic thirty-mark," while

Women discovered this way
of keeping skin youthful

LISTERINE as an ASTRINGENT

SO many women have written us enthusiastically about Listerine used as an astringent,
we feel duty bound to pass the suggestion on to
you. Furthermore, beauty doctors and derma-
tologists tell us that Listerine is almost ideal for this purpose.
Next time you use an astringent in connection with your
toilette, give Listerine a trial.

Note how it closes pores, how it tends to tighten sagging
muscles and how wonderfully cool and smooth your skin
feels after you have used it.

You will find that it accomplishes results equal to those
performed by special astringents costing from two to six
times as much. Moreover, Listerine protects you against infection. Though gentle in action and healing in effect, full
strength Listerine kills even the stubborn Staphylococcus
Aureus (pus) germ in 15 seconds. Lambert Pharmacal
Company, St. Louis, Mo., U. S. A.

GREAT AFTER SHAVING
Tell your husband it's great after shaving. Doused on the
skin full strength, it produces a delightful sensation of in-
vigoration and coolness. And ends all smarting and burning.

Surgical antiseptic, mouthwash and, in 1929, another use for Listerine: as a facial astringent.

she remained "often a bridesmaid but never a bride." Or Smedley, a man with good marriage prospects until women caught a whiff of his breath. Halitosis could even threaten the mother-child bond: an ad titled "Are you unpopular with your own children?" shows a scowling little boy resisting his mother's embrace. The most worrying thing about halitosis (and the most lucrative for the makers of Listerine) was that no one was likely to tell you that you had it, nor could you discover it for yourself. And, according to the ads, it was a nationwide epidemic, attested to by hotel clerks, who declared that one in three people seeking a room had halitosis, and by dentists, 83 per cent of whom said they encountered it frequently in patients.

Listerine's claim that it eliminated local, non-organic halitosis by halting "food fermentation" in the mouth remains unproved. But with almost no change to the bottle or its contents, Lambert turned its forty-year-old formula into an overnight success. Gargling became part of America's morning routine, and Lambert's annual profits rose from $115,000 in 1921 to more than $8 million in 1928. "Often a bridesmaid, but never a bride," which is still one of the twentieth century's best-known slogans, epitomizes the advertising technique known as "whisper copy" or "advertising by fear." Inspired by Listerine's success, marketers tried using technical, medical-sounding names for other ailments or conditions—comedone for blackhead, bromodosis for smelly feet, tinea trichophyton for athlete's foot.

As it turned out, no one duplicated the magnitude of Listerine's success, but it suggested the depths of people's insecurity about their physical appeal and their readiness to seek remedies. Perhaps most important, the ad campaign changed unpleasant breath from a piece of bad luck to an example of antisocial behaviour. As an ad

"If I were starting life over again, I am inclined to think that I would go into the advertising business in preference to almost any other. . . . It is essentially a form of education; and the progress of civilization depends on education."

—Franklin D. Roosevelt

for breath mints announced in 1925, "A few years ago, bad breath was condoned as an unavoidable misfortune. Today it is judged one of the gravest social offenses."

"So you fly off back home. Wash your hands. Why, surely. You've got so much soap in the United States."

—Marlene Dietrich, playing a Berlin singer, to an American lover in Billy Wilder's *A Foreign Affair*, 1948

From the 1920s on, the onus was on everybody to gargle, deodorize and clean oneself vigilantly, because unsuspected transgressions would not be treated lightly.

Although deodorants had been available since the 1880s, the first generation worked by attempting to close the pores with wax. (Shades of Francis Bacon's seventeenth-century bath, but with a different goal.) Aside from not being terribly effective, they were rarely advertised because of their "unpleasant" nature. On a hot day in 1907, a Cincinnati doctor became conscious of his own perspiration while performing surgery. As a result, he invented Odorono ("Odour? Oh, no!"), a formula that inhibited perspiration with aluminum chloride. Outside of a sultry operating theatre, a little body odour was no bad thing for a man, and the doctor had no wish to capitalize on his invention. But his daughter, Edna Alfred, wanted to sell the new deodorant to women.

In 1919, James Webb Young, a copywriter for the J. Walter Thompson advertising agency, wrote one of the century's most sensational ads, for the doctor's formula. Under a picture of an attractive, well-dressed couple, the woman with her arm in a thin short sleeve gracefully extended not too far from the man's nose, the headline reads, "Within the Curve of a Woman's Arm." In the "frank discussion of a subject too often avoided," as the subtitle promises, the word "underarm" never appears. It begins lyrically, "A woman's arm! Poets have sung of its grace: artists have painted its beauty." But it proceeds to plainspoken truths about the active perspiration glands under the arm, accompanied with the ominous warning that the resulting odour may be "unnoticed by ourselves, but distinctly noticeable to others." Deftly handled as it was, the ad disgusted several women of Young's acquaintance, who threatened never to speak to him again. Two hundred readers of the *Ladies' Home Journal,* which carried the ad, cancelled their subscriptions in protest. But sales for Odorono rose 112 per cent within a year of the ad's appearance.

The success of the Odorono ad and the deluge of deodorant advertisements that followed say much about the decade's willingness to broach taboo subjects and its growing intolerance of secretions and smells. Advertising promised that the body and its embarrassments could be held at arm's length, disciplined and made acceptable. For the consumers of the day, devoted to "scientific" or at least systematic methods of getting ahead in life, that was essential.

In 1923, William M. Handy published a four-volume book called *The Science of Culture.* In spite of its high-toned title, Handy's book is a detailed and practical guide to gentility. His cultivated man or woman understands that cleanliness is the first requirement for "the attractive bodily expression of innate Culture." For those still on the road to Culture (always capitalized), Handy devotes about fifteen pages to advice about hygiene. Without a daily bath, "no one can be really clean, nor either feel or express Culture." (So much for Michelangelo, Beethoven and Jane Austen.) Actually, two baths a day are ideal, Handy writes: a warm cleansing one in the evening and a stimulating cold one in the morning. "Scented soaps, unless the most delicate, are taboo to persons of Culture," and they rarely clean as well as the unscented variety. Without warm water and lots of soap, Handy writes, it's impossible to remove "the evaporated remnants of the pint and a half of perspiration, virtually the same as urine, that exudes through the pores of your skin each day."

The Science of Culture is really about worldly success, and cleanliness is a crucial step toward it. "It costs a little time and perhaps a little money to keep fresh and clean," Handy writes, "but from a purely mercenary standpoint of increasing your business and social efficiency, it is a good investment." A man who wants to make a good impression needs a clear, healthy skin, shaved at least once a day. Successful men, we read, are quick to note the condition of other people's hands. He who neglects them will not be tolerated, "except for the strongest business reasons."

Handy writes forthrightly about underarm hair and other delicate matters, but he is reserved compared with Sophie Hadida, also American and the author of *Manners for Millions: A Correct Code of Pleasing Personal Habits for Everyday Men and Women*. The important words in the title of her 1932 book are "Millions" and "Everyday": even more than Handy's work, this is a volume for ambitious people without

> "We are all glowing, and sparkling, and snapping, and tingling with health, by way of the toothbrush, and the razor, and the shaving cream, and the face lotion, and the deodorant, and a dozen other brightly packaged gifts of the gods."
>
> —Theodore MacManus, "The Nadir of Nothingness," 1928

Even more sensitive a subject than deodorant, menstrual pads appeared and became a success in the 1920s. Before the invention of Kotex, women used cotton cloths or rags, which they washed and reused. During the First World War, a Wisconsin company called Cellucotton made bandages from wood fibre for use in the army hospitals in France, and the nurses began using these "cellucotton" bandages as disposable sanitary pads. Once the war was over, the company renamed them Kotex (short for "cotton-like texture") and hired a Chicago advertising agency to market this awkward product.

Bizarrely, its first ad showed two wounded soldiers with an attendant nurse, and two other soldiers in the background. Accepted by the *Ladies' Home Journal* but never printed, the ad was recalled by the agency, which had second thoughts about spotlighting men in connection with such an unmentionable female function. But the product's wartime origin—perhaps some sense that if it was good enough for heroic soldiers, it would serve for a woman's monthly inconvenience—was apparently too compelling to forgo entirely. The next attempt, which was published in the *Journal* in 1921 and is pictured here, shows a wounded veteran seen from the back in his wheelchair in a garden, attended by a nurse and another woman. A third woman sits behind them on the grass. The copy fills in the "romantic background" of this "wonderful absorbent," which is now manufactured by machinery that makes and seals it completely without contact from human hands. The sanitary pads became so successful that the company changed its name from Cellucotton to Kotex.

a refined upbringing. In America, this is a perennial subject and, in spite of significant social changes brought about by the Depression and the Second World War, Hadida's book was still being reprinted in 1950.

Her chapter called "Odors" begins with a breezy preface:

> If you are going to be insulted, don't read this chapter. But there is really no reason for your taking offense if you have that dreadful thing

known to all the world as "B.O." (Body Odor)! It is not you who should be offended, but your friends, if by this time you have not lost them all. Of course, you do as you like, for after all it is your book—not mine.

The frankness of deodorant manufacturers, Hadida writes, has brought a formerly forbidden subject out in the open. Now men and women are being told that unless we bathe daily and use deodorant, "we are guilty of B.O." It's obvious why this reprimand is necessary: "You need only to go into a dressing room of a department store, depot, theatre, office building, or any other room frequented by women to know that more attention should be paid to the subject of baths."

Never underestimate the unpleasant aroma that stems from the neglect of cleanliness: B.O. has been the cause of rupture of friendships, of the breaking of engagements, of exclusion from definite social groups, of disgusted expressions of the face, of quarrels between husbands and wives, friends, brothers and sisters—and how unnecessary—when for ten cents the difficulty can be removed.

Although Hadida claims that a ten-cent box or bottle or jar of deodorant can last a lifetime, that is doubtful given the frequency and range of applications she suggests. After bathing, it should coat "ANY PART of the body that is likely to have an odor—under the arms, between the toes, around the edge of the hair, in the groin, the palms of the hands." Because nerves and excitement provoke B.O., it's a good practice to carry a small package of deodorant in your purse for extra applications when needed.

Most odours are unwelcome in Hadida's world. She cautions women not to appear for job interviews wearing a fragrant powder or perfume, because the prospective employer will probably believe she is trying to disguise a bad odour of her own: "The one who smells of clean unperfumed soap indicates that she has no odor to conceal." In addition to the usual causes of halitosis, a cold may cause unpleasant breath, but the remedy—antiseptic mouth wash or sprays—is also offensive to many, so Hadida's solution is "KEEP YOUR DISTANCE." That applies also to the person who eats the most apparently innocuous foods, such as bread and butter. "All food odors are offensive," so when eating, don't come near anyone who is not also eating.

Because cleanliness and freedom from bad smells are essential social assets, parents owe it to their children to make sure they form the proper habits early. In particular, the boy or girl who bathes daily makes a powerful appeal to the teacher.

> Of course there are some teachers who love
> their charges whether they are clean or dirty, but
> your child may have an instructor who is partial
> to the privileged classes. In such case, no matter
> how modest your means may be, no matter how
> poor are the facilities for bathing in your little
> home, you are wise if you make an appeal to her,
> for the child's sake, through his cleanliness.

Dirty boys and girls of any age will "repel desirable friends," but adolescents are particularly smelly. Even for the girl who is menstruating (when bathing was not usually recommended), the daily bath is a must. Hadida suggests lathering completely while standing at the sink, then jumping in and immediately out of a tub filled with warm water for rinsing.

She sums up her chapter with the admonition "Odors are unnecessary and those who have them are violating rules of courtesy." It's tempting to conclude that when she says "odors," Hadida doesn't mean only obviously bad smells. She means odour, period. The most courteous person, who intrudes least on other people, is as odourless as humanly possible.

Judging from the deluge of etiquette and self-help books, magazine articles and advertisements that urged Americans to wash themselves with as much soap and water as possible, the 1920s should have been a fine time for soap makers. Instead, they anticipated a drop in sales. A buyer's market of goods was overwhelming and distracting the consumer. At the same time, Americans were getting less and less dirty. Paved streets and roads, the automobile and electricity all made for people who were cleaner than those who lived with dirt roads, horses, coal stoves and kerosene lamps. More efficient central heating made the wearing of heavy woollen clothes unnecessary. Thanks to more mechanized factories and labour-saving devices, workers and housewives did not get as dirty as before. What concerned soap makers most, however, was the Roaring Twenties' booming cosmetics industry. The most successful advertising campaigns for soap had promised that cleanliness would bring beauty. Unfortunately for them, lipstick, rouge and mascara produced the illusion of beauty more effectively than the most luxurious soap.

In 1927 the soap makers retaliated by founding the Cleanliness Institute, a trade organization devoted to inculcating in Americans a belief in the supreme value of hygiene. Eighty per cent of soap manufacturers supported the new organization, and the *New York Times* welcomed its initiative. Happy that "the slovenly folk, who have been going on the theory that they can take a bath or leave it, are to be brought to their senses," the *Times* saw the Institute as meeting a genuine social need. Using magazine advertisements, radio ads and "public service announcements," and a battery of classroom teaching aids, the Institute aimed at making Americans feel that there was no such thing as "clean enough." To do that, they were willing to play the germ card, in publications such as *Hitchhikers: Patrolling the Traffic Routes to the Mouth and Nose,* a deliberately worrying book addressed to doctors, nurses, health workers, bureaucrats and teachers. But for the general public, in an advertising campaign for which they paid $350,000 over three years, the Institute bypassed health issues as usual to concentrate on the ability of soap to deliver status, money and romance.

Homing in on a man's anxieties about the work world, one of their magazine ads shows a silver-haired, well-groomed man looking skeptically at an unkempt fellow. The grubby man, who has sullied the elder one's tidy desk with a worn briefcase and fedora, turns away to look at a huge, surreal version of himself, biting his fingernails. The headline reads, "He had to fight himself so hard . . . *he didn't put it over.*" Admitting to himself that he's his own worst enemy, the slovenly man asks himself, "Oh why had he neglected the bath that morning, the shave, the change of linen? Under the other fellow's gaze it was hard to forget that cheap feeling. . . . The clean-cut chap can look any man in the face, and tell

Lifebuoy soap made bathing fun, while its "searching, super-cleansing power" emulsified odour-causing waste matter and carried it away.

him the facts—for when you're clean, your appearance fights *for* you." The conclusion, in large letters: "There's self-respect in SOAP & WATER."

In another advertisement, a woman stares pensively out of the window at a group of children playing between her house and the neighbours'. The woman and her husband, who looks up at her quizzically from his newspaper, are a handsome, prosperous couple. But the headline asks, "What do the neighbours think of *her* children?" Naturally every mother, the ad tells us, considers her children ideal. "But what do the neighbours think? Do *they* smile at happy, grimy faces acquired in wholesome play? For people have a way of associating unclean clothes and faces with other questionable characteristics." It's not clear from this ever-so-slightly menacing message whether the well-intentioned mother should interrupt her children's play with soapy washcloths and a change of clothes. The ad ends, "There's CHARACTER—IN SOAP AND WATER."

The Cleanliness Institute tried to touch as many bases as possible. But it concentrated its efforts in the schools, aiming not just to make children clean, "but to make them love to be clean." To that end, it produced and sold at cost hundreds of thousands of stories, along with leaflets, posters and teachers' guides. It devised a cleanliness curriculum, with clearly stated objectives, that stretched from the earliest grades to high school. Conditioning began in grade one, with Health Town, a toy town made by the teacher. Each child made a house of paper, labelled it with his name and placed it on a street. If he was found deficient in the daily "Keep Clean Parade," his house was removed from Health Town until he redeemed himself. But cleaning should never be seen as punitive, the Institute stressed, and the morning check-up should be "a period of rejoicing over cleanliness rather than searching for dirt."

The declining sales that had worried the soap industry did not materialize, or not in the way they imagined. The price of soap held firm throughout the 1920s, as the supply increased. What hurt its business, as it hurt everyone's business, was the Depression. Just as the Cleanliness Institute closed its doors in 1932, a casualty of the stalled economy, Aldous Huxley published his satire of a sanitized utopia, *Brave New World*. It's doubtful that Huxley, living in England, had heard of the Institute, although naturally enough there are parallels between its emphasis on indoctrination and social pressure and the vastly more extreme measures taken in the novel's odour- and germ-phobic future civilization.

Scornful of a world he saw as mindlessly hedonistic and devoted to synthetic pleasures, Huxley created a society where children are conceived in and born from test tubes and where nursing a baby is even more disgusting than wearing old clothes or using the words "mother" and "father." One of the cardinal sins in the brave new world is retaining one's natural aroma. The Controller's scathing picture of the old order—a place

AN ENGLISH VIEW OF
AMERICAN HYGIENE

"With a steady hand Aimée fulfilled the prescribed rites of an American girl preparing to meet her lover—dabbed herself under the arms with a preparation designed to seal the sweat glands, gargled another to sweeten the breath, and brushed into her hair some odorous drops from a bottle labelled: 'Jungle Venom.'"

—Evelyn Waugh, *The Loved One*, 1948

called "home," stuffy, unsterilized and smelly—contrasts with a scene of Lenina Crowne, bathing, massaging and scenting herself in the Girls' Dressing Room. "Torrents of hot water were splashing into or gurgling out of a hundred baths," as Lenina, after a day's work in the Central London Hatchery and Conditioning Centre, unzips herself out of her clothes. For an Englishman like Huxley, the prospect of a hundred baths generously supplied with hot water was still a futuristic vision in 1932; in America, it was much closer to reality.

In both countries, the after-bath facilities were the stuff of fantasy. Once she has bathed and dried herself, Lenina

> took hold of a long flexible tube plugged into the wall, presented the nozzle to her breast, as though she meant to commit suicide, pressed down the trigger. A blast of warmed air dusted her with the finest talcum powder. Eight different scents and eau-de-Cologne were laid on in little taps over the wash-basin. She turned on the third from the left, dabbed herself with chypre and, carrying her shoes and stockings in her hand, went out to see if one of the vibro-vacuum machines were free.

Lenina returns from the vibro-vac "like a pearl illuminated from within, pinkly glowing."

With Bernard Marx, a young man whose orthodoxy is rightly suspected, Lenina visits a Savage Reservation in New Mexico, one of the remnants of the old order left unreformed as an exotic and slightly revolting tourist destination. Lenina finds its squalor disorienting, and the smell of their native guide is the last straw. When Bernard tries to make light of the body odour, the dirt and dust, and the insects, she protests with one of the mantras drilled into them, sleeping and waking, as children.

"But cleanliness is next to fordliness."

"Yes, and civilization is sterilization," Bernard went on, concluding on a tone of irony the second hynopaedic lesson in elementary hygiene. "But these people have never heard of Our Ford, and they aren't civilized."

Linda, who was raised in the new world but accidentally left behind on the reserve for decades, agrees with Bernard. She tells the couple about the horror of a place where "nothing is aseptic." In vain she tried to teach the natives the slogans she had been conditioned with as a child, including "Streptocock-Gee to Banbury-T, to see a fine bathroom and W.C." But, she says, "they didn't understand. How should they? And in the end I suppose I got used to it. And anyhow, how *can* you keep things clean when there isn't hot water laid on?"

Linda's question was a good one, and still relevant in Europe. By the 1930s in America, almost all urban houses and apartments were supplied with hot water, as were a smaller majority in Britain. Fifty-five per cent of all American houses had a complete bathroom in 1940. On the Continent it was more difficult to keep clean. Only 10 per cent of Italians had a

"We are the first great nation in which all individuality, all sweetness of life, all saline and racy earthiness has with success been subordinated to a machine-ruled industrialism."

—American novelist Sinclair Lewis

bathroom in 1931. Twenty years later in France, in 1954, only one house or apartment in ten had a shower or bath. America remained the pioneer of personal cleanliness, and every time Americans went a step further—decreeing that people should bathe or shower and apply deodorant daily, or that women should shave their underarms to inhibit body odour—Europeans reacted with incredulity, scorn or both. Gradually, their plumbing improved and their washing increased, although outside the largest cities it often did not meet American standards.

By the late 1930s and the '40s, millions of Americans had a healthy respect for the evils of malodorous mouths, underarms, feet and genital areas. They knew about the products that promised to solve those problems. Movie stars, from Bette Davis to Joan Crawford to Rosemary Clooney, recommended soap ("9 out of 10 Screen Stars are Lux Girls") as the way to lovelier skin. Dewy-looking brides, who had realized every woman's ambition, vouched for the efficacy of Listerine ("Till BREATH do us part"), soap ("Skin that says 'I do!'"), and deodorant ("You can say 'yes' to Romance because Veto says 'no' to Offending!"). The advertisers had largely succeeded in what they liked to think of as their educational mission. What could they do next?

NINE

THE HOUSEHOLD SHRINE

1950 TO THE PRESENT

In 1956, a University of Michigan professor named Horace Miner published a paper in the *American Anthropologist* called "Body Ritual among the Nacirema." A little-studied group, the Nacirema had a sophisticated market economy but were most notable for their extraordinary focus on their health and appearance. Their fundamental belief, Miner wrote, is "that the human body is ugly and that its natural tendency is to debility and disease." Imprisoned in these treacherous bodies, the Nacirema resorted to elaborate rituals and extreme behaviours that took place in a household shrine or shrines.

"The more powerful individuals in the society have several shrines in their houses," Miner reported, "and, in fact, the opulence of a house is often referred to in terms of the number of such ritual centers it possesses." The centre of the shrine was a chest built into the wall, full of charms and potions. Underneath this charm box was a small font, into which flowed holy waters whose purity was guarded by a priestly class. The Nacirema entered the shrine daily, one by one, bowing the head before the charm box and performing a brief ablution ritual. These practices, although critically important to them, were enacted not as a family but privately and surreptitiously: "The rites are normally only discussed with children," Miner wrote, "and then only during the period when they are being initiated into these mysteries."

> "America is the only country that passed from barbarism to decadence without civilization in between."
>
> —Oscar Wilde

Nacirema, of course, spells "American" backwards, and Miner's classic spoof is still taught in universities as a satire aimed at anthropological method and Western condescension toward the "others" they study. Miner devoted much of his attention to the Nacirema's masochistic faith in dentists and hospitals, but it is his description of the household shrine, the bathroom, that is most prophetic. As with *Brave New World*, reality has overtaken the satirical fantasy, and if Miner were writing today, half a century later, he would have to describe the shrine as a far more excessive site of luxury, complicated rituals and miracle-working potions.

The phenomenon Miner noted, that the Nacirema gauged the magnificence of a house by the number of its ritual shrines, or bathrooms, has recently reached new extremes. In January 2006, the *New York Times Magazine* ran an advertisement for the luxurious apartments being built in the Stanhope Hotel, across Fifth Avenue from the Metropolitan Museum. An eight-bedroom apartment has no fewer than eleven bathrooms, including two for the master bedroom. At the Stanhope, Harriet Beecher Stowe's futuristic dream of a bathroom for every two or three inhabitants has nearly been turned on its head: this apartment could well accommodate an inhabitant for every two or three bathrooms. In the nineteenth and early twentieth centuries, bathrooms were rarely built on the first floor of a house because no lady wanted to be seen entering one. Now, if we can afford it, bathrooms are ubiquitous, and our idea of delicacy has gone in a different direction: ideally, as at the Stanhope, no one would ever have to share a bathroom, even a married couple.

An apartment at the Stanhope is beyond the reach of most people, but 24 per cent—almost one in four—of the U.S. houses built in 2005 had three or more bathrooms. And quantity is only the beginning of what Americans want from their bathrooms. In the twenty-first century, these rooms have become the inner sanctum, the place where hedonism, narcissism, over-the-top luxury and hygienic scrupulosity meet. At the end of the nineteenth century, the French found the American bathroom as clinical as an operating theatre. Things began to shift in the 1920s when towel companies such as Cannon and Martex and fixture manufacturers such as Kohler and Crane realized there was money to be made from the newest, smallest room in the house. Cannon supplied several "bathing recipes" that advised a generous use of towels. "Because the first towel absorbs impurities from the skin," Cannon warned the bather, "it must never (under any circumstances) be used again before washing." Towels, which had come only in white and white with red or blue borders, now bloomed in pistachio, orange and rose, which coordinated with the new, exotically coloured fixtures. Kohler's Imperator Bath was available in lavender, and Standard Sanitary made tubs, sinks and toilets in Clair de Lune Blue and Vincennes Orchid.

But the bathroom reached its current sybaritic levels only in the 1990s. Often, it's no longer the smallest room in the house. The average size of the American bathroom tripled between 1994 and 2004, and it's not uncommon to sacrifice a bedroom to make an extra-large bathroom. Previously undreamed-of luxuries—oversized tubs that fill in sixty seconds, waterproof plasma TV screens and bathroom scales that calculate muscle/fat ratios—are becoming standard items in high-end bathrooms. Other features hark back to ancient Rome and the golden age of bathing. If your floor, and your wallet, can support it, an 1,800-pound marble tub with animal feet can be had for US $20,000 without fixtures. It actually resembles a sarcophagus more than the bronze individual tubs used in Rome, but the Imperial fantasy is what's important here. Like the rec rooms of the 1950s, the contemporary bathroom is the space where make-believe is allowed the fullest expression—perhaps a Japanese-style "wet room," where the shower is not in a cubicle but sprays the whole room, or, for a period look, a four-poster bathtub. It can be a retreat where no one else is welcome, a "meditation room" or a new kind of family room—one the Romans would have understood, a place to reconnect with your family after the stresses of the day are past.

As in the nineteenth century, hotels are leading the way. Once travellers to five-star hotels experience fogless mirrors, a shower that imitates a rainforest downpour and a bathtub built for four, chances are it won't be long before those amenities are available for the domestic market. Eros plays a prominent part in these hotel designs, as seen in the "romantic getaway" room that features a transparent glass shower in the bedroom. Half of the more than three hundred rooms of the Hotel Puerto America in Madrid, designed by a battery of celebrity architects, have open-plan bathroom-bedrooms. The rooms in one of Montreal's newest hotels, W, have a wall between the bedroom and bathroom—almost a retro step in some quarters—but only to heighten the naughtiness potential: there is a cutout in the wall, offering what the president of W Hotels, Ross Klein, calls a "voyeuristic opportunity." He adds, "It's a sexy transmission between the grooming, bathing and sleeping areas." The Hotel on Rivington on New York City's Lower East Side takes the titillation a notch higher with floor-to-ceiling windows in the shower that make it visible to the hotel's neighbours. (If exhibitionism is not to your taste, the hotel will obscure the window with a plastic film.) These kinds of saucy self-indulgences, applied to what was an everyday chore in the not-so-distant past, cry out for the appraising eye of a

"As we know it, dirt is essentially disorder. There is no such thing as absolute dirt: it exists in the eye of the beholder. Dirt offends against order."

—anthropologist Mary Douglas, *Purity and Danger: An Analysis of Concepts of Pollution and Taboo,* 1966 modern Martial: he would sometimes jeer at their vulgarity, and in other moods celebrate their carnal possibilities.

Miner singled out a part of the body that particularly worried the Nacirema. They had "an almost pathological horror of and fascination with the mouth," he wrote, "the condition of which is believed to have a supernatural influence on all social relationships. Were it not for the rituals of the mouth, they believe that their teeth would fall out, their gums bleed, their jaws shrink, their friends desert them, and their lovers reject them." Miner was prescient, but again, the ante has been upped significantly since 1956. In the eighteenth century, Lord Chesterfield wanted his son to preserve his own teeth into old age and not offend others with his bad breath. Twenty-first-century North Americans would consider that a ludicrously meagre demand: now teeth must be perfectly straight, even and preternaturally white. (Even prosperous Britons and Europeans do not share this obsession, and the easiest way to pick out the non-American actors in a movie with an international cast is to look at their teeth.)

Many of the potions used by the twenty-first-century Nacirema to forestall the toothless, shrunken-jawed, friendless and loveless fate they fear would look familiar to their grandparents, although the toothpastes, brushes, dental flosses and mouthwashes have diversified into a bewilderment of choices. Forget mint and spearmint toothpaste; some of the flavours for Crest sound like sorbets—Lemon Ice, Cinnamon Ice and Refreshing

Vanilla Mint. Dental floss, which also offers a range of flavours, comes in waxed, unwaxed and "whitening."

Since floss goes between the teeth, it doesn't sound as if much of that whitening would be visible, but whitening is the current *sine qua non* in the Nacirema's oral obsession. Even battery-operated power brushes promise a "whitening bristle system." The bandwagon these products are hoping to mount dates from 2002, when Crest Whitestrips, an expensive ($50-plus) collection of strips impregnated with hydrogen peroxide or a peroxide-type chemical, appeared on drugstore shelves. Delighted retailers saw sales in the powder-polish-whitener category shoot up 263 per cent in that year alone, and by 2005, whitening strips had become a $500 million industry. Dentists repeat that our teeth are not intended to be bright white, but ivory or cream or even—yes—yellow-white, and that repeated use of the whiteners may damage the gums as well as enamel. But sales continue to boom, and dentists are seeing increasing numbers of patients who overuse the strips because their teeth are never "white enough." They liken the fad to anorexia, where the patient is never "thin enough," and predict that this compulsion could end in every tooth needing a crown.

If paper-white teeth are the latest necessity, that does not mean that previous hygienic goals have become irrelevant. New demands are added on constantly, without subtracting anything. For more than a century, cleanliness has been a definitive part of the American way, and

CLEANING UP THE PENIS: NON-RITUAL CIRCUMCISION

The cultures that ritually circumcised their males—Jews, Muslims, Australian aborigines, various African tribes—thought of it as a purification rite, or as a sign of their covenant with God. But starting in America in the nineteenth century, doctors saw the removal of the foreskin as progressive hygiene. In the 1870s, a New York City surgeon claimed that circumcising paralyzed boys cured them. From this bizarre beginning, doctors looked to the uncircumcised penis when there were problems elsewhere, and the more they looked, the more apparent abnormalities they found. The new germ theory also encouraged circumcision, in that the only defence against the hordes of microscopic enemies was prevention, which included surgery. The foreskin, which harboured potentially infectious secretions called smegma, looked eminently operable. In fact, smegma in classical Greek means soap, and the substance needs only to be rinsed off with warm water, but by 1894, the most common reason given for circumcision was hygiene.

Non-ritual circumcision was a twentieth-century phenomenon, limited to the English-speaking world and particularly popular in America. By 1970, it was clear that most of the conditions of the foreskin that doctors had interpreted as disorders were normal, and that an intact penis was no barrier to cleanliness. In 1971 the American Academy of Pediatrics announced that there was no medical rationale for routine circumcision. Circumcisions dropped to 3.8 per cent in Britain and 12 per cent in Canada. The country where rates have remained highest is the United States, where circumcisions have dropped from 85 per cent to about 60 per cent.

a signal divider between those who belonged and those who didn't. At the time of the Civil War, dirty faces and hands and dingy collars and cuffs indicated that you were a farmer, a manual worker or simply poor. By the twentieth century, the visual evidence of dirtiness was rare, and smell became the telltale sign. As marketers and advertisers of soaps and deodorizers refined their skills and drove hygienic standards upwards, their messages fell on constantly fertile ground. Smelling someone's real body or allowing your own real body to be smelled has become an intrusion, a breach of a crucial boundary.

At the end of the nineteenth century, Jolyon Forsyte in John Galsworthy's *The Forsyte Saga* flosses his teeth with sewing thread. Nylon floss became available during World War Two

In North America today, there seems to be no resting place, no point at which we can feel comfortable in our own skins for more than a few hours after our last shower. "Clean" keeps receding into the distance. Although our dream of a perfect body can sound like the ancient Greeks' glorification of the physical self, Miner is closer to the mark when he describes the Nacirema's "pervasive aversion to the natural body and its functions." In some ways, we are as repulsed by our real bodies as were the medieval saints, although without their religious motivation. Or, to put it another way, our religion is bodily perfection and any deviation from that unreachable goal is deplorable.

The North American wish to replace our real aroma with one we've bought doesn't surprise Sissel Tolaas, but that doesn't mean she likes it. Tolaas, who calls herself a professional provocateur but is more often described as an odour artist, is on a one-woman crusade to lead the "smell-blinded," as she calls us, back to the valuable, grounding sense we've diminished. Although she has never made a commercial fragrance, Tolaas heads a research lab in Berlin for International Flavours and Fragrances Inc., a company that produced perfumes for Ralph Lauren and Prada. At IFF, Tolaas originated the smells of Ikea, Volvo and H&M, but she sees her role more as a gadfly, a perpetual challenge to our conventional ideas about smell.

In her office at IFF, Tolaas closes her eyes, flares her elegant nostrils and takes a deep whiff from a bottle holding the smell of unregenerate, skunky male sweat. She pronounces it "*fab-ulous*," and pats a spot on each wrist. She grew up in Iceland and Norway, smelling the air for rain, storms and snow. One day she asked herself why we have so many words for describing what we see and hear, and so few for the nuances of smell, why we undervalue our sense of smell while exalting sight and hearing. She trained herself to experience odour the way our ancestors did—not primarily to be delighted or disgusted but to gain valuable facts or clues. An autodidact because there was no one to teach her, she amassed a "smell archive" of 7,630 jars of different aromas, from dried fish to soiled fabric.

Why is Tolaas so passionate about wanting us to stop and think again about the information we take in through our noses? Because our noses connect us to the most basic reality: we smell our mothers, she points out, before we see them. And the way back to that basic reality begins with our own undeodorized bodies. Another reason, she says, is that disliking the smell of other classes, races and countries is a cheap and fatally easy way to bolster our illusion of superiority. She's outraged by a 2005 law that allows the public librarians in San Luis Obispo County, California, to eject smelly readers, i.e., street people. Taking a leaf from George Orwell, whom she admires, Tolaas says we're usually too politically correct to articulate that aversion: "We express it by the way we move around the other people and their neighbourhoods, by the space we give them."

Tolaas has various stratagems for destabilizing our normal expectations and educating our olfactory illiteracy. Having synthesized the rank sweat of nine men with intense phobias, she chose one and wore it, along with her party clothes, to a reception given by the Brazilian ambassador in Berlin. As Tolaas hoped, confusion ensued, "because the way I looked and the way I smelled did not fit at all." Last year, she impregnated nine walls in the art centre at the Massachusetts Institute of Technology with her synthetic sweat smells; in a unique scratch-and-sniff experience, the gallery-goers activated the pungent odours by touching the walls.

Tolaas's hopes for more intelligent smelling also hinge on her educational work with children in elementary school, where she encourages them to talk about, draw and dramatize their reactions to odours. The more words and spontaneous, unsocialized associations they have for smells, she believes, the less vulnerable they'll be to advertising for cover-ups. This kind of rethinking is easier in Europe, according to Tolaas, where Europeans are used to crossing a border and encountering a different language and culture. "Europe is more open," she says, "more tolerant of individuality and differences."

Sissel Tolaas, at work in her Berlin office.

Tolaas may be idealizing European tolerance, but it is true that Europeans as a whole have resisted any headlong rush into over-cleanliness. At the same time, they have travelled a long way since 1954, when only one French dwelling in ten had a shower or bathtub. The percentage of houses and apartments with a bath or shower is now very high in western Europe: 100 per cent in the Netherlands, Sweden and Malta and percentages in the high 90s in most other western European countries. (The anomaly is Portugal, with only 65 per cent in 2001.) In some of the countries in the former Soviet bloc, full bathrooms are still relatively rare, with Lithuania, Latvia and Estonia all reporting percentages in the 60s in the early years of this century.

How much use those baths and showers see is another question. As always, mentality is more important than plumbing, and an anecdote reported by Antoine Prost in *A History of Private Life* underscores the longevity of traditional French attitudes. Just before the Second World War, when a school principal in Chartres suggested to a working-class mother that her teenaged

Seven hundred new antibacterial products were launched in the United States between 1992 and 1998. One of them was the "oral-care strip," pieces of antimicrobial tape designed to be stuck to the tongue.

daughter was now menstruating and that her personal hygiene needed improvement, the incensed mother replied, "I am fifty years old, Madame, and I have never washed down there!" It does not sound as if an available bath or shower would have made a great difference to this woman's frame of mind, and she was probably typical of her class and generation.

Still, habits were gradually changing. When North Americans in the 1960s and '70s returned from European trips, they were almost guaranteed to have a wide-eyed story or two about strange encounters with middle-class Europeans whose hair was greasy and whose underarms were stinky. Those encounters are far less frequent today. In 1998, *Francoscopie,* a French publication that reports social trends, claimed that the average French person showered or bathed 4.4 times a week, compared with 3.7 times a week for Britons and 3.8 for Italians. (The same study announced that the French lead Europe in the amount of perfume, deodorants, makeup, and face and hand creams they buy.) More recently, a number of polls and studies reported that 51 per cent of French women and 55 per cent of French men do not shower or bathe every day and that half of the men and 30 per cent of the women don't use deodorant. As for putting on fresh underwear every day, 40 per cent of French men and one in four French women don't. News like that makes North Americans either guffaw or

"Not so very long ago—perhaps within 40 years—more than a few UK homes did not have a bathroom. It was shocking then, because compared with our American cousins, we seemed to be the great unwashed. It is shocking now, because not since Roman times has a nation elevated the room in which it bathes to such temple-like status."

—Lisa Freedman, *Financial Times,* 5 September 2003

shake their heads at what they consider the unsavoury habits of Europeans, but for sedentary workers whose houses are filled with labour-saving devices, four baths or showers a week is not unreasonable. Besides, it shows a nice resistance to the ploys of advertisers.

⌣⌒

Compared with Europe, Sissel Tolaas says, "In America, everything is more extreme, and everything turns into a rule." Ironically, the product that most epitomizes the extremes to which the American deodorizing imperative could go was invented by the Swiss. In the early 1960s, the Swiss combined hexachlorophene, an emollient, a scent and a propellant into a spray for cleansing and deodorizing women's external genitalia. Moist tissues for the same purpose had been around for decades, but the use of a spray was something new. Unlike the heavy, sticky sprays then available, the Swiss product added fluorocarbon 12, which made it dry and warm. The first American version, which was rushed into production by Alberto-Culver and flatly named FDS, for "feminine deodorant spray," was launched in 1966. Although the Swiss spray was never more than moderately popular, FDS, thanks to the canny marketers and willing consumers of America, was a wildfire success. Twenty brands followed Alberto-Culver into the market, and in 1973, more than twenty million women were using the sprays, with sales of $40 million.

Not everybody welcomed the new product. Psychiatrists, therapists and feminists charged that the sprays and their ads exploited women's insecurities. Noting that "I smell bad. That's why no one likes me" is a classic paranoid statement, the psychoanalyst Natalie Shainess criticized the ads' "horrendous image, of women being inherently smelly creatures. It undermines the sense of self and ego even as it's supposed to do something about it." To which the manufacturer had ready answers, usually a simple repetition of the irrefutable—to them—fact that women had a "problem," and it was "down there." As one of the manufacturers explained to Nora Ephron in her 1973 *Esquire* article, "Dealing with the, uh, Problem":

> Our whole approach was, women have a vaginal-odor problem and here is a product that will solve the problem. They do, you know. And panty hose contribute to it. Women's liberation says that advertising is creating a need that isn't there. They say it's a nice, natural smell. That's their right. But I would go back and ask them, do women have a vaginal-odor problem? I keep going back to the problem. The problem is there.

Other men involved in the making or marketing of the sprays bypassed the question of whether the odour actually existed and congratulated themselves on helping a woman feel more assured and attractive. Jerry Della Femina, the advertising executive whose company managed the campaign for a spray called Feminique, had his own dramatic fantasy:

> Somewhere out there, there is a girl who might be hung up about herself, and one day she goes

out and buys Feminique and shoots up with it, and she comes home and that same night she feels more confident and she jumps her husband and for the first time in her life she has an orgasm. If I can feel I was responsible for one more orgasm in the world I feel I deserve the Nobel Peace Prize.

By the late 1960s, as the sexual revolution followed the development of the birth control pill, orgasms were definitely on the agenda. Unfortunately, there were times when the revolution felt more constraining and inhibiting than freeing for women. The message conveyed by the feminine hygiene ads was puzzling: Sex is natural and wonderful, but the "natural you" needs to be sprayed to be wonderful. Sex is natural and wonderful, but it leaves a woman in urgent need of washing, powdering, spraying and douching. Sex is natural and wonderful, but it means that the natural you can be rejected on the most intimate level. As an ad for Demure spray put it, over a picture of a girlhood bedroom, "Your Teddy Bear loved you, no matter what. It's only when you marry somebody that you have to think about things you never thought about before."

If spraying something on a woman's external genitalia was so successful, why not go further, into the vagina? Douches had existed for millennia, but adding flavour—raspberry and champagne, in the case of the suggestively named Cupid's Quiver—was an innovation. The magazine ad for Cupid's Quiver showed an unclad model, who urged, "Relax. And enjoy the revolution." The flavoured douche's obvious connection with oral sex made some magazines and all television networks nervous, but within two months of its introduction in 1969, Cupid's Quiver had sold $250,000 worth of liquid douche concentrate. Kate Kane, a feminist who surveyed the gamut of advertisements for douches and sprays, seemed to echo "Body Ritual among the Nacirema" when she wrote, "Taken together, these commercials form a picture of a people obsessed with physical intimacy, yet unable to achieve it without performing many elaborate, expensive daily purifications."

After a brilliant start, sales of the sprays stalled in the early 1970s with reports of irritation and a ban on the use of hexachlorophene from the U.S. Food and Drug Administration. Somewhere between the 1970s and the '80s, the sprays lost their cachet. Doubts about their efficacy, worries about aerosol cans, consumerism, the women's movement—all contributed. Since the second wave of feminism began in the 1960s, at least two generations of feminists have tried to raise savvy, self-confident daughters, and it would be nice to conclude that women have become more skeptical about products that promise to smother their real aroma with a chemical "freshness."

> "Deep at the bottom of all our sense of uncleanness, of dirt, is the feeling, primitive, irresolvable, universal, of the sanctity of the body. Nothing in the material sphere can properly be dirty except the body. We speak of a 'dirty road,' but in an uninhabited world moist clay would be no more dirty than hard rock; it is the possibility of clay adhering to a foot which makes it mire."
>
> —Edwyn Bevan, "Dirt," 1921

Eve Ensler's acclaimed 1996 play *The Vagina Monologues* devotes a monologue to the question "What does a vagina smell like?" The answers include "earth," "spicy, musky jasmine forest," "a brand-new morning," "no smell, I've been told," "damp moss," "somewhere between fish and lilacs" and "me." But the people who take heart from *The Vagina Monologues* are far fewer than those who relentlessly spray their pillows with Febreze and plug in air fresheners wherever they spot an available outlet. In this climate, anxieties about what a friend calls, ironically, "the gamy filth of womanhood" are all too easy to rouse. In 2003, sales of feminine sprays at Wal-Mart rose 30 per cent from the previous year. In the year that ended in September 2005, the "intimate hygiene" category had grown by 9.4 per cent.

These days, wipes—moistened disposable cloths like those used to clean a baby's bottom—are more popular than sprays and are being manufactured by the makers of both condoms and sanitary napkins. Within the past few years, Procter & Gamble, Johnson & Johnson, Vagisil and Playtex have all launched their own wipes. Elexa, a condom brand, markets a package for women that contains three premium latex condoms and six "freshening cloths," presumably one wipe for before sex and another for after.

Freshening cloths and other feminine hygiene products have little interest for Sissel Tolaas, but she admits that living in an un-deodorized body is unsettling. "What is the body without the smell of mango? You don't know," she says. "And before mango, it was lemon, and before that, rose. People are so used to fictions that reality is difficult to react to. And people are afraid of smelling like themselves, because that means being naked. It's dangerous today, to go out without any external smell." When it feels right, by all means wear an external smell, but be conscious of the effect you're trying to produce. (Tolaas, for example, created an aroma

Some of the research techniques used by Alberto-Culver when testing the effectiveness of FDS sound more like material for a Monty Python or an early Woody Allen sketch than credible product tests. To determine the effectiveness of the new spray, the company recruited housewives as research subjects and told them to report to the Institute for Applied Pharmaceutical Research in Yeadon, Pennsylvania.

There the subject removed her clothes, covering the top part of the body, and allowed a "judge" to apply a nosepiece to her vulva. The judge smelled the subject's vulva at intervals over a four-day period, during which the subject bathed with soap and water alone, and then bathed with soap and water before applying FDS. (The subject, who could return home during the intervals but not have intercourse, was paid $150 for the four-day period. The judge, who also smelled subjects for underarm odour, could make up to $1,000 a week.)

The results of the testing justified Alberto-Culver's optimism. Six hours after applying FDS, the subjects were judged 74 to 78 per cent more odour-free than after bathing with plain soap and water; after twelve hours they were 53 to 59 per cent more odour-free, and after twenty-four hours, 38 to 40 per cent more odour-free.

that resembles the metallic smell of money to see if it would make the wearer more successful in business, which it did.) For women today, with increasingly powerful positions in society, she thinks the innocuous florals and baby powders of hygiene products and perfumes are silly: "No sweet rose. That's over."

The future of fragrance, as Tolaas sees it, would begin with a ground or base of your own unique body smell. Then, "you could choose different molecules to add to it. Maybe you'd have one perfume for sex, one for business, whatever." Our natural smell reminds us of our animality, something we usually prefer to forget, but Tolaas doesn't. "The more body smell you have, the more you relate to sex and the more others relate to you sexually," she says. "Animals do that; look at them." It's true that increasing numbers of companies advertise pheromones in fragrances and gels to enhance sexual appeal, but we prefer our animality as sanitized as possible: it's unthinkable that these substances would be accompanied by the body odours that attend them in nature.

We have come to expect that the people we encounter walking down city streets or sitting on subways are showered, mouthwashed and deodorized as much as possible, with the goal of eradicating all natural smells. Then, onto their odourless bodies, they import carefully chosen scents. These people are listening to their own private musical repertoire on their iPods, messaging people on their BlackBerries or talking on their cell phones. The illusion that they exist in their own individual, hygienically sealed bubbles is so strong that, paradoxically, they forget the presence of others and talk loudly of private matters on their cell phones.

The building of these individual bubbles has been a long process. The cultural critic Ivan Illich believed that the French Revolution, when the idea circulated that every man deserved his own bed, was an important starting point in that evolution. In a world where people regularly slept in the same bed with their family or co-workers or fellow guests at an inn, where you emptied your bowels at a public latrine with no dividers between you and the other users, and might expect to be buried in a mass grave, that was a radical step toward dignity and privacy. As gradually it became possible for people to sleep, defecate and be buried in a private space, the desire for privacy grew. Most drastically in twentieth-century North America, it intensified beyond a point that was reasonable or desirable. In 1986, in his book *H$_2$O and the Waters of Forgetfulness,* Illich described the end result, as seen by the modern bourgeois: "Each citizen has the right to be surrounded by a buffer zone that protects him from the aura of others, while keeping his own to himself."

The word "bathroom" appeared in the *Oxford English Dictionary* for the first time in 1972, in the *Supplement.*

Dignity and privacy are good things, but it looks as if America, especially, doesn't know where to stop. Perhaps above all, it's about control: to smell like a body, which alters on its own with time, physical exertion, anxiety, and climatic and hormonal variations, demonstrates that we're not completely in charge, something we increasingly expect of ourselves. As more of the world spins out of control, it seems there is a greater drive to manage what we can, however pointless it may be.

Horace Miner noted that the Nacirema's distrust of the body went in two directions: they were convinced not only that they were ugly but also that they were doomed to illness and infirmity. If North Americans find it difficult to control the look and smell of their bodies, their attempt to control their health is even more stressful—and particularly so in the last few decades.

Fears about disease are unquestionably exacerbating our twenty-first-century preoccupation with hygiene, whether the disease is the Norwalk virus, bird flu, SARS, a new disease called community-associated methicillin-resistant *Staphylococcus aureus* (community-associated MRSA) or problems associated with the bacillus *E. coli*. In 2003, SARS struck 8,096 people and killed 774. Thirty-one of those deaths occurred in Toronto, more than anyplace outside Asia, and that taught Torontonians in short order the virtues of face masks, Purell and handwashing.

According to Vincent Lam and Colin Lee, Toronto emergency room doctors and the authors of *The Flu Pandemic and You*, those straightforward low-tech practices are about the only hygienic steps that might protect us in the next epidemic or pandemic. Get a flu shot by all means, they say, exercise caution with live birds, and cook turkey and chicken well. But during a pandemic or even a normal flu outbreak, wash your hands often and properly, cover your face when sneezing or coughing, and keep a distance of at least one metre from sick people. If you're taking care of a sick person, wear gloves and a mask. And keep some rubber gloves and containers of hand sanitizer with your emergency supplies.

For normal life, the one hygienic measure Drs. Lam and Lee advise is handwashing, to protect ourselves and other people from the spread of germs. If you're a farmer or a manual labourer—jobs with lots of contact with the ground and potential for cuts—or if you play contact sports, washing your body could prevent organisms from entering through a "portal of entry," a cut or a microcut. Otherwise, as far as health is concerned, the most you have to fear from not washing anything but your hands is skin problems, such as yeast or fungal infections.

Charles Gerba, a microbiologist at the University of Arizona who writes and broadcasts as Dr. Germ, agrees that the only parts of the body that need washing for serious health reasons are the hands, but he stresses the wily stubbornness of the thousands of microbes that regularly coat our hands. "Microbes never give up," Dr. Gerba says admiringly. "They adapt and they follow our new habits." He itemizes some of our new habits in the age of information: we spend most of our time in an office, surrounded by electronic equipment that loves to collect germs, where the janitors are told not to interfere with our personal space, that is, not to clean our desks. We travel more and in enclosed spaces such as airplanes, where the toilet will be used by an average of fifty people per flight and is exceptionally germy. And by travelling, we spread diseases all over the world.

Although Gerba says "we have to reinvent hygiene because our world has changed so much," his mantra is an ancient one—clean hands, clean hands, clean hands. He washes his own whenever he leaves his desk, when he goes to the bathroom, after he teaches. When asked, people in movie theatres swear they washed their hands in the restroom, but Gerba and his gimlet-eyed researchers say only 65 per cent do, only half of those who wash use soap, and only half of the ones who use soap wash long enough—it should be for fifteen to twenty seconds. By contrast, he says, to get to a sink in the restroom at a sanitarians' conference, "you have to wait in line." We spoke on the phone, and just before we hung up, I asked Dr. Gerba if he would have shaken my hand if we had met in person. "Sure, unless you had a cold," he said, and then paused for a beat. "And after we shook hands, within a few minutes I'd be looking to sanitize my hands with an alcohol gel."

Gerba denies that he's afraid of germs, because, he says, he knows where to find them, and his basic message is a sensible one. But with his gleeful counts of germs on sinks and fecal bacteria in clean laundry, he is contributing to the anxious sense that we live in a world populated by billions of unseen enemies. We all know people who go to extraordinary lengths never to shake hands or touch a tap in a public washroom, and whose cupboards are filled with antibacterial soaps. Inventions that address their fears are multiplying. One new product, a plastic box to be installed above the doorknob in a public toilet, sprays a disinfectant mist on the knob every fifteen minutes. (However, Dr. Gerba says, "Never fear a doorknob." Unlike a sink, it is not moist, and moisture supplies the most hospitable breeding ground for germs.) Another innovation, the Sanitgrasp, replaces traditional door pulls in restaurants and other public places with a big U-shaped object that allows the door to be opened by a forearm.

Your hands can open the door to all of life's experiences. Like E. Coli.

Your hands can carry thousands of infection-causing germs that are spread through contact, including E. Coli and Salmonella. That's why it's important to thoroughly wash your hands for at least 15 seconds with soap and water or use an alcohol-based hand rub. In fact, cleaning hands often can significantly reduce your chances of getting sick. For more information, please visit health.gov.on.ca/handwashing

Practise proper handwashing. Because your health is in your hands.

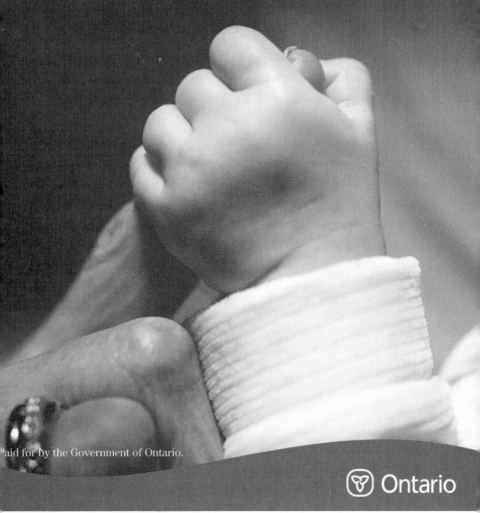

Paid for by the Government of Ontario.

⟲ Ontario

A poster from Ontario's 2006 campaign to encourage handwashing.

The list of these new products stretches from the plausible to the wilder shores of paranoia. You can buy a portable subway strap so your hands never have to come into contact with the overhead bar, as well as a strip of vinyl that covers supermarket cart handles. You can store your toothbrush in a $50 holder that kills germs with ultraviolet light. Imagine the fun Horace Miner would have had with the Nacirema's inability to go anywhere without their personal subway strap, their reverent attitude to the sacred mist sprayed four times an hour on doorknobs, and their clumsy but ritualized use of the forearm to open doors.

People who were once normally hygiene-conscious are behaving more and more like mysophobes (the technical term for those with an inordinate fear of germs). Others whose horror of germs was considered seriously eccentric, such as the obsessive-compulsive TV detective Monk or the television host Howie Mandel, now seem closer to the norm. A decade ago, the editorial writers at a large Canadian newspaper were amused when the germ-conscious editor-in-chief urged them to write an editorial against shaking hands. (He suggested crossing your arms and nodding instead.) The editorial never appeared. It's doubtful that the editor's suggestion would strike them as outlandish or exaggerated today.

On a very real level, germs concern us because the world has become a significantly more perilous place of

The Clean Shopper prevents babies from touching germ-laden supermarket carts.

late. In recent years, many normal activities, such as eating beef and chicken, travelling on public transit and being treated in a hospital, have turned out to be extremely dangerous in certain places. Arrogantly and ignorantly, we assumed that epidemics such as the Spanish flu of 1918 could not happen again. SARS proved us wrong, and now we dread bird flu or a yet unnamed pandemic. Our fearfulness is heightened rather than lessened by the abundance of information and misinformation available at our fingertips on the Internet.

On a more symbolic level, since September 11, 2001, we know that we live in a world that harbours deadly, hidden dangers—terrorists are like germs in that way. The American writer Allen Salkin asks, "Is it only a coincidence that the same places where Americans most fear terrorism—airplanes, schools, mass transit, water supplies and computers—they also fear germs?" Probably not, and what at least some of this overwrought avoidance of germs really demonstrates is our wish to be protected, to be safe in a world that seems increasingly unsafe.

In 2006, the Museum of Modern Art in New York City was selling some unlikely stuffed toys in its gift shop. Not lambs or bunnies, they were microbes—a dust mite, a bedbug, a stomach-ache virus and a common cold virus. These cuddly playthings in bright colours were perplexing: are microbes our friends? For 125 years, educated opinion would have said no. Now, surprisingly and with increasing frequency, the answer seems to be "some of them" and "sometimes."

Cleanliness in the twenty-first century has more than one face. While some of its aspects, such as the new germ phobia, are charging ahead in one direction, others stand still or take some steps in the opposite direction. The most unexpected example in the last category began surfacing almost twenty years ago. In 1989, a British epidemiologist, D. P. Strachan, published a groundbreaking article in the *British Medical Journal* called "Hay Fever, Hygiene, and Household Size." In it, he suggested that unhygienic contact and infections, both of which are facilitated by large families, might prevent the development of allergies. The so-called Hygiene Hypothesis, first voiced by Strachan, is that our immune system needs a certain amount of bacteria on which to flex its muscles. Deprived of it, the white cells that are designed to fight bacteria, called Th1 lymphocytes, fail to develop, and the other white cells, Th2 lymphocytes—those designed to make antibodies to defend the body against microbial dangers as well as to produce allergic reaction—will take over.

That imbalance in the two types of white cells is "like a set of scales that sometimes tips sharply enough to send a person's health tumbling," as a science writer, Siri Carpenter, put it. Without the check of healthy Th1 lymphocytes, "the Th2 system flourishes and the immune system teeters toward allergic responses." In the view of Strachan and the dozens of researchers who followed him in trying to understand the late twentieth century's baffling rise in asthma and other allergies, the likely culprit is the scrupulous cleanliness of the developed world. Unlike Dr. Gerba, who seeks to eliminate or avoid bacteria as much as possible, these scientists see value in bacteria.

Also in the late 1980s, a German doctor, Erika von Mutius, compared the incidence of allergies and asthma in children from East Berlin and West Berlin. She expected to find that children living in unhygienic, polluted and economically disadvantaged East Berlin would have higher rates than the children from the same genetic background who lived in clean, prosperous West Berlin. She found just the opposite. The West Berlin children had significantly more asthma and allergic reactions.

The research of von Mutius, Strachan and others interested in the Hygiene Hypothesis began to fill in a picture of those who were most and least at risk. Children who had lots of brothers and sisters, especially older ones and more especially brothers, who lived on a farm, who went to daycare in their first year or who had a cat were discovered to do better at avoiding allergic diseases than children in none of these circumstances. These factors provided the "dirty" triggers that are needed to spur the Th1 lymphocytes into action, thus preventing the Th2 lymphocytes from taking over. Even children whose mother had lived on a farm during her pregnancy were less likely to become allergic. The children most likely to develop allergies and asthma were only children who lived in cities, did not go to daycare, had no pets, washed their hands more than five times a day and bathed more than once a day.

The list of diseases possibly contracted in this way came to include rheumatoid arthritis, diabetes, Crohn's disease, multiple sclerosis and even heart disease. Rats living in normally germy environments turned out to be less susceptible to arthritis and diabetes than rats raised in germ-free environments. When people emigrated to Europe and North America from Africa, Asia and Latin America, where multiple sclerosis, Crohn's disease and asthma are extremely rare, their children, who were born and raised in the cleaner developed world, showed the same incidence of those diseases, or even higher, as children with European or North American parents.

The Hygiene Hypothesis remains a hypothesis but an increasingly respected one. There is both contrary evidence (the presence of dust mites and cockroaches has been associated with the development of asthma) and growing corroboration of the theory. So far there are no proven practical applications, although experiments are being conducted in several countries. In Perth, Australia, some asthmatic children are taking a "dirt pill," with the probiotic bacteria they presumably missed out on as babies and toddlers, and antioxidants. Other children with asthma will receive a placebo, and all will be monitored for

WISHFUL THINKING
Germs Are Not for Sharing is the title of a children's book published in 2006 by Elizabeth Vendick that instructs children to play without touching each other. No more ring-around-the rosy, holding hands or high-fives.

frequency of attacks, tolerance for exercise and breathing capacity. Japanese children who were given mycobacteria, a weakened form of tuberculosis bacteria that is related to soil bacteria, were found to have a significantly lower incidence of asthma and allergies than other children.

When I was a child, my playmates and I knew the old saying "You eat a peck of dirt before you die," but we thought of it as a prophecy, not a command. (There are, in fact, places in the world where folk medicine does prescribe eating clay.) So far, no one has suggested feeding children actual dirt or relaxing hygienic standards to any great extent. The possibility that North Americans and Europeans would continue their usual hygienic routines while taking some kind of dirt pill to beef up their immune systems is a solution Aldous Huxley might have found worthy of *Brave New World*. Eventually asthmatic and allergic children may take some kind of bacterial medication, but for the rest of us, Tore Midtvedt, a microbiologist at the Karolinska Institute in Sweden and an expert on indigenous flora, advises a more moderate approach. He wants to see an end to "war on germs" thinking and an understanding that reflects our often fruitful coexistence with germs. "Find the mechanisms that are at work in those few people that have a disease," he says. "And use that to eradicate the disease without eradicating the bug." Midtvedt isn't advocating that we live close to rats and fleas or drink polluted water, just that we stop trying to live in sanitized houses and bodies. "I'm not saying that we should be more dirty," he says. "I'm saying we should be less clean." In other words, we could loosen our currently scrupulous regimen quite a bit before it reached dirtiness.

Appraising contradictory information about hygiene has become one of the everyday conundrums of modern life. At times, the quest for cleanliness at the end of the century's first decade echoes Stephen Leacock's panic-stricken horseman, who mounted his charger and rode off in all directions at once. Some people are attempting to live in laboratory-clean conditions, as far from contact with anyone else's germs as possible, while others urge a more laissez-faire approach. We are concerned about the environment, but we avoid thinking very much about the gallons of clean hot water we use every day and the toxins in our cleansers that we pour down the drain. Living up to our hygienic standards takes huge amounts of energy, but cleanliness is such a sacred cow that to be told "cut down on your washing" would be even more repugnant than being urged to restrict our driving. In his London shower, the hero of Ian McEwan's novel *Saturday* reflects on the everyday extravagance we take for granted and the probability that we won't be able to sustain it:

> When this civilisation falls, when the Romans, whoever they are this time round, have finally left and the new dark ages begin, this will be one of the first luxuries to go. The old folk crouching by their peat fires will tell their disbelieving grandchildren of standing naked midwinter under jet streams of hot clean water, of lozenges of scented soaps and of viscous amber and vermilion liquids they rubbed into their hair to make it glossy and more voluminous than it really was, and of thick white towels as big as togas, waiting on warming racks.

Both dependent on large cultural and natural forces and intensely personal, because it concerns the body, cleanliness is always debatable. The ancient Greeks argued about cold- and hot-water bathing, sixteenth-century Europeans shunned water as much as possible except for the fortunate few who immersed themselves in spa waters, and nineteenth-century peasants (who now look like early believers in the Hygiene Hypothesis) clung to the proverbial powers of dirt as sanitarians tried to mend their ways.

The way a culture approaches and achieves cleanliness always says something interesting about that culture. The French often seem to have a perverse national pride in their own unconcern about cleanliness. As Alain Corbin, the French historian of aroma, describes his compatriots, they enjoy a "somatic culture" that appreciates the strong smells and sensory communications of the human body. Even while the French reformers called for better hygiene, their claim that their people washed less than most Europeans has a whiff of something self-congratulatory. It is as if they were saying, yes, more washing would be good, but our taste for bodies *au naturel* is another example of our Gallic relish for the earthy and sensual.

How differently the Americans do cleanliness. The middle-class North American has never had less need to wash beyond the wrists and has never scrubbed more obsessively. Horace Miner got the Nacirema's vanity and fear of disease right. He didn't dwell on their Puritan beginnings, their extreme individualism and their conviction that they can control every aspect of their lives, but those too mark the American definition of cleanliness. Comparatively new at hedonism, we North Americans are throwing ourselves headlong into our own peculiar version of it. Unlike the French, we are still leery of our visceral, animal side and prefer to smell like tea or cupcakes.

Little is fundamentally new about cleanliness, and yet its definition shifts constantly. In 2007, as in most of the years since our ancestors pulled up an abrasive plant to scour their teeth or waded into a stream, clean is a moving target. There's no upward line of progress to be graphed here. By fretting and deliberating for a century and a half, from the end of the eighteenth century to about 1950, agonizing over full immersion versus piece-meal cleaning, over soap or not soap, over almost every aspect of hygiene, we managed to get ourselves back to roughly where the Romans were two millennia ago. The one cleansing practice canonized by modern science is the one that has never gone out of fashion—a prelude to prayer, symbolic of respect and civility as well as a practical routine, handwashing was practised by Homer's characters, medieval knights and ladies, and seventeenth-century people who washed no other part of themselves. Now public health campaigns celebrate the virtues of handwashing, and the U.S. Centers for Disease Control and Prevention has annointed it as "the single

"Bath, *n*. A kind of mystic ceremony substituted for religious worship, with what spiritual efficacy has not been determined."

—Ambrose Bierce, *The Devil's Dictionary*, 1906

most important means of preventing the spread of infection."

The future of cleanliness is a mystery, dependent as it always is on resources as well as mentality. Nothing, for example, would change our bathing habits more quickly and thoroughly than a serious water shortage. One thing is certain. A century from now, people will look back in amusement if not amazement at what passed for normal cleanliness at the beginning of the twenty-first century.

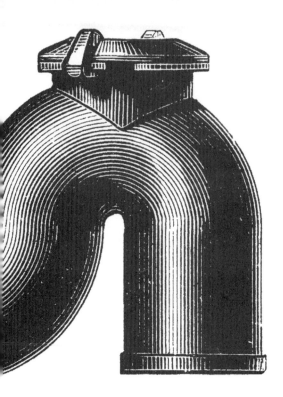

ACKNOWLEDGMENTS

The subject of cleanliness inspired a wealth of words and pictures—everything from French postcards, soap ads and plumbers' catalogues to stories about dirty boyfriends and the first literary appearance of dental floss. My benefactors include Barbara and Buzz Ashenburg, Beth Ashenburg, Sybil Carolan, Mimi Divinsky, Robert Everett Green, Ruth Kaplan, Dagmar LeFrancois, Alberto Manguel, Philip Marchand, Leah McLaren, Erna Paris and Andrea Weinstein. Special thanks to Barbara Ashenburg for introducing me to the Nacirema.

For translations, thank you to Harald Bohne, Birgit Deir, John Ganze and Jose Latour. For expert readings, I am grateful to James Carley, Roger Hall, Ann Hutchinson, Sandra Martin, Tom Robinson and Stephen Strauss. Good counsel came from Robert

Fulford, Mary Hanson, Marni Jackson, Val Ross, Geraldine Sherman, Susan Swan and—especially— from my indefatigable agent, Bella Pomer.

Writing a book demands occasional stretches of solitude, and friends and family generously lent me houses and cottages, including Bob and Alicia Ashenburg, Carole Ashenburg, Hannah Carolan and Bruce Townson, Moira Farr, Jane O'Hara and Helen Ryane, and Elizabeth Wilson and Ian Montagnes. I also benefited enormously from residences at Yaddo and the MacDowell Colony. The Canada Council, the Ontario Arts Council and the Toronto Arts Council all provided welcome funding. It was Rebecca Saletan, then at Farrar, Straus and Giroux, who initially smiled on this project. Thanks also to Ayesha Pande and John Glusman, Jim Guida and especially to Jonathan Galassi, who has been unfailingly resourceful and warmly enthusiastic. My first thanks at Knopf Canada go to Louise Dennys, who welcomed the book with open arms, strategy and wisdom. Thank you to Diane Martin for intelligence and encouragement; to Michelle MacAleese and Frances Bedford for efficiency and good cheer; to Freya Godard for excellent questions and a fine eye for commas; and to Kelly Hill for a beautiful book design. To Gary Ross (as usual) for the subtitle, and to Sarah Tanzini for the title. Apparently it is possible to write a book without relying on Barbara Czarnecki's formidable knowledge and care, but I wouldn't want to risk it. And, finally, to my editor Angelika Glover, who challenged, provoked and very occasionally flattered me into writing a much better book—thank you.

NOTES

PREFACE
"BUT DIDN'T THEY *SMELL*?"

2   As St. Bernard said: Roy Bedichek, *The Sense of Smell* (Garden City, NY: Doubleday, 1960), 125.

6   The ancient Egyptians: Mandy Aftel, *Essence and Alchemy: A Book on Perfume* (New York: Farrar, Straus & Giroux, 2001), 164.

6   Napoleon and Josephine: Lyall Watson, *Jacobson's Organ and the Remarkable Nature of Smell* (London: Penguin Press, 1999), 90.

9   young women in Renaissance Germany: Hannelore Sachs, *The Renaissance Woman*, trans. D. Talbot Rice (New York: McGraw-Hill, 1971), 22.

CHAPTER ONE
THE SOCIAL BATH: GREEKS AND ROMANS

15   etiquette demanded: Emile Mireaux, *Daily Life in the Time of Homer*, trans. Iris Sells (London: George Allen and Unwin, 1959), 70.

16   "Accordingly Arete": Homer, *Odyssey* (New York: Mentor/New American Library, 1963), 96–97.

17 Telemachus emerges: Homer, *Odyssey*, 42.

17 Odysseus gains height: Homer, *Odyssey*, 256.

17 Laertes' clothes . . . "stronger than I saw you before!": Homer, *Odyssey*, 265–68.

19 Hippocrates: Ralph Jackson, "Waters and Spas in the Classical World," in *Medical History of Waters and Spas*, ed. Roy Porter (London: Wellcome Institute for the History of Medicine, 1990), 1–2.

19 Sanctuaries normally had fonts: Robert Parker, *Miasma: Pollution and Purification in Early Greek Religion* (Oxford: Clarendon, 1983), 19–21.

19 like almost all peoples: Arnold van Gennep, *Rites of Passage*, trans. Monika B. Vizedom and Gabrielle Caffee (London: Routledge and Kegan Paul, 1965), 20.

19 The first bath: Parker, *Miasma*, 50–51.

20 Both the Greek bride and groom: Anne Carson, "Putting Her in Her Place: Woman, Dirt, and Desire," in *Before Sexuality: The Construction of Erotic Experience in the Ancient Greek World*, ed. David Halperin, John J. Winkler and Froma I. Zeitlin (Princeton: Princeton University Press, 1990), 151–53; H. Blümner, *The Home Life of the Ancient Greeks*, trans. Alice Zimmern (London: Cassell, 1910), 137.

20 And when someone died: Parker, *Miasma*, 35–42.

20 When Achilles: Homer, *The Iliad*, trans. Ennis Rees (New York: Oxford University Press, 1991), 383.

20 An upper-middle-class: Blümner, *Home Life*, 188, 192–94; Peter Connolly and Hazel Dodge, *The Ancient City: Life in Classical Athens and Rome* (Oxford: Oxford University Press, 1998), 55.

22 make an occasional visit . . . wine and probably snacks: Fikret Yegül, *Baths and Bathing in Classical Antiquity* (Cambridge, MA: MIT Press, 1992), 25–29; T. G. Tucker, *Life in Ancient Athens: The Social and Public Life of a Classical Athenian from Day to Day* (London: MacMillan, 1907), 88–89; Blümner, *Home Life*, 192–94.

23 One of the central Athenian institutions . . . before the Roman period: Yegül, *Baths and Bathing*, 7–24.

24 The playwright Aristophanes: Aristophanes, *The Clouds*, trans. H. J. Easterling and P. E. Easterling (Cambridge: W. Hoffer, 1961), 2, 31, 36 (lines 43–45, 835–40, 995 ff.).

25 Edward Gibbon: Edward Gibbon, *The Decline and Fall of the Roman Empire* (New York: Modern Library, 1932), 1:360, 1:539, 2:192.

25 modern German expression: Doug Saunders, "Gyno-politics 101: Germany Tries a Woman's Touch," *Globe and Mail*, 17 Sept. 2005, F3.

25 *The Laws:* Hans Licht, *Sexual Life in Ancient Greece,* trans. J. H. Freese, ed. Lawrence H. Dawson (London: Routledge, 1932), 101.

25 militaristic, ascetic Spartans: H. Michell, *Sparta* (Cambridge: Cambridge University Press, 1964), 166, 281–82, 173–74.

26 Theophrastus . . . "no thanks to you for that!": *The Characters of Theophrastus,* ed. and trans. J. M. Edmonds (Cambridge: Harvard University Press, 1961), 51, 65, 87–89, 95, 121.

28 the characteristic Roman bath: Garrett G. Fagan, *Bathing in Public in the Roman World* (Ann Arbor: University of Michigan Press, 1999), 44–45.

29 After his exercise: Françoise de Bonneville, *The Book of the Bath,* trans. Jane Brenton (New York: Rizzoli, 1998), 24.

30 Roman men adopted: Yegül, *Baths and Bathing,* 32–35.

32 (box) A mixture of animal fats: Terence McLaughlin, *Coprophilia; or, A Peck of Dirt* (London: Cassell, 1971), 42–43; John A. Hunt, "A Short History of Soap," *Pharmaceutical Journal* 263, no. 7076 (18/25 Dec. 1999): 985–89.

33 When Agricola became: Peter Jones and Keith Sidwell, eds. *The World of Rome: An Introduction to Roman Culture* (Cambridge: Cambridge University Press, 1997), 78.

34 The great age of Imperial baths . . . Oratory of Saint Bernard: Yegül, *Baths and Bathing,* 128–72; Fagan, *Bathing in Public,* 14–19, 104–23.

37 The most famous anecdote: Jerome Carcopino, *Daily Life in Ancient Rome,* trans. E. O. Lorimer (New York: Penguin, 1991), 285.

39 (box) nine aqueducts: Yegül, *Baths and Bathing,* 391–95; Alev Lytle Croutier, *Taking the Waters: Spirit, Art, Sensuality* (New York: Abbeville Press, 1992), 82.

39 (box) hypocaust: Yegül, *Baths and Bathing,* 356–65.

39 (box) Roman concrete: Fagan, *Bathing in Public,* 83–84; Yegül, *Baths and Bathing,* 492.

40 Pliny the Younger: J. P. V. D. Balsdon, *Roman Women: Their History and Habits* (London: Bodley Head, 1962), 265.

40 Trimalchio and his guests: Petronius, *The Satyricon,* trans. Alfred R. Allinson (New York: Panurge Press, 1930), 84–85, 150–52.

41 Seneca's famous account . . . "Of the army, of farm work, and of manliness!": Lucius Annaeus Seneca, *17 Letters,* trans. C. D. N. Costa (Warminster, UK: Aris and Phillips, 1988), letter 56, pp. 37–39; letter 86, p. 311.

43 Aper decried: Martial, *Epigrams,* trans. Walter C. A. Kerr, 2 vols. (Cambridge, MA: Harvard University Press, 1961), ep. 12.70, 2:271.

44 Poor pathetic Selius: Martial, *Epigrams*, ep. 2.14, 1:117–19.

44 "I defy you": *Martial in English*, ed. J. P. Sullivan and A. J. Boyle (London: Penguin, 1996), ep. 12.82, trans. Philip Murray, 321–22.

44 anecdotes of ladies bathing: Martial, *Epigrams*, ep. 11.75, 2:291–92; ep. 11.82, 2:295–96; ep. 11.95, 2:305; ep. 12.19, 2:333.

44 When the poet gripes: Martial, *Epigrams*, ep. 3.36, 1:185.

45 his friend Ligurinus: Martial, *Epigrams*, ep. 3.44, 1:189.

45 Take poor Thais: Martial, *Epigrams*, ep. 6.93, 1:417.

45 "It's easy to tell": *Martial in English*, ep. 9.33, trans. Donald C. Goertz, 329.

46 "Naked I shall please you": Martial, *Epigrams*, ep. 3.51, 1:195.

46 Saufeia says: Martial, *Epigrams*, ep. 3.72, 1:209–11.

46 "A gymnasium": Martial, *Epigrams*, ep. 3.68, 1:207.

46 "a taverner": Martial, *Epigrams*, ep. 2.48, 1:139.

MARGINALIA IN CHAPTER ONE

17 Stephanie A. Nelson, *God and the Land: The Metaphysics of Farming in Hesiod and Vergil and 'Works and Days,'* trans. (Works and Days) David Grene (New York: Oxford University Press, 1998), 27.

19 Hippocrates: Lawrence Wright, *Clean and Decent: The History of the Bath and Loo and of Sundry Habits, Fashions and Accessories of the Toilet, Principally in Great Britain, France and America* (London: Routledge and Kegan Paul, 1980), 15.

20 Mary Kingsley, *Travels in West Africa: Congo Français, Corisco and Cameroons* (London: Virago, 1982), 469–70.

23 Herodotus: Lionel Casson, *The Horizon Book of Life in Ancient Egypt* (New York: American Heritage, 1975) 23.

28 Fagan, *Bathing in Public*, 319.

30 Fagan, *Bathing in Public*, 93–100; Audrey Cruse, *Roman Medicine* (Brimscombe Port Stroud, UK: Tempus Publishing, 2004), 59.

33 Fagan, *Bathing in Public*, 324.

34 Petronius, *Satyricon*, 61.

37 Scott Clark, *Japan: A View from the Bath* (Honolulu: University of Hawaii Press, 1994), 73.

38 Ovid, *The Erotic Poems*, trans. Peter Green (Harmondsworth, UK: Penguin, 1982), 181–82.

38 The accumulated sweat: Personal communication, Judith Gorman, Royal Ontario Museum, Toronto.

40 Ovid, *Erotic Poems*, 219.

44 Yegül, *Baths and Bathing*, 40.

49 "They never wash": The Book of the Thousand Nights and One Night, trans. Powys Mathers from the French of J. C. Mardrus (London: Routledge & Kegan Paul Ltd., 1953), 2:57.

50 Reginald Reynolds: Reginald Reynolds, *Cleanliness and Godliness* (Garden City, NY: Doubleday, 1946), 2–3.

51 During the time of Christ: Thomas Kazen, *Jesus and Purity Halakhah: Was Jesus Indifferent to Purity?* (Stockholm: Almqvist and Wiksell International, 2002), 7.

52 Scholars have advanced: Kazen, *Jesus and Purity Halakhah*, 342–47.

54 By the end: Kazen, *Jesus and Purity Halakhah*, 347–48.

54 Early Christian brides: Stefanie Hoss, *Baths and Bathing: The Culture of Bathing and the Baths and Thermae in Palestine from the Hasmoneans to the Moslem Conquest* (Oxford: Archaeopress, 2005), 82.

55 "We live with you": Christoph Markschies, *Between Two Worlds: Structures of Earliest Christianity*, trans. John Bowden (London: SCM Press, 1999), 120.

56 Cyprian, the bishop of Carthage: Hoss, *Baths and Bathing*, 89.

56 Clement of Alexandria: John Ferguson, *Clement of Alexandria* (New York: Twayne, 1974), 96; Hoss, *Baths and Bathing*, 88.

57 Chrysostom's ascetic credentials . . . with the same aim in mind: Palladius, *Dialogue on the Life of St. John Chrysostom* (New York: Newman Press, 1985), trans. and ed. Robert T. Meyer, 1–2, 61–62, 72; Hoss, *Baths and Bathing*, 83–84, 88.

58 St. Jerome: Joyce E. Salisbury, *Church Fathers, Independent Virgins* (London: Verso, 1991), 35.

59 His dear friend Paula: Elizabeth A. Clark, *Jerome, Chrysostom, and Friends: Essays and Translations* (New York: Edward Mellen Press, 1979), 58.

59 Particularly in the East: Yegül, *Baths and Bathing*, 318.

59 "the washing of regeneration": Palladius, *Chrysostom*, 35.

59 St. Agnes: McLaughlin, *Coprophilia*, 11.

60 Godric: Mary-Ann Stouck, *Medieval Saints* (New York: Broadview, 1999), 66.

61 St. Francis: Reynolds, *Cleanliness and Godliness*, 2.

61 St. Olympias . . . her "immaterial body": "Life of Olympias," trans. and ed. Elizabeth Clark, in Clark, *Jerome, Chrysostom*, 127–42, esp. 129, 137–38, 139–40.

62   St. Radegund: Jo Ann McNamara and John E. Halborg, eds. and trans.,
      Sainted Women of the Dark Ages (Durham, NC: Duke University
      Press, 1992), 454.

64   In the sixth century: Yegül, *Baths and Bathing*, 319–20.

64   In Italy and the western part: Yegül, *Baths and Bathing*, 321, 315.

65   The Romans thought: Constance Classen, David Howes and Anthony
      Synnot, *Aroma: The Cultural History of Smell* (New York:
      Routledge, 1994), 51.

65   The baths lasted longer: Yegül, *Baths and Bathing*, 321, 326, 329, 350–51.

66   They devised complicated: Paul B. Newman, *Daily Life in the Middle
      Ages* (Jefferson, NC: McFarland, 2001), 140.

67   they performed their ablutions: Hans-Werner Goetz, *Life in the Middle
      Ages from the Seventh to the Thirteenth Century* trans. Albert
      Wimmer, ed. Steven Towan (Notre Dame: Notre Dame
      University Press, 1993), 102.

67   The Rule of St. Benedict: *The Rule of St. Benedict*, trans. Cardinal
      Gasquet (London: Chatto and Windus, 1925), 69.

67   The baths taken: C. H. Lawrence, *Forms of Religious Life in Western
      Europe in the Middle Ages* (London: Longman, 1989), 119–20;
      Jeffrey Singman, *Daily Life in Medieval Europe* (Westport, CT:
      Greenwood Press, 1999), 159.

69   A *niddah:* Rahel R. Wasserfall, "Introduction: Menstrual Blood into
      Jewish Blood," in *Women and Water: Menstruation in Jewish Life
      and Law,* ed. Rahel R. Wasserfall (Hanover, NH: Brandeis
      University Press, 1999), 4–6.

69   The *mikveh* had other uses: Therese and Mendel Metzger, *Jewish Life
      in the Middle Ages: Illuminated Hebrew Manuscripts of the
      Thirteenth to the Sixteenth Centuries* (Secaucus, NJ: Chartwell,
      1982), 75.

69   The *niddah*, including her hair: Tirzah Meacham (leBeit Yoreh), "An
      Abbreviated History of the Development of the Jewish Menstrual
      Laws," in Wasserfall, *Women and Water*, 34; Shaye J. D. Cohen,
      "Purity, Piety, and Polemic: Medieval Rabbinic Denunciations of
      'Incorrect' Purification Practices," in Wasserfall, *Women and
      Water*, 84–85.

70   all Jews were commanded: Hoss, *Baths and Bathing*, dedication page
      (unnumbered), 68; Metzger, *Jewish Life*, 75–76.

70   Arab Spain . . . destroy the Moorish baths: Erna Paris, *The End of Days:
      A Story of Tolerance, Tyranny, and the Expulsion of the Jews from
      Spain* (Toronto: Lester, 1995), 40; John A. Crow, *Spain: The Root
      and the Flower* (New York: Harper and Row, 1963), 32–34, 61.

MARGINALIA IN CHAPTER TWO

50 St. Jerome: Yegül, *Baths and Bathing,* 314.

51 Gibbon, *Decline and Fall,* 2:526.

55 Gibbon, *Decline and Fall,* 1:569.

56 Hoss, *Baths and Bathing,* 85.

57 Sissinius: Hoss, *Baths and Bathing,* 88.

58 Caroline Walker Bynum, *Holy Feast and Holy Fast: The Religious Significance of Food to Medieval Women* (Berkeley: University of California Press, 1987), 15, 5; McNamara and Halborg, *Sainted Women,* 109.

59 Fernando Henriques, *Prostitution and Society* (New York: Grove Press, 1966), 16.

61 William Dalrymple, *From the Holy Mountain: A Journey in the Shadow of Byzantium* (London, HarperCollins, 1997), 326.

64 Fagan, *Bathing in Public,* 320–21.

67 Christopher Brooke, *The Monastic World, 1000–1300* (London: Elek, 1974), 69.

70 Jean de Blainville, *Travels through Holland, Germany, Switzerland, but Especially Italy* (London: John Noon and Joseph Noon, 1757), 1:127.

CHAPTER THREE

A STEAMY INTERLUDE: 1000–1550

73 *The Romance of the Rose* . . . "chamber of Venus" clean: Guillaume de Lorris and Jean de Meun, *The Romance of the Rose,* trans. and ed. Frances Horgan (Oxford: Oxford University Press, 1994), 220, 33, 205.

75 "Wash yourself ": *Ancrene Wisse: Guide for Anchoresses,* trans. Hugh White (London: Penguin, 1993), 196.

76 Sone of Nansay: Danielle Regnier-Bohler, "Imagining the Self," in *Revelations of the Medieval World,* ed. Georges Duby, vol. 2 of *A History of Private Life,* ed. Philippe Ariès and Georges Duby, trans. Arthur Goldhammer (Cambridge: Belknap Press of Harvard University Press, 1988), 363–64.

76 *The Romance of Flammenca: The Romance of Flammenca,* trans. Merton Jerome Hubert, ed. Marion E. Porter (Princeton: Princeton University Press, 1962), 53, 57.

76 medieval baby-care manuals: Shulamith Shahar, *Childhood in the Middle Ages,* trans. Chaya Galai (London: Routledge, 1992), 83–86.

77 A gallon of water: Newman, *Daily Life in the Middle Ages,* 152.

77 St. Thomas Aquinas: Annick Le Guérer, *Scent: The Mysterious and Essential Powers of Smell*, trans. Richard Miller (London: Chatto and Windus, 1993), 205.

77 "When he took a bath": Goetz, *Life in the Middle Ages*, 186–87.

78 a deceitful woman named Lydia: Giovanni Boccaccio, *The Decameron*, trans. John Payne (New York: Random House, 1930), 561 (day 7, story 9).

78 the return of the public bath: De Bonneville, *Book of the Bath*, 34.

80 *Badegeld:* De Bonneville, *Book of the Bath*, 36.

80 Fourteenth-century London: Georges Vigarello, *Concepts of Cleanliness: Changing Attitudes in France since the Middle Ages*, trans. Jean Birrell (Cambridge: Cambridge University Press, 1988), 21; Lynn Thorndike, "Sanitation, Baths, and Street-Cleaning in the Middle Ages and Renaissance," *Speculum*, 1924, 197–98.

80 Public baths enjoyed: Georges Duby and Philippe Braunstein, "The Emergence of the Individual," in *Revelations of the Medieval World*, ed. Georges Duby, vol. 2 of *A History of Private Life*, ed. Philippe Ariès and Georges Duby, trans. Arthur Goldhammer (Cambridge: Belknap Press of Harvard University Press, 1988), 602.

80 A miniature: De Bonneville, *Book of the Bath*, 36; Henriques, *Prostitution and Society*, 57.

81 Gian-Francesco Poggio: Duby and Braunstein, "Emergence of the Individual," 603–7.

82 A French manuscript: De Bonneville, *Book of the Bath*, 34; Fernando Henriques, *Prostitution in Europe and the New World* (London: McGibbon and Kee, 1963), 97.

83 "All who want": Sachs, *Renaissance Woman*, 29.

83 *The Romance of Flammenca* . . . "No longer maids": *The Romance of Flammenca*, 95, 313, 353.

85 Lovers bathe: Boccaccio, *Decameron*, 658–60.

86 In fifteenth-century France: Jacques Rossiaud, "Prostitution, Sex and Society in French Towns in the Fifteenth Century," in *Western Sexuality: Practice and Precept in Past and Present Times*, ed. Philippe Ariès and André Béjin, trans. Anthony Foster (Oxford: Basil Blackwell, 1985), 76–77.

87 Henry II: Henriques, *Prostitution and Society*, 59–61; Ruth Mazo Karras, *Common Women: Prostitution and Sexuality in Medieval England* (New York: Oxford University Press, 1996), 17–18.

87 The grandest of residences: Mark Girouard, *Life in the French Country House* (New York: Knopf, 2000), 220.

88 John Russell: John Russell, "The Boke of Nurture," ed. Frederick J. Furnivall, in *The Babees Book* (London: Early English Text Society, 1868), 176–78, 182–85, 249–59.

90 A story from late medieval Germany: Joachim Bumke, *Courtly Culture: Literature and Society in the High Middle Ages*, trans. Thomas Dunlap (Woodstock, NY: Overlook Press, 2000), 120–21.

90 In the sixteenth century: Bumke, *Courtly Culture*, 121.

91 Beginning in 1347: Joan Acocella, "The End of the World: Interpreting the Plague," *New Yorker*, 21 Mar. 2005, 82.

92 Boccaccio gives a dispassionate . . . without ceremony or attendants: Boccaccio, *Decameron*, 8–16.

93 Marchionne di Coppo Stefani: Colin Platt, *King Death: The Black Death and Its Aftermath in Late-Medieval England* (Toronto: University of Toronto Press, 1996), 4.

93 In Avignon: Acocella, "End of the World," 83.

93 Philippe VI . . . "as has frequently been observed": Vigarello, *Concepts of Cleanliness*, 8, 11, 22, 33.

94 *Pulex irritans:* Acocella, "End of the World," 82.

95 clothing should be smooth: Vigarello, *Concepts of Cleanliness*, 10.

95 "Twenty-five years ago": Vigarello, *Concepts of Cleanliness*, 27.

MARGINALIA IN CHAPTER THREE

74 Nicholas Orme, *Medieval Children* (New Haven: Yale University Press, 2001), 76.

75 "On Good Manners for Boys," *Collected Works of Erasmus*, ed. J. K. Sowards (Toronto: University of Toronto Press, 1985), 25:276–77.

78 Orme, *Medieval Children*, 76.

78 Singman, *Daily Life in Medieval Europe*, 49.

79 Avicenna, *Treatise on the Canon of Medicine of Avicenna, Incorporating a Translation of the First Book*, trans. and ed. O. Cameron Gruner (London, Luzac and Co., 1930), 389.

80 Thorndike, "Sanitation, Baths," 198.

82 Sachs, *Renaissance Woman*, 29.

83 Nickie Roberts, *Whores in History: Prostitution in Western Society* (London: HarperCollins, 1993), 82.

87 Thorndike, "Sanitation, Baths," 197–98.

90 Barbara Tuchman, *A Distant Mirror: The Calamitous 14th Century* (New York: Knopf, 1978), 159.

90 Elizabeth Burton, *The Elizabethans at Home* (London: Secker & Warburg, 1958), 243–44.

93 Sachs, *Renaissance Woman,* 29.

94 Shahar, *Childhood in the Middle Ages,* 84.

CHAPTER FOUR

A PASSION FOR CLEAN LINEN: 1550–1750

97 Elisabeth Charlotte . . . "those who lived there": Vigarello, *Concepts of Cleanliness,* 89.

99 Elizabeth I: Reynolds, *Cleanliness and Godliness,* 74.

99 James I: Olwen Hufton, *The Prospect before Her: A History of Women in Western Europe,* vol. I, 1500–1800 (New York: HarperCollins, 1995), 80.

99 Louis XIII: Vigarello, *Concepts of Cleanliness,* 66.

99 Michel de Montaigne: Michel de Montaigne, *The Complete Works,* trans. Donald M. Frame (New York: Everyman's Library, Knopf, 2003), 715.

100 One hundred thousand Londoners: Ragnhild Hatton, *Europe in the Age of Louis XIV* (London: Thames and Hudson, 1969), 10.

100 "The bath": Vigarello, *Concepts of Cleanliness,* 13.

101 Francis Bacon: Classen, Howes and Synnot, *Aroma,* 70, n. 68.

101 "only with the greatest caution": Vigarello, *Concepts of Cleanliness,* 83.

102 Daniel Roche: Daniel Roche, *The Culture of Clothing: Dress and Fashion in the Ancien Régime,* trans. Jean Birrell (Cambridge: Cambridge University Press, 1994), 372–73.

102 Fynes Moryson: Antoni Maczak, *Travel in Early Modern Europe,* trans. Ursula Phillips (Cambridge: Polity Press, 1995), 102.

103 Travellers agreed: Paul Zumthor, *Daily Life in Rembrandt's Holland,* trans. Simon Watson Taylor (London: Weidenfeld and Nicolson, 1962), 53–54.

103 Leonhard Rauwulf: Karl H. Dannenfeldt, *Leonhard Rauwulf: Sixteenth-Century Physician, Botanist, and Traveler* (Cambridge, MA: Harvard University Press, 1968), 47–49.

104 Henry Blount: Henry Blount, *A Voyage into the Levant* (Amsterdam: Theatrum Orbis Terrarum, 1977), 100–101.

105 the Sun King's halitosis: Louis Bertrand, *The Private Life of Louis XIV,* trans. Paul Morin (New York: Louis Carrier, 1929), 99–100.

105 the same Princess Palatine: Duchess of Orleans, Elizabeth-Charlotte of Bavaria, Princess Palatine, *The Letters of Madame,* trans. and ed. Gertrude Scott Stevenson (London: Arrowsmith, 1925), 2:208.

105 future Louis XIII: Hufton, *Prospect before Her*, 200, n. 38; Vigarello, *Concepts of Cleanliness*, 16, n. 50.

106 When Louis XIV arose: Louis de Rouvroy, Duke of Saint-Simon, *Memoirs of Louis XIV and the Regency*, trans. Bayle St. John (New York, M. Walter Dunne, 1901), 3:30–31; Henri Carré, *The Early Life of Louis XIV (1638–1661)*, trans. Dorothy Bolton (London: Hutchinson, 1951), 228–29.

107 "We understand why linen": Vigarello, *Concepts of Cleanliness*, 60.

107 Louis Savot: Vigarello, *Concepts of Cleanliness*, 60.

107 Samuel Johnson: James Boswell, *Life of Johnson* (London: Oxford University Press, 1966), 281.

108 "white and fine linen": Fynes Moryson, *The Itinerary of Fynes Moryson* (Glasgow: James MacLehose and Sons, 1907), 3:452.

108 Marie Adelaide: Lucy Norton, *First Lady of Versailles: Marie Adelaide of Savoy, Dauphine of France* (London: Hamish Hamilton, 1978), 143.

108 Since Englishwomen: C. Willett and Phillis Cunnington, *The History of Underclothes* (London: Michael Joseph, 1951), 52.

108 Mary of Cleves: D. Michael Stoddart, *The Scented Ape: The Biology and Culture of Human Odour* (Cambridge: Cambridge University Press, 1990), 63.

109 the man's shirt . . . "ruffled down to his middle": Willett and Cunnington, *History of Underclothes*, 53–62, 75.

110 "I work at literature" . . . "dress himself elegantly": Jacques Casanova, *The Memoirs of Jacques Casanova de Seingalt* (London: Chapman and Hall, 1902), 2:141, 145.

110 A French household manual: Vigarello, *Concepts of Cleanliness*, 15.

111 Many of the Moorish baths . . . turned tawny-coloured: Crow, *Spain*, 33–34, 149.

112 Fernand Braudel: Fernand Braudel, *The Structures of Everyday Life: The Limits of the Possible*, vol. 1, *Civilization and Capitalism 15th to 18th Century*, trans. Sian Reynolds and Miriam Kochan (London: Collins, 1981), 330.

112 German, Austrian and Swiss . . . traditional remedies associated with them: Martin Widman, "Krise und Untergang der Badstube," *Gesnerus* 56 (1999): 220–40. (Translated for the author by Harald Bohne.)

114 Thomas Platter: Thomas Platter, *Journal of a Younger Brother*, trans. Sean Jennett (London: Frederick Muller, 1963), 95.

114 Anne of Austria: De Bonneville, *Book of the Bath*, 41.

114 Guy Patin: Vigarello, *Concepts of Cleanliness*, 14.

114 King Henri IV: Vigarello, *Concepts of Cleanliness*, 12.

115 Louis XIV: Vigarello, *Concepts of Cleanliness*, 13.

116 But in the Renaissance . . . "like unto ducks": Richard Palmer, "'In This Our Lightye and Learned Tyme': Italian Baths in the Era of the Renaissance," in Porter, *Medical History of Waters and Spas*, 14–22; L. W. B. Brockliss, "The Development of the Spa in Seventeenth-Century France," in Porter, *Medical History of Waters and Spas*, 23–38.

117 Fynes Moryson: Moryson, *Itinerary*, 1:55.

117 Michel de Montaigne: Montaigne, *Complete Works*, 1063, 1207–08.

117 Italian doctors' campaign: Palmer, "'In This Our Lightye and Learned Tyme,'" 21–22; Brockliss, "Development of the Spa," 26, 30–32, 38, 43.

118 Madame de Sévigné: *Letters of Madame de Sévigné*, ed. Richard Aldington (New York: Brentano's, 1927), 2:216–23; Frances Massiker, *Madame de Sévigné: A Life and Letters*, letters trans. Frances Massiker (New York: Knopf, 1983), 363.

120 (box) Letters of Madame de Sévigné, ed. Aldington, 1:219–20.

122 Like many visitors to Bath: Celia Fiennes, *The Illustrated Journeys of Celia Fiennes 1685-c.1712*, ed. Christopher Morris (London: MacDonald & Co., 1982), 44–46.

MARGINALIA IN CHAPTER FOUR

98 Sachs, *Renaissance Woman*, 29.

100 Burton, *Elizabethans at Home*, 242.

101 William Ian Miller, *The Anatomy of Disgust* (Cambridge, MA: Harvard University Press, 1997), 286, n. 64.

102 *The Complete Letters of Lady Mary Wortley Montagu*, ed. Robert Halsband (Oxford: Clarendon Press, 1965), 1:248.

103 E. S. Bates, *Touring in 1600: A Study in the Development of Travel as a Means of Education* (London: Constable, 1911), 190.

106 Miller, *Anatomy of Disgust*, 153.

107 Maczak, *Travel in Early Modern Europe*, 101.

108 Stoddart, *The Scented Ape*, 63.

111 Classen, Howes and Synnot, *Aroma*, 71, n. 2.

116 Ivan Illich, H_2O *and the Waters of Forgetfulness* (London: Marion Boyars, 1986), 46.

117 Duchess of Orleans, Elizabeth-Charlotte of Bavaria, Princess Palatine, *The Letters of Madame*, trans. and ed. Gertrude Scott Stevenson (London: Arrowsmith, 1925), 1:256.

118 Palmer, "'In This Our Lightye and Learned Tyme,'" 19, n. 28.

119 Platter, *Journal*, 50–51.

122 Massiker, *Madame de Sévigné*, 224.

123 Samuel Pepys, *The Shorter Pepys*, ed. Robert Latham (London: Bell & Hyman, 1958), 925.

CHAPTER FIVE

THE RETURN OF WATER: 1750–1815

125 Lady Mary Wortley Montagu . . . Although she attributed: Montagu, *Complete Letters*, 1:312–15, 407; Robert Halsband, *The Life of Lady Mary Wortley Montagu* (Oxford: Clarendon Press, 1957), 68.

127 "How dirty your hands are": *The Habits of Good Society: A Handbook for Ladies and Gentlemen* (New York: Rudd & Carlton, 1860), 108; Halsband, *Mary Wortley Montagu*, 150, 204, 281.

127 Women wore leather or bone stays: Lawrence Stone, *The Family, Sex and Marriage in England 1500–1800* (London: Weidenfeld and Nicolson, 1977), 488.

127 Thomas Turner: Derek Jarrett, *England in the Age of Hogarth* (London: Hart-Davis, MacGibbon, 1974), 170.

127 James Boswell: Aline Ribeiro, *The Art of Dress: Fashion in England and France 1750 to 1820* (New Haven: Yale University Press, 1995), 151.

127 Duke of Norfolk's servants: Rosamond Bayne-Powell, *Housekeeping in the Eighteenth Century* (London: John Murray, 1956), 119.

128 The traditional departure: Kristen Olsen, *Daily Life in 18th-Century England* (Westport, CT: Greenwood Press, 1999), 268.

128 Lord Chesterfield: Olsen, *Daily Life*, 269.

128 John Locke's 1693 treatise: John Locke, *Some Thoughts Concerning Education and of the Conduct of the Understanding*, ed. Ruth W. Grant and Nathan Tarcov (Indianapolis: Hackett, 1996), 12–13.

129 Sir John Floyer: John Floyer and Edward Baynard, *The History of Cold Bathing: Both Ancient and Modern* (London: Samuel Smith and Benjamin Walford, 1706), 78.

129 "A cold regimen": Floyer and Baynard, *Cold Bathing*, unpaginated introduction.

130 (box) Dr. Edward Baynard: Floyer and Baynard, *Cold Bathing*, pt. 2, 79, 80.

130 John Wesley: Stanley Ayling, *John Wesley* (London: Collins, 1979), 168.

130 For Wesley . . . hands and feet needed to be immersed: John Wesley, *Primitive Physick; or, An Easy and Natural Method of Curing Most Diseases* (Bristol: William Pine, 1770), xvii, xix, 150 ff., 46.

131 people regarded the sea: Sarah Howell, *The Seaside* (London: Collier and Collier Macmillan, 1974), 7–8, 43, 45–46.

132 (box) In 1789: Howell, *The Seaside*, 30–31.

133 Dr. Richard Russell: Richard Russell, *A Dissertation on the Use of Sea-water in the Diseases of the Glands* (London: W. Owen, 1760).

133 pirated English version: Howell, *The Seaside*, 14–17.

133 *Sanditon:* Jane Austen, *Sanditon, The Watsons, Lady Susan and Other Miscellanea* (London: J. M. Dent, 1934), 19.

134 Tobias Smollett's satirical novel . . . "every sinew of the human frame": Tobias Smollett, *The Expedition of Humphry Clinker* (London: J. M. Dent, 1943), 13–14, 16, 43–44, 174–75, 169–70.

135 *An Essay* . . . "the Element itself": Tobias Smollett, *An Essay on the External Use of Water*, ed. Claude E. Jones (Baltimore: Johns Hopkins Press, 1935), 53, 61, 64, 55.

136 He spent two years . . . "my spirits have been more alert": Tobias Smollett, *Travels through France and Italy*, ed. Frank Felsenstein (Oxford: Oxford University Press, 1979), 83, 276, 13–14, 192–93.

137 Smollett's 1766 account: Howell, *The Seaside*, 55–56.

137 the apartments at Versailles . . . a city renowned for its uncleanliness: Smollett, *France and Italy*, 40, 47, 107–8.

138 "I am attached": Smollett, *France and Italy*, 341.

140 Madame de Pompadour: Christine Previtt Algrant, *Madame de Pompadour: Mistress of France* (New York: Grove Press, 2002), 117.

140 Even Marie Antoinette: Antonia Fraser, *Marie Antoinette: The Journey* (New York: Anchor Books, 2002), 169.

141 As a young man: Jean-Jacques Rousseau, *The Confessions and Correspondence, Including the Letters to Malesherbes*, vol. 5 of *The Collected Writings of Rousseau*, ed. Christopher Kelly, Roger D. Masters and Peter G. Stillman, trans. Christopher Kelly (Hanover, NH: University Press of New England, 1995), 305–6.

141 When a urinary complaint: J. H. Huizinga, *The Making of a Saint: The Tragi-Comedy of Jean-Jacques Rousseau* (London: Hamish Hamilton, 1976), 50.

142 Again and again in *The Confessions:* Rousseau, *Confessions*, 113, 437, 516, 133.

142 Praising Thetis . . . "more than clean, she is pure": Rousseau, *Emile*, trans. Barbara Foxley (London: J. M. Dent, 1993), 16, 30–31, 26, 428.

145 a water mill: D. C. Charlton, *New Images of the Natural in France* (Cambridge: Cambridge University Press, 1984), 30.

146 Helen Maria Williams: Aileen Ribeiro, *Fashion in the French Revolution* (London: Batsford, 1988), 70.

146 the Duchesse d'Abrantes: Ribeiro, *French Revolution*, 128.

146 the Margravine of Bayreuth: Adrien Faucher-Magnan, *The Small German Courts in the Eighteenth Century*, trans. Mervyn Savill (London: Methuen, 1958), 92.

147 Holy Roman Emperor: Olivier Bernier, *Pleasure and Privilege: Life in France, Naples and America 1770–1790* (Garden City, NY: Doubleday, 1981), 191.

147 Princess Josephine: Antonia Fraser, *Marie Antoinette: The Journey* (New York: Anchor, 2002), 96.

147 Caroline of Brunswick: Kathleen Campbell, *Beau Brummell: A Biographical Study* (London: Hammond, Hammond & Co., 1948), 40.

148 Samuel Johnson: Boswell, *Life of Johnson*, 188.

148 Lord Chesterfield: Philip Dormer Stanhope, Earl of Chesterfield, *The Letters of Philip Dormer Stanhope, Earl of Chesterfield with The Characters*, ed. John Bradshaw (London: George Allen and Unwin, 1926), 1:56, 126, 221.

148 *Le Tableau de Paris:* Vigarello, *Concepts of Cleanliness*, 136–37.

149 Louis XIV's reign: De Bonneville, *Book of the Bath*, 40, 42–43.

149 *Le médecin des dames:* Jean-Pierre Goubert, *The Conquest of Water: The Advent of Health in the Industrial Age*, trans. Andrew Wilson (Princeton: Princeton University Press, 1989), 27.

149 Elizabeth Montagu: Elizabeth Montagu, *Elizabeth Montagu: The Queen of the Bluestockings, Her Correspondence from 1720 to 1761*, ed. Emily Climenson (London: John Murray, 1906), 88–89.

150 Marie Antoinette: Jeanne Louise Henriette Campan, *The Private Life of Marie Antoinette* (New York: Brentano's, 1917), 1: 96.

150 The Continental habit: Arthur Young, *Travels in France and Italy during the Years 1787, 1788 and 1789* (London: J. M. Dent, 1927), 259–60, 324.

151 it was the Italians . . . a silver bidet: Goubert, *Conquest of Water*, 88–90; Vigarello, *Concepts of Cleanliness*, 105.

152 When fifteen-year-old Marie Antoinette: Fraser, *Marie Antoinette*, 42.

152 cabinetmakers designed: Goubert, *Conquest of Water*, 88–89.

152 An English writer: Stone, *Family, Sex and Marriage*, 486.

153 *Le médecin des dames:* Vigarello, *Concepts of Cleanliness*, 107.

154 Napoleon and Josephine . . . it stretched to six hours: Andrea Stuart, *The Rose of Martinique: A Life of Napoleon's Josephine* (London: Macmillan, 2003), 206, 328, 331, 334; Alan Schom, *Napoleon Bonaparte* (New York: HarperCollins, 1997), 377; Evangeline Bruce, *Napoleon and Josephine: The Improbable Marriage* (New York: Scribner, 1995), 137, 316, 393.

154 Lord Byron: Samuel Tenenbaum, *The Incredible Beau Brummell* (South
  Brunswick, NJ: A.S. Barnes, 1967), 8.

154 Brummell, in the words: William Jesse, *The Life of George Brummell, Esq.,*
  Commonly Called Beau Brummell (London: Nimmo, 1886), 2:349.

156 "If John Bull": Jesse, *George Brummell,* 1:69.

156 He travelled everywhere: Jesse, *George Brummell,* 1:70–71, 89.

157 debtors' prison in Caen: Jesse, *George Brummell,* 2:192–96.

158 Sixteen months before he died: Ian Kelly, *Beau Brummell: The Ultimate*
  Man of Style (New York: Free Press, 2006), 192–95, 333;
  Tenenbaum, *Incredible Beau Brummell,* 270; Campbell, *Beau*
  Brummell, 204.

158 At the beginning of Brummell's career: Jesse, *George Brummell,* 2: 349.

MARGINALIA IN CHAPTER FIVE

126 Stone, *Family, Sex and Marriage,* 486.

127 James Boswell, *Boswell on the Grand Tour: Germany and Switzerland*
  1764, ed. Frederick A. Pottle (London: Heinemann, 1953), 16.

129 Henriques, *Prostitution and Society,* 122.

130 Wesley, *Primitive Physick,* 51.

132 Howell, *The Seaside,* 44–45.

133 Howell, *The Seaside,* 15.

134 Guy Williams, *The Age of Agony: The Art of Healing, c. 1700–1800*
  (London: Constable, 1975), 142.

136 Vigarello, *Concepts of Cleanliness,* 97.

138 César de Saussure, *A Foreign View of England in the Reigns of George I*
  and George II, trans. and ed. Madame van Muyden (London: John
  Murray, 1902), 157.

141 Jay Barrett Botsford, *English Society in the Eighteenth Century As*
  Influenced from Overseas (New York: Macmillan, 1924), 96.

142 Vigarello, *Concepts of Cleanliness,* 141.

147 Vigarello, *Concepts of Cleanliness,* 102.

148 Earl of Chesterfield, Philip Dormer Stanhope, *The Letters of Philip*
  Dormer Stanhope Earl of Chesterfield with The Characters, ed. John
  Bradshaw, 3 vols.(London: George Allen and Unwin, 1926),
  1:375.

151 De Bonneville, *Book of the Bath,* 86.

151 Goubert, *Conquest of Water,* 89.

153 Elisabeth Donaghy Garrett, *At Home: The American Family 1750–1870*
  (New York: Abrams, 1990), 132.

155 Virginia Woolf, "Beau Brummell," in *Collected Essays* (London:
  Hogarth Press, 1967), 3:189.

161 Charles Dickens . . . "as it is set up here!": Charles Dickens, *The Letters of Charles Dickens,* ed. Graham Storey and K. J. Fielding (Oxford: Clarendon Press, 1981), 5:583; 6:520, 502, 543, 574.

164 "Baths and How to Take Them": Harriet N. Austin, M.D., quoted in Jacqueline S. Wilkie, "Submerged Sensuality: Technology and Perceptions of Bathing," *Journal of Social History* 19 (Summer 1986): 661, n. 15.

164 the skin's respiratory function . . . crucial to health and even to life: Vigarello, *Concepts of Cleanliness,* 169–72.

165 Hippolyte Taine: Hippolyte Taine, *Notes on England,* trans. Edward Hyams (London: Thames and Hudson, 1957), 148–50.

166 London's Common Council: Wright, *Clean and Decent,* 138.

166 The master of a Cambridge college: Reynolds, *Cleanliness and Godliness,* 117–18.

166 Queen Victoria: Wright, *Clean and Decent,* 139.

167 When personal daintiness: Mark Girouard, *Life in the English Country House: A Social and Architectural History* (New Haven: Yale University Press, 1979), 256.

167 Hot piped water: Judith Flanders, *The Victorian House* (New York: HarperCollins, 2003), 286–88.

167 Lord Ernest Hamilton . . . an occasional aquarium: David Rubinstein, ed., *Victorian Homes* (London: David and Charles, 1974), 85–86.

168 *The Habits of Good Society* . . . "should be so": *The Habits of Good Society,* 110–14, 119.

170 Lady Buckingham: Girouard, *English Country House,* 241.

171 Church Lane: M. W. Flinn, "Introduction," to Edwin Chadwick, *Report on the Sanitary Condition of the Labouring Population of Great Britain* (Edinburgh: Edinburgh University Press, 1965), 4–5.

171 Chadwick quoted a doctor . . . "as black as your hat": Chadwick, *Report on the Sanitary Condition,* 214, 316, 315.

172 (box) *The Water Babies:* Charles Kingsley, *The Water Babies* (London: Macmillan, 1886), 3–4, 17, 28–32, 65, 371.

175 Kitty Wilkinson . . . private bath compartments and a laundry: Marcus Binney, Hana Laing and Alastair Laing, *Taking the Plunge: The Architecture of Bathing* (London: Save Britain's Heritage, n.d.), 12–14.

175 Within six years: Agnes Campbell, *Report on Public Baths and Wash-Houses in the United Kingdom* (Edinburgh: Edinburgh University Press, 1918), 4.

175 In the first few decades . . . "the needful strength": Campbell, *Report on Public Baths,* 4–6, 20, 37–38.

176 Beyond religious affiliation: Witold Rybczynski, *Home: A Short History of an Idea* (New York: Penguin, 1987), 143.

176 Lady Diana Cooper . . . "faded away into the elements": Rubinstein, *Victorian Homes,* 48–50.

178 Lady Fry: Jill Franklin, *The Gentleman's Country House and Its Plan 1835–1914* (London: Routledge and Kegan Paul, 1981), 112.

178 Between 1800 and 1850 . . . going out to bathe: Brian K. Ladd, "Public Baths and Civic Improvement in Nineteenth-Century German Cities," *Journal of Urban History* 14, no. 3 (May 1988), 375–80, 389.

179 Stuttgart's bathhouse: Marilyn Thornton Williams, *Washing "the Great Unwashed": Public Baths in Urban America, 1840–1920* (Columbus: Ohio State University Press, 1991), 9.

179 Cologne's Hohenstaufenbad: Ladd, "Public Baths," 378–80.

182 one turn-of-the-century survey . . . 66 million marks a year: Ladd, "Public Baths," 382–88. See also Siegfried Giedion, *Mechanization Takes Command: A Contribution to Anonymous History,* trans. Siegfried Giedion and Martin James (New York: Oxford University Press, 1948), 676–81.

182 An American sanitary engineer: William Gerhard, *On Bathing and Different Forms of Baths* (New York: William Comstock, 1895), 21.

182 Vienna, Frankfurt: Ladd, "Public Baths," 386–87.

183 establishment of a chair: Vigarello, *Concepts of Cleanliness,* 180–81.

184 Frances Trollope: Vigarello, *Concepts of Cleanliness,* 180.

184 Charles François Mallet: Vigarello, *Concepts of Cleanliness,* 181.

186 Stéphane Mallarmé: De Bonneville, *Book of the Bath,* 100–103.

186 Hector Berlioz: Vigarello, *Concepts of Cleanliness,* 187.

186 Edmée Renaudin: Goubert, *Conquest of Water,* 240–41.

186 Chinese Baths: De Bonneville, *Book of the Bath,* 46; Vigarello, *Concepts of Cleanliness,* 188–89.

186 public baths in Paris: Vigarello, *Concepts of Cleanliness,* 285–86.

187 Beginning in the 1860s: De Bonneville, *Book of the Bath,* 104.

187 (box) In 1819: De Bonneville, *Book of the Bath,* 104.

188 *On Politeness and Good Taste:* Philippe Perrot, *Fashioning the Bourgeoisie: A History of Clothing in the Nineteenth Century,* trans. Richard Bienvenu (Princeton: Princeton University Press, 1994), 125.

188 "No-one in my family": Vigarello, *Concepts of Cleanliness,* 175.

188 Mademoiselle Moisset: De Bonneville, *Book of the Bath*, 96, 108–9.

189 Many convent-educated girls: Vigarello, *Concepts of Cleanliness*, 174–75.

190 Baroness Staffe . . . into the primordial sludge: La Baronne Staffe, *Le Cabinet de Toilette*, 15, 18, 19, 20, 23, 28, 30, 51–54. (Translation by the author.)

192 Edouard Dainville: Girouard, *French Country House*, 233.

192 Château d'Armainvilliers: Girouard, *French Country House*, 239.

192 Roquetaillade: Girouard, *French Country House*, 237.

192 Before 1850 . . . warned Bourgeois d'Orvanne: Vigarello, *Concepts of Cleanliness*, 190, 200, 198–99.

193 Ministry of Public Education . . . "he died in the big baths": Goubert, *Conquest of Water*, 157, 217–18, 23, 138.

195 *Encyclopédie de la santé:* Vigarello, *Concepts of Cleanliness*, 195.

195 Jules Ferry . . . who were ill took full baths: Goubert, *Conquest of Water*, 146, 150–51, 153, 156–57.

196 importation of the German shower: De Bonneville, *Book of the Bath*, 58.

MARGINALIA IN CHAPTER SIX

162 Norman and Jeanne MacKenzie, *Dickens: A Life* (New York: Oxford University Press, 1979), 243.

164 De Bonneville, *Book of the Bath*, 120.

167 Jan Read, *The Moors in Spain and Portugal* (London: Faber and Faber, 1974), 234.

168 L. W. Cowie, *A Dictionary of British Social History* (London: Bell, 1973), 19.

170 Stone, *Family, Sex and Marriage*, 486.

173 George Orwell, *The Road to Wigan Pier* (London: Penguin, 1989), 121.

174 Casanova, *Memoirs*, 2:148.

178 Ladd, "Public Baths," 391, n. 21.

181 Giedion, *Mechanization Takes Command*, 678, n. 78.

184 Perrot, *Fashioning the Bourgeoisie*, 125.

188 Goubert, *Conquest of Water*, 90.

190 De Bonneville, *Book of the Bath*, 116.

191 De Bonneville, *Book of the Bath*, 112.

193 Illich, H_2O, 2.

195 Emile Zola, *Germinal*, trans. Peter Collier (Oxford: Oxford University Press), 1993, 114–16.

199 Elizabeth Drinker: Elizabeth Drinker, *The Diary of Elizabeth Drinker*, ed. Elaine Forman Crane (Boston: Northeastern University Press, 1991), 2:1185.

202 hydropathy, which seized the country . . . Elizabeth Blackwell: Susan E. Cayleff, *Wash and Be Healed: The Water-Cure Movement and Women's Health* (Philadelphia: Temple University Press, 1987), 21–23; Giedion, *Mechanization Takes Command*, 660–62.

203 Americans welcomed it: Cayleff, *Wash and Be Healed*, 3, 15–16, 76.

204 Harriet Beecher Stowe . . . should circulate to every chamber: Cayleff, *Wash and Be Healed*, 144, 148.

205 Duc de Doudeauville: Girouard, *French Country House*, 233.

205 American hotels: Jefferson Williamson, *The American Hotel: An Anecdotal History* (New York: Knopf, 1930), 9, 13–28.

206 John Jacob Astor: Williamson, *American Hotel*, 29, 33.

206 *Illustrated London News:* Giedion, *Mechanization Takes Command*, 694.

206 In the decades: Williamson, *American Hotel*, 55, 61–62; Giedion, *Mechanization Takes Command*, 693–97.

207 Andrew Jackson Downing: Andrew Jackson Downing, *Victorian Cottage Residences* (New York: Dover, 1981), 131.

207 Sarah Josepha Hale: Esther B. Aresty, *The Best Behaviour: The Course of Good Manners—from Antiquity to the Present—As Seen through Courtesy and Etiquette Books* (New York: Simon and Schuster, 1970), 223; Wilkie, "Submerged Sensuality," 650.

208 Florence Nightingale's success: Suellen Hoy, *Chasing Dirt: The American Pursuit of Cleanliness* (New York: Oxford University Press, 1996), 30–35.

208 the Union government: Hoy, *Chasing Dirt*, 36–45.

209 The Union Army: Hoy, *Chasing Dirt*, 58, 38, 57, 53.

210 Dirt was seen: Hoy, *Chasing Dirt*, 70, 59ff., 51–53.

211 Booker T. Washington . . . that student's future: Booker T. Washington, *Up from Slavery: An Autobiography* (Garden City, NY: Doubleday, 1963), 31, 37, 88, 126–27; Hoy, *Chasing Dirt*, 89–92.

213 37 per cent: M. T. Williams, *Washing "the Great Unwashed,"* 17. On American immigration, see also Hoy, *Chasing Dirt*, 87–122.

213 The public bath: David Glassberg, "The Public Bath Movement in America," *American Studies* 20 (Fall 1979): 9.

214 *How the Other Half Lives:* Jacob A. Riis, *How the Other Half Lives: Studies among the Tenements of New York* (New York: Hill and Wang, 1968), 80–81.

214 When New York: Jacob A. Riis, *The Battle with the Slum* (Montclair, NJ: Patterson Smith, 1969), 281.

214 paper published in *Science:* Joseph Hall, "The Macbeth Effect: Is Cleansing Theory Spot-On?" *Toronto Star,* 8 Sept. 2006, A16.

216 Sol Meyerowitz: Neil M. Cowan and Ruth Schwartz Cowan, *Our Parents' Lives: The Americanization of East European Jews* (New York: Basic, 1989), 100–101.

216 one complained to Riis: Riis, *How the Other Half Lives,* 83–84.

218 The country's first bathhouse: M. T. Williams, *Washing "the Great Unwashed,"* 16.

218 Simon Baruch: M. T. Williams, *Washing "the Great Unwashed,"* 42–44.

219 People's Baths: M. T. Williams, *Washing "the Great Unwashed,"* 32.

219 New York State legislature: M. T. Williams, *Washing "the Great Unwashed,"* 37–39.

219 The Americans followed the German model: M. T. Williams, *Washing "the Great Unwashed,"* 35–36; Glassberg, *Public Bath Movement,* 10, 14–16.

220 Model Tenement House Reform Law: Glassberg, *Public Bath Movement,* 18; M. T. Williams, *Washing "the Great Unwashed,"* 65–67.

221 Their model house . . . thirty-one dollars in food annually: Catharine E. Beecher and Harriet Beecher Stowe, *The American Woman's Home; or, Principles of Domestic Science: Being a Guide to the Formation and Maintenance of Economical, Healthful, Beautiful, and Christian Homes* (New York: Arno Press and New York Times, 1971), 269–70, 150–57.

222 study of bathing habits: Hoy, *Chasing Dirt,* 65.

223 Susanna Moodie: Susanna Moodie, *Roughing It in the Bush; or, Forest Life in Canada* (Toronto: McClelland and Stewart, 1962), 199.

223 Ella Sykes: Ella C. Sykes, *A Home-Help in Canada* (London: Smith, Elder, 1912), 258, 117, 132.

224 Five out of six Americans: Hoy, *Chasing Dirt,* 65.

224 In mid-century . . . from $33.90 to $51.10: Susan Strasser, *Never Done: A History of American Housework* (New York: Pantheon, 1982), 96, 100; Wilkie, *Submerged Sensuality,* 653.

225 (box) During the sixteenth: McLaughlin, *Coprophilia,* 42–43: Hunt, "A Short History of Soap," 985–89; Richard L. Bushman and Claudia Bushman, "The Early History of Cleanliness in America," *Journal of American History* 74 (March 1988): 1232–33.

225 Emily Thornwell . . . "should put ladies on their guard": Emily
     Thornwell, *The Lady's Guide to Perfect Gentility* (New York:
     Derby and Jackson, 1859), 13–15.

MARGINALIA IN CHAPTER SEVEN

200 Strasser, *Never Done*, 92.
203 Cayleff, *Wash and Be Healed*, 137.
205 Goubert, *Conquest of Water*, 87.
213 Washington, *Up from Slavery*, 126.
214 Hoy, *Chasing Dirt*, 17.
218 M. T. Williams, *Washing "the Great Unwashed,"* 49.
219 Hugh Cortazzi, *Victorians in Japan: In and Around the Treaty Ports*
     (London: Athlone Press, 1987), 264.
220 Riis, *Battle with the Slum*, 54.
221 Catharine E. Beecher, *A Treatise on Domestic Economy for the Use of
     Young Ladies at Home and at School* (Boston: Marsh, Capen, Lyon,
     and Webb, 1841), 100.
223 Jeanne Minhinnick, *At Home in Upper Canada: Toronto* (Toronto:
     Clarke, Irwin, 1983), 103.
224 Mary Wood-Allen, *What Every Young Woman Should Know*
     (Philadelphia: Vir, 1913), 80–81.
226 Thornwell, *Lady's Guide*, 12–13.

CHAPTER EIGHT
SOAP OPERA: 1900–1950

229 Eliza Doolittle . . . throwing a towel over it: George Bernard Shaw,
     "Pygmalion," *Collected Plays with Their Prefaces* (London: Bodley
     Head, 1970–74), 4:698–705, 713–15.
232 A London social worker . . . attendance at big-city baths: Campbell,
     Report on Public Baths, 36–37, 27, 78–81, 7–8; diagram II.
235 habit of bathing publicly: Campbell, *Report on Public Baths*, 22; Binney
     et al., *Taking the Plunge*, 9.
236 Orwell . . . "despise the 'lower classes.'": Orwell, *Road to Wigan Pier*,
     119–20, 121, 123.
237 Louis Heren . . . "to live without a bathroom": Louis Heren, *Growing
     Up Poor in London* (London: Hamish Hamilton, 1973), 33, 39, 51,
     158, 192, 205.
240 Procter & Gamble . . . "It floats!": Oscar Schisgall, *Eyes on Tomorrow: The
     Evolution of Procter & Gamble* (Chicago: Doubleday, 1981), 24–28.

241 (box) By the beginning: Merritt Ierley, *The Comforts of Home: The American House and the Evolution of Modern Convenience* (New York: Three Rivers Press, 1999), 172–76.

241 high profit margin in soap: Vincent Vinikas, *Soft Soap, Hard Sell: American Hygiene in an Age of Advertisement* (Ames: Iowa State University Press, 1992), 80.

242 Pears' Soap: Vinikas, *Soft Soap*, 81; Lori Anne Loeb, *Consuming Angels: Advertising and Victorian Women* (Oxford: Oxford University Press, 1994), 131; Vincent Vinikas, "Lustrum of the Cleanliness Institute," *Journal of Social History* 22, no. 4 (1989): 623.

242 B. T. Babbitt: Vinikas, *Soft Soap*, 81.

244 A favourite case study . . . Lambert's annual profits rose: Vinikas, *Soft Soap*, 21–22; Tom Reichert, *The Erotic History of Advertising* (Amherst, NY: Prometheus Books, 2003), 120–27; Roland Marchand, *Advertising the American Dream* (Berkeley: University of California Press, 1986), 18–20; Juliann Sivulka, *Soap, Sex and Cigarettes* (Belmont, CA: Wadsworth, 1998), 160–61; Daniel Delis Hall, *Advertising to the American Woman 1900–1999* (Columbus: Ohio State University Press, 2002), 121.

246 technical, medical-sounding names: Sivulka, *Soap, Sex and* Cigarettes, 160; Marchand, *Advertising the American Dream*, 20.

247 "A few years ago": Vinikas, *Soft Soap*, 30.

247 On a hot day . . . sales for Odorono rose: Stephen Fox, *The Mirror Makers: A History of American Advertising and Its Creators* (New York: William Morrow, 1984), 87–88; Sivulka, *Soap, Sex and Cigarettes*, 158–59.

248 *The Science of Culture* . . . "except for the strongest business reasons": William M. Handy, *The Science of Culture* (Garden City, NY: Nelson Doubleday, 1923), 1:57, 58, 59, 60, 61, 62, 65, 67, 68.

249 *Manners for Millions* . . . "violating rules of courtesy": Sophie C. Hadida, *Manners for Millions: A Correct Code of Pleasing Personal Habits for Everyday Men and Women* (New York: Sun Dial Press, 1932), 98, 99–100, 101–2, 103, 104.

252 A buyer's market of goods . . . Cleanliness Institute closed its doors in 1932: Vinikas, *Soft Soap*, 79–94; Juliann Sivulka, *Stronger Than Dirt: A Cultural History of Advertising Personal Hygiene in America, 1875 to 1940* (Amherst, NY: Humanity, 2001), 229–43; Marchand, *Advertising the American Dream*, 211, 246.

253 (box) Even more sensitive: Fox, 99; Silvulka, *Soap, Sex and Cigarettes*, 163–64.

258 *Brave New World* ... "when there isn't hot water laid on?": Aldous
      Huxley, *Brave New World* (New York: HarperCollins, 1998),
      36–37, 108–10, 120–21.
260 By the 1930s: Ierley, *Comforts of Home*, 220; Goubert, *Conquest of Water*,
      87, 218.
261 Movie stars: W. J. Reader, *Fifty Years of Unilever, 1930–1980* (London:
      Heinemann, 1980), 30–31; Hall, *Advertising to the American
      Woman*, 72.

MARGINALIA IN CHAPTER EIGHT

230 Watson, *Jacobson's Organ*, 137.
233 Watson, *Jacobson's Organ*, 134.
235 John Kenneth Galbraith, *The Scotch* (Toronto: McClelland and Stewart,
      1985), 87–88.
237 Fox, *Mirror Makers*, 101.
240 Vinikas, *Soft Soap*, 42.
243 Illich, H_2O, 53–54, n. 33.
246 Fox, *Mirror Makers*, 117.
249 Fox, *Mirror Makers*, 117.
258 Evelyn Waugh, *The Loved One* (London: Penguin, 1951), 89.

CHAPTER NINE

THE HOUSEHOLD SHRINE: 1950 TO THE PRESENT

263 Horace Miner ... "initiated into these mysteries": Horace Miner,
      "Body Ritual among the Nacirema," *American Anthropologist* 58
      (1956): 503–7.
265 Stanhope Hotel: *New York Times Magazine*, 22 Jan. 2006, 17.
265 24 per cent: Paul Grobman, Vital Statistics website, http://www
      .vitalstatistics.info/stat2.asp?id=3202&cid=4&scid=929.
265 Things began to shift: Marchand, *Advertising the American Dream*, 122–25.
266 The average size: Ted Geatros, "Haute Hotels Redo the Loo," *Globe
      and Mail*, 27 Mar. 2004, T5.
266 an 1,800-pound marble tub: Wendy Goodman, "Bathing Beauties," *New
      York*, 3 Apr. 2006, 45.
266 Japanese-style "wet room": Lisa Freedman, "Bathrooms to Soak the
      Rich," *Financial Times*, 5 Sept. 2003, FT.com.
267 Hotel Puerto America: Denny Lee, "The Latest Splash? Baths and
      Pools," *New York Times*, 25 June 2006, TR 9.
268 Miner singled out: Miner, "Body Ritual," 504.

269 "Crest Whitestrips: Demand for Whiter Teeth Transcends Cost, Age Limits," *Drug Store News*, 4 Mar. 2002, www.drugstorenews.com.

269 by 2005, whitening strips: Simon Pitman, "Health and Beauty Dominate New Launches," 22 Mar. 2005, http://www .cosmeticsdesign.com/news/ng.asp?id=58899-health-and-beauty.

270 (box) New York City surgeon: David L. Gollaher, *Circumcision: A History of the World's Most Controversial Surgery* (New York: Basic, 2000), 86–99, 105–8, 84. "Cleaning up the penis" is Gollaher's phrase.

271 Miner is closer: Miner, "Body Ritual," 506.

271 Sissel Tolaas . . . a spot on each wrist: Susie Rushton, "The Sweat Hog," *New York Times Magazine*, 27 Aug. 2006, 150–52.

272 She grew up . . . "by the space we give them": Sissel Tolaas, telephone conversation with the author, 24 Feb. 2007.

273 Having synthesized the rank sweat: Rushton, "Sweat Hog," 150–52.

273 educational work with children: Tolaas, telephone conversation with the author, 24 Feb. 2007.

274 The percentage of houses: *Housing Statistics in the European Union 2004* (Falun, Sweden: Intellecta Strålins, 2005), table 2.3, http://www.uepc.org/statistics/en/uepc-statistics-3.pdf.

274 school principal in Chartres: Antoine Prost, "The Family and the Individual," in *Riddles of Identity in Modern Times*, ed. Antoine Prost and Gerard Vincent, vol. 5 of *A History of Private Life*, ed. Philippe Ariès and Georges Duby, trans. Arthur Goldhammer (Cambridge, MA: Harvard University Press, 1991), 85–87.

275 *Francoscopie:* Scripps Howard News Service, "Study: French Smell Better Than Brits," 23 Oct. 1998, http://www.coastalbendhealth.com/autoconv/newsworld98/ newsworld53.html.

276 Compared with Europe: Tolaas, telephone conversation with the author, 24 Feb. 2007.

276 invented by the Swiss: Nora Ephron, "Dealing with the, uh, Problem," *Esquire*, Mar. 1973, 91–93.

276 Noting that "I smell bad": Ephron, "Dealing with the, uh, Problem," 184.

277 women had a "problem" . . . "I deserve the Nobel Peace Prize": Ephron, "Dealing with the, uh, Problem," 90, 184, 91.

278 "Your Teddy Bear . . . things you never thought of before": Elana Levine, "'Having a Female Body Doesn't Make You Feminine': Feminine Hygiene Advertising and 1970s Television," *Velvet Light Trap*, no. 50 (Fall 2002): 36.

278 raspberry and champagne: "The Unlikeliest Product," *Time,* 26 Dec. 1969, 49.

279 Kate Kane: Kate Kane, "The Ideology of Freshness in Feminine Hygiene Commercials," *Journal of Communications Inquiry* 14 (1990): 292.

279 sales of the sprays stalled: Kane, "Ideology of Freshness," 184, 186.

279 *The Vagina Monologues:* Eve Ensler, *The Vagina Monologues* (New York: Villard, 1998), 77–79.

280 sales of feminine sprays: "RM/AC Neilsen HBC Category Performance Study," *Retail Merchandiser* 43, no. 6 (June 2003): 27; www.drugstorenews.com, 10 Oct. 2005.

280 "What is the body": Tolaas, telephone conversation with the author, 24 Feb. 2007.

281 (box) recruited housewives as research subjects: Ephron, "Dealing with the, uh, Problem," 91.

281 metallic smell of money: Rushton, "Sweat Hog," 152.

281 For women today: Tolaas, telephone conversation with the author, 24 Feb. 2007.

282 The future of fragrance: Rushton, "Sweat Hog," 152.

282 "The more body smell": Tolaas, telephone conversation with the author, 24 Feb. 2007.

282 Ivan Illich: Illich, H_2O, 58.

284 Vincent Lam and Colin Lee: Diane Peters, "Preparing for a Pandemic," *Globe and Mail,* 16 Dec. 2006, F9.

285 For normal life: Vincent Lam and Colin Lee, telephone conversation with the author, 10 Jan. 2007.

285 Charles Gerba . . . "with an alcohol gel": Charles Gerba, telephone conversation with the author, 21 Feb. 2007.

286 One new product: Allen Salkin, "Germs Never Sleep," *New York Times,* 5 Nov. 2006, http://nytimes.com.

286 "Never fear": Maggie Fox, "Teachers' Pets: Germs Just Love Them," *Globe and Mail,* 4 May 2006, A17.

286 Sanitgrasp . . . covers supermarket cart handles: Salkin, "Germs Never Sleep."

288 You can store your toothbrush: Vauhini Vara, "High-Tech Bathrooms Know How Hot You Like Your Shower," *Wall Street Journal Online,* 2 Mar. 2005, http://online.wsj.com/public/article_print/SB110919097334562337–84aekEQhhxhJYbkDLa_c2nvF2ho_2005 0331.html.

289 Allen Salkin: Salkin, "Germs Never Sleep."

290 Museum of Modern Art: Marianne Rohrlich, "Babes in Germ Land," *New York Times,* 29 Jan. 2006, ST 3.

290 "Hay Fever, Hygiene, and Household Size" . . . growing corroboration
of the theory: Bianca Schaub, Roger Lauener, Erika von Mutius,
"The Many Faces of the Hygiene Hypothesis," *Journal of Allergy
and Clinical Immunology* 117 (2006): 969–77; Siri Carpenter,
"Modern Hygiene's Dirty Tricks," 14 Aug. 1999, http://www
.sciencenews.org; Garry Hamilton, "Why We Need Germs," *The
Ecologist Report,* June 2001, http://www.mindfully.Org/Health/
We-Need-Germs.htm; Timothy Begany, "Hygiene Hypothesis
Gains Support in the United States and Europe," Jan. 2003,
http://www.respiratoryreviews.com.

292 In Perth, Australia: Ean Higgins, "Dirt Pills May Help to Ease Kids'
Asthma," *Australian,* 27 Apr. 2006.

293 Japanese children: Edward Willett, "The Hygiene Hypothesis," 2000,
www.edwardwillett.com/Columns/hygienehypothesis.htm.

293 Tore Midtvedt: Hamilton, "Why We Need Germs."

294 *Saturday:* Ian McEwan, *Saturday* (London: Jonathan Cape, 2005),
149–50.

295 Alain Corbin: Alain Corbin, *The Foul and the Fragrant: Odor and the
French Social Imagination,* trans. Miriam L. Kochan, Roy Porter
and Christopher Prendergast (Cambridge, MA: Harvard
University Press, 1986), p. 173.

MARGINALIA IN CHAPTER NINE

267 Mary Douglas, *Purity and Danger: An Analysis of Concepts of Pollution
and Taboo* (Harmondsworth, UK: Penguin, 1970), 12.

271 http://www.toothbrushexpress.com/html/floss_history.html.

274 Hamilton, "Why We Need Germs," 1.

279 Edwyn Bevan, *Hellenism and Christianity* (London: George Allen and
Unwin, 1921), 154.

288 Hamilton, "Why We Need Germs," 2.

292 Salkin, "Germs Never Sleep."

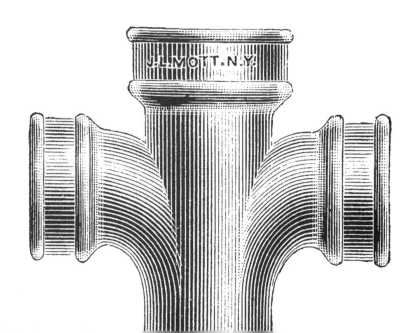

SELECTED BIBLIOGRAPHY

Binney, Marcus, Hana Laing and Alastair Laing. *Taking the Plunge: The Architecture of Bathing*. London: Save Britain's Heritage, n.d.

Brue, Alexia. *Cathedrals of the Flesh: My Search for the Perfect Bath*. New York: Bloomsbury, 2003.

Bushman, Richard L. and Claudia Bushman. "The Early History of Cleanliness in America." *Journal of American History* 74 (March 1988): 1213–38.

Campbell, Agnes. *Report on Public Baths and Wash-Houses in the United Kingdom*. Edinburgh: Edinburgh University Press, 1918.

Carcopino, Jerome. *Daily Life in Ancient Rome*. Trans. E. O. Lorimer. New York: Penguin, 1991.

Cayleff, Susan E. *Wash and Be Healed: The Water-Cure Movement and Women's Health*. Philadelphia: Temple University Press, 1987.

Chadwick, Edwin. *Report on the Sanitary Condition of the Labouring Population of Great Britain*. Edited, with an introduction by M. W. Flinn. Edinburgh: University of Edinburgh Press, 1965.

Clark, Scott. *Japan: A View from the Bath*. Honolulu: University of Hawaii Press, 1994.

Classen, Constance, David Howes and Anthony Synnot. *Aroma: The Cultural History of Smell*. New York: Routledge, 1994.

Connolly, Peter, and Hazel Dodge. *The Ancient City: Life in Classical Athens and Rome.* Oxford: Oxford University Press, 1998.

Corbin, Alain. *The Foul and the Fragrant: Odor and the French Social Imagination.* Trans. Miriam L. Kochan, Roy Porter and Christopher Prendergast. Cambridge, MA: Harvard University Press, 1986.

Croutier, Alev Lytle. *Taking the Waters: Spirit, Art, Sensuality.* New York: Abbeville Press, 1992.

Daly, Mary. *Purity and Danger: An Analysis of Concepts of Pollution and Taboo.* Harmondsworth, Middlesex: Penguin, 1970.

De Bonneville, Françoise. *The Book of the Bath.* Trans. Jane Brenton. New York: Rizzoli, 1998.

Duby, Georges, ed. *A History of Private Life, II: Revelations of the Medieval World.* Trans. Arthur Goldhammer. Cambridge, MA: Harvard University Press, 1988.

Duby, Georges, and Philippe Braunstein. "The Emergence of the Individual," in *A History of Private Life, II: Revelations of the Medieval World.* Ed. George Duby. Trans. Arthur Goldhammer. Cambridge, MA: Harvard University Press, 1988, pp. 507–632.

Elias, Norbert. *The Civilizing Process: The History of Manners.* Trans. Edmund Jephcott. Oxford: Basil Blackwell, 1978.

Ephron, Nora. "Dealing with the, uh, Problem," *Esquire,* March 1973.

Fagan, Garrett G. *Bathing in Public in the Roman World.* Ann Arbor: University of Michigan Press, 1999.

Flanders, Judith. *The Victorian House.* New York: HarperCollins, 2003.

Garrett, Elisabeth Donaghy. *At Home: The American Family 1750–1870.* New York: Harry N. Abrams, 1990.

Giedion, Sigfried. *Mechanization Takes Command: A Contribution to Anonymous History.* New York: W. W. Norton, 1969.

Girouard, Mark. *Life in the English Country House: A Social and Architectural History.* New Haven: Yale University Press, 1978.

———. *Life in the French Country House.* New York: Knopf, 2000.

Glassberg, David. "The Public Bath Movement in America." *American Studies* 20 (Fall 1979): 5–21.

Gollaher, David L. *Circumcision: A History of the World's Most Controversial Surgery.* New York: Basic Books, 2000.

Goubert, Jean-Pierre. *The Conquest of Water: The Advent of Health in the Industrial Age.* Trans. Andrew Wilson. Princeton: Princeton University Press, 1989.

Hamilton, Garry. "Why We Need Germs," *The Ecologist Report* (June 2001), http://www.mindfully.Org/Health/We-Need-Germs.htm

Henriques, Fernando. *Prostitution and Society.* New York: Grove Press, 1966.

——. *Prostitution in Europe and the New World.* London: McGibbon and Kee, 1963.

Hoss, Stefanie. *Baths and Bathing: The Culture of Bathing and the Baths and Thermae in Palestine from the Hasmoneans to the Moslem Conquest.* Oxford: Archaeopress, 2005.

Howell, Sarah. *The Seaside.* London: Collier and Collier Macmillan, 1974.

Hoy, Suellen. *Chasing Dirt: The American Pursuit of Cleanliness.* New York: Oxford University Press, 1996.

Ierley, Merritt. *The Comforts of Home: The American House and the Evolution of Modern Convenience.* New York: Three Rivers Press, 1999.

Illich, Ivan. *H₂O and the Waters of Forgetfulness.* London: Marion Boyars, 1986.

Jackson, Ralph. "Waters and Spas in the Classical World," in *Medical History of Waters and Spas.* Ed. Roy Porter. London: Wellcome Institute for the History of Medicine, 1990, pp. 1–13.

Kazen, Thomas. *Jesus and Purity Halakhah: Was Jesus Indifferent to Purity?* Stockholm: Almqvist and Wiksell International, 2002.

Ladd, Brian K. "Public Baths and Civic Improvement in Nineteenth-Century German Cities." *Journal of Urban History* 14, no. 3 (May 1988): 372–93.

Le Guérer, Annick. *Scent: The Mysterious and Essential Powers of Smell.* Trans. Richard Miller. London: Chatto and Windus, 1993.

Marchand, Roland. *Advertising the American Dream: Making Way for Modernity, 1920–1940.* Berkeley: University of California Press, 1986.

Martial. *Epigrams.* Trans. Walter C.A. Kerr. 2 vols. Cambridge, MA: Harvard University Press, 1961.

——. *Martial in English.* Ed. J.P. Sullivan and A.J. Boyle. London: Penguin Books, 1996.

McLaughlin, Terence. *Coprophilia, or a Peck of Dirt.* London: Cassell, 1971.

Miner, Horace. "Body Ritual among the Nacirema." *American Anthropologist* 58 (1956): 503–7.

Orwell, George. *The Road to Wigan Pier.* London: Penguin Books, 1989.

Palmer, Richard, "'In this our lightye and learned tyme': Italian baths in the era of the Renaissance," in *Medical History of Waters and Spas.* Ed. Roy Porter. London: Wellcome Institute for the History of Medicine, 1990, pp. 14–22.

Perrot, Michelle, ed. *A History of Private Life IV: From the Fires of Revolution to the Great War.* Trans. Arthur Goldhammer. Cambridge, MA: Harvard University Press, 1990.

Perrot, Philippe. *Fashioning the Bourgeoisie: A History of Clothing in the Nineteenth Century.* Trans. Richard Bienvenu. Princeton: Princeton University Press, 1994.

Porter, Roy, ed. *Medical History of Waters and Spas*. London: Wellcome Institute for the History of Medicine, 1990.

Prost, Antoine. "Public and Private Spheres in France," in *A History of Private Life, V: Riddles of Identity in Modern Times*. Ed. Antoine Prost and Gerard Vincent. Trans. Arthur Goldhammer. Cambridge, MA: Harvard University Press, 1991, pp. 1–144.

Regnier-Bohler, Danielle. "Imagining the Self," in *A History of Private Life II: Revelations of the Medieval World*. Ed. Georges Duby. Trans. Arthur Goldhammer. Cambridge, MA: Belknap Press of Harvard University Press, 1988, pp. 311–94.

Reynolds, Reginald. *Cleanliness and Godliness*. Garden City, NJ: Doubleday, 1946.

Riis, Jacob A. *The Battle with the Slum*. Montclair, NJ: Patterson Smith, 1969.

————. *How the Other Half Lives: Studies among the Tenements of New York*. New York: Hill and Wang, 1968.

Roche, Daniel. *The Culture of Clothing: Dress and Fashion in the Ancien Régime*. Trans. Jean Birrell. Cambridge: Cambridge University Press, 1994.

Rousseau, Jean-Jacques. *The Confessions and Correspondence, Including the Letters to Malesherbes*, vol. 5, *The Collected Writings of Rousseau*. Ed. Christopher Kelly, Roger D. Masters and Peter G. Stillman. Trans. Christopher Kelly. Hanover, NH: University Press of New England, 1995.

————. *Emile*. Trans. Barbara Foxley. London: J.M. Dent, 1993.

Rubinstein, David, Ed. *Victorian Homes*. London: David and Charles, 1974.

Salisbury, Joyce E. *Church Fathers, Independent Virgins*. London: Verso, 1991.

Salkin, Allen. "Germs Never Sleep." *The New York Times*, 5 Nov. 2006 (http://nytimes.com).

Sarti, Raffaella. *Europe at Home: Family and Material Culture 1500–1800*. Trans. Allan Cameron. New Haven: Yale University Press, 2002.

Schama, Simon. *The Embarrassment of Riches: An Interpretation of Dutch Culture in the Golden Age*. New York: Vintage, 1997.

Schaub, Bianca, Roger Lauener and Erika von Mutius. "The Many Faces of the Hygiene Hypothesis." *Journal of Allergy and Clinical Immunology* 117 (2006): 969–77.

Shaw, Bernard. "Pygmalion," in *Collected Plays with Their Prefaces*, vol. IV. London: The Bodley Head, 1970–74.

Singman, Jeffrey. *Daily Life in Medieval Europe*. Westport, CN: Greenwood Press, 1999.

Sivulka, Juliann. *Soap, Sex, and Cigarettes: A Cultural History of American Advertising.* Belmont, CA: Wadsworth, 1998.

———. *Stronger Than Dirt: A Cultural History of Advertising Personal Hygiene in America, 1875–1940.* Amherst, NY: Humanity Books, 2001.

Stouck, Mary-Ann. *Medieval Saints.* New York: Broadview, 1999.

Strasser, Susan. *Never Done: A History of American Housework.* New York: Pantheon, 1982.

Thorndike, Lynn. "Sanitation, Baths, and Street-Cleaning in the Middle Ages and Renaissance," *Speculum*, 1924, pp. 193–203.

Urbain, Jean-Didier. *At the Beach.* Trans. Catherine Porter. Minneapolis: University of Minnesota Press, 2003.

Vigarello, Georges. *Concepts of Cleanliness: Changing Attitudes in France since the Middle Ages.* Trans. Jean Birrell. Cambridge: Cambridge University Press, 1988.

Vinikas, Vincent. *Soft Soap, Hard Sell: American Hygiene in an Age of Advertisement.* Ames: Iowa State University Press, 1992.

Wilkie, Jacqueline S. "A Submerged Sensuality: Technology and Perceptions of Bathing." *Journal of Social History* 19 (Summer 1986): 649–64.

Williams, Marilyn Thornton. *Washing "The Great Unwashed": Public Baths in Urban America, 1840–1920.* Columbus: Ohio State University Press, 1991.

Williamson, Jefferson. *The American Hotel: An Anecdotal History.* New York: Knopf, 1930.

Wright, Lawrence. *Clean and Decent: The History of the Bath and Loo and of Sundry Habits, Fashions and Accessories of the Toilet, Principally in Great Britain, France and America.* London: Routledge and Kegan Paul, 1980.

Yegül, Fikret. *Baths and Bathing in Classical Antiquity.* Cambridge, MA: MIT Press, 1992.

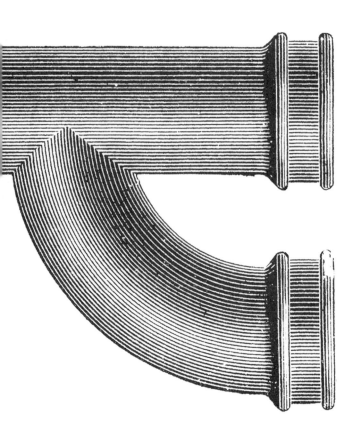

INDEX

comparison to other continents,
2, 10–11, 139, 273
decline of Roman bath culture
in, 64–65
emigrants to America from,
213–16
late Middle Ages through mid-
1800s
bathing in spas, 116–19,
120–21, 122–23
bathing or swimming in
rivers and lakes, 113–14,
192
belief in cleanliness of linen,
106–11
outward elegance but dirty
bodies, 98–99
royal cleanliness or lack of,
105–6
water avoided for fear of disease, 94–95, 100–101, 105
Middle Ages
revival of public baths, 78–80
soaps, *32*
resistance to over-cleanliness in,
274
tooth-cleaning today in, 268
therapeutic baths in, 10
view of American deodorant
efforts in, 226
view of Turkish baths in, 126–27
See also specific countries
Eustadiola, Saint, *58*
exercise
in ancient Greece, 23–24, 295
in ancient Rome, 28, 295
in the Bozerian shower bath, *163*
in England of 1800s, *163*, 169
and production of bad odour,
226

face
dry wiped in 1600s, 101

gladiator sweat as cream for, *38*
religious prescriptions for, 63
washing of
1500–1839, 97–98, 102
in Middle Ages, 66, 76, 87–88
Fagon, Guy-Crescent, 116
Fausta, *55*
feet
of travellers, 62, 66, 87
washing of, in 1600s, 110
washing of, in 1800s, 196
Wesley's recommendations for
cleaning of, 131
feminine hygiene products,
276–81
Ferdinand IV, King of Naples, 147
Ferdinand V of Castile, 111
Ferry, Jules, 195
Fiennes, Celia, 119, 122–23
Finland, 10, 30, *37*
fleas, 94, *98*, 99
Floyer, John, 129, 131, 134
flu, 284, 289
food in public baths, 23, 36, 41, 44,
83, 86
Ford, Richard, 71–72, *167*
Forges, France, 118
France
bathrooms in 1900s in, 274
belief in danger of bathing in 1600s
in, 114–16
bidets in, 150–54
cleanliness in art and literature
in, 140, 142–44
cleanliness standards in
in 1600s, 105
in 1700s, 98–99, 137, 139–54
in 1800s, 165, 178, 183–84,
186–97
in 1900s, 274–75, 295
in Middle Ages, *93*
history of soap in, *32*
hygiene manuals of 1500–1839,
102, 110

saints
   who accepted some need for
      washing, 57–58, 62–63
   who saw uncleanliness as badge
      of holiness, 59–62
   who washed lepers and others,
      60, 62–63
   whose saliva or chewings were
      healing, 58
   whose washwater was healing,
      58
   See also Christianity; and indi-
      vidual saints' names
Salkin, Allen, 289
Sapolio Soap, 243
SARS, 284, 289
Sartre, Jean-Paul, 230
saunas 30, 37, 80. See also steam
   baths
Savot, Louis, 107
Scarborough, England, 119
schools and hygiene education,
      193, 195–96, 216, 218, 233,
      257–58
Scipio Africanus, 42–43
Scotland, 138, 232–33
sea bathing, 131–33, 136–37
Semmelweis, Ignaz, 239–40
Seneca, 41–42
servants
   at public baths
      in ancient Rome, 31, 37
      in Middle Ages, 79
   attending at bath
      in 1800s, 178, 197
      in Middle Ages, 87–90
   changing linens in 1600s,
      110
   inappropriate for early Christian
      bathers, 57, 59
   unappetizing bodies of, in early
      1900s, 236
Sévigné, Madame de, 118–19, 120,
      122, 122–23

sexual activity
   and benefits of cold water, 130
   and body odour, 6, 78, 282
   and Jewish purity laws, 51, 69
   and medieval bathhouses, 83,
      86–87
   of Christians, bathing afterward,
      54
   and orgasms, 73
   and Roman bathhouses, 31, 33,
      36, 43
   and vaginal odour, 278–79
Shainess, Natalie, 277
shampoos, 5
Shaw, George Bernard, 229, 232
Shebbeare, John, 126
showers
   considered dangerous, 168
   private
      Bozerian shower bath, 163
      Dickens,' 161–62
      in France, 234–35
      in North America in 1700s,
         199
   public
      in ancient Greece, 22
      in France in 1800s, 196–97
      in Germany in 1800s, 181–82
      in North America in 1800s, 219
Silesia, 202
sin, 51
Sissinius, Pope, 57
skin
   open pores seen as healthy, 100,
      135–36, 203, 221
   plugged pores seen as
      protective, 94–95, 100–101
slaves
   freed, and North America's
      cleanliness, 211–13
   in ancient Roman baths, 31, 37
Smart, Christopher, 107
smoking, 3
Smollett, Tobias, 134–39

TEXT PERMISSIONS

ILLUSTRATION CREDITS

P. 16 Greek woman, © Royal Museums of Art and History—Brussels; p. 19 earliest bathtub, *Clean and Decent*, Lawrence Wright, © 1980 Routledge and Kegan Paul. Reproduced by permission of Taylor & Francis Books UK; p. 21 Archimedes, Ann Ronan Picture Library / Heritage Images; p. 22 Athenian baths, Photo: akg-images / Peter Connolly; p. 29 strigil, Glyptothek (Munich), courtesy of Wikipedia.org; p. 36 Baths of Diocletian, Paulin, Les Thermes de Dioclétien, envoi 1880, Bibliothèque Nationale Supériore des Beaux Arts à Paris; p. 50 *The Birth of the Virgin*, Scala / Art Resource, NY; p. 53 baptism of Jesus, Mary Ann Sullivan, Bluffton University; p. 60 St. Francis, Harvard University Art Museums, Fogg Art Museum, Friends of the Fogg Art Museum Fund, 1929.234; p. 68 Bathsheba, Erich Lessing / Art Resource, NY; p. 81 bath at Baden, Württembergische Landesbibliothek Stuttgart, HBb 725; p. 84 Polish monks, author's collection; p. 88 private tub, Württembergische Landesbibliothek Stuttgart, HBb 725; p. 89 knight, Ms 648/404 f.415v Bathing Scene in a Castle Courtyard (vellum) by French School (15th century) © Musée Condé, Chantilly, France/ Giraudon / The Bridgeman Art Library; p. 92 plague, Toggenburg Bible, courtesy of Wikipedia.org; p. 99 woman with flea, © Musée Lorrain, Nancy / photo. P. Mignot; p. 104 ablutions, Bonnart, 1690 engraving, Bibiothèque National de France, Paris; p. 108 Holbein, The State Hermitage Museum, St. Petersburg;

p. 119 Montaigne, Portrait of Montaigne by Thomas de Leu (1608) (H. 14,5 x L. 9,1 cm). Bibliotheca Desaniana, Chicago; p. 121 baths at Vichy, Base Liber Floridus, Bibiothèque Mazarine, Ms 3243, p. 62; p. 145 Marie Antoinette, Réunion des Musées Nationaux / Art Resource, NY; p. 147 Marat, Assassinat de Jean-Paul Marat par Charlotte Corday (13 juillet 1793). Gravure, B.N.F. © Roger-Viollet; p. 152 bidet, Getty Images "Woman at Her Toilette," Louis-Léopold Boilly; p. 163 shower bath, © The British Library (Design & Work); p. 166 bath cabinet, The British Library, C12112-08, p. 6; p. 180 travelling trunk, The British Library, C1211-07, p. 208; p. 183 man in device, gta Archiv / ETH Zürich; p. 185 bébé learns to wash, author's collection; p. 188 steam bath, gta Archiv / ETH Zürich; p. 189 bathroom, author's collection; p. 193 soldiers, author's collection; p. 202 outdoor shower, gta Archiv / ETH Zürich; p. 210 hospital, Collection of The New-York Historical Society; p. 211 Washington, Cheynes Studio, Hampton, Va, 1903; p. 215 washing up, "Newsboys Washing for Dinner," Museum of the City of New York, The Jacob A. Riis Collection, Riis #167; p. 217 bathtub, "Bath-tub in Airshaft," c. 1890, Museum of the City of New York, The Jacob A. Riis Collection, Riis #ST5; p. 230 woman in bathroom, gta Archiv / ETH Zürich; p. 234 makeshift shower, author's collection; p. 242 Pears' soap, author's collection; p. 245 Listerine, author's collection; p. 255 Kotex, Wisconsin Historical Society, WHi-49898; p. 256 Lifebuoy, author's collection; p. 274 Tolaas, © Matti Hillig; p. 287 Ontario poster, Text and Advertisement © Queen's Printer for Ontario, 2006. Reproduced with permission. Photograph: © Getty Image Library; p. 289 Clean Shopper, photo courtesy of Babe Ease, LLC.